IN A FREE
REPUBLIC

IN A FREE REPUBLIC

Life in Cromwell's England

ALISON PLOWDEN

SUTTON PUBLISHING

First published in the United Kingdom in 2006 by
Sutton Publishing Limited · Phoenix Mill
Thrupp · Stroud · Gloucestershire · GL5 2BU

British Library Cataloguing in Publication Data
A catalogue record for this book is available from the British
Library.

ISBN 0-7509-1883-7

Typeset in 11/14pt Sabon.
Typesetting and origination by
Sutton Publishing Limited.
Printed and bound in England by
J.H. Haynes & Co. Ltd, Sparkford.

Contents

List of Illustrations

Chronology

1640
November   The Long Parliament meets.

1641
November   Grand Remonstrance passed.

1642
January   The King attempts to arrest the Five Members.
August   Civil War breaks out.

1643
December   Death of John Pym.

1645
January   Parliament approves a Presbyterian Directory of Worship to replace the Book of Common Prayer.
August   Parliamentary Ordinance regulating the election of parish elders, aimed at setting up a Presbyterian chuch in England.

1646
March   End of the Civil War fighting.
May   The King surrenders to the Scots at Newark.
October   Parliament abolishes the episcopacy and authorises the sale of bishops' lands.

1647
January   The King handed over to parliament and confined at Holmby House, Northants.

May	The Commons vote to disband the infantry regiments, with only eight weeks' arrears of pay.
June	The King taken from Holmby House by soldiers of the New Model Army. The army musters in a general rendezvous at Newmarket. It refuses to disband and issues *A Solemn Engagement* and a *Declaration of the Army* setting out its demands.
August	The army marches on London and publishes the *Heads of Proposals* as a basis for a settlement with the King.
October	The Levellers publish *The Case of the Army Truly Stated* and *The Agreement of the People*.
October/ November	The Putney Debates take place.
November	The King escapes from Hampton Court to the Isle of Wight and an army mutiny inspired by the Levellers at Corkbush Field is suppressed.

1648

April/ August	The Second Civil War takes place.
August	A Presbyterian system of church government established in England.
November	The Council of Officers demands that the King be brought to justice but is refused by parliament.
December	The King is brought back towards London and the army again occupies the capital.
6 December	Members of the Commons considered hostile to the army are forcibly excluded in the so-called Pride's Purge.

1649

January	The trial and execution of the King.
March	The monarchy and the House of Lords abolished by the Purged or 'Rump' Parliament.

April	The Diggers attempt to set up a self-sufficient commune on wasteland at St George's Hill in Surrey.
May	England declared a Commonwealth or Republic by Act of Parliament. Leveller mutiny in the army crushed at Burford.

1650

January	All adult males ordered to swear an Oath of Engagement to the Commonwealth.
March	An Act of Parliament passed making adultery a capital offence.
August	The Blasphemy Act passed against nonconformist sects in general but the Ranters in particular.

1651

January	Charles II crowned in Scotland.
September	Charles II defeated at Worcester.

1653

April	The Rump Parliament expelled by Cromwell.
July	Barebone's Parliament meets.
September	Parliament introduces civil marriage.
November	Formation of the Sealed Knot.
December	Parliament resigns its jurisdiction to the army. The Protectorate established with Cromwell as Lord Protector by the terms of the Instrument of Government.

1654

September	First Protectorate Parliament meets.

1655

January	First Protectorate Parliament dissolved by Cromwell.
March	Penruddock's Rising suppressed.

August	Establishment of a system of regional government by major-generals, to be funded by a Decimation Tax on royalist estates.
December	The Jews readmitted to England.

1656

September	First session of the second Protectorate Parliament.
October	The Quaker James Nayler enters Bristol and is arrested and accused of blasphemy.

1657

January	The major-generals abolished.
May	Cromwell accepts the Commons' Humble Petition and Advice, including the right to nominate his successor, but refuses the Crown. A second chamber or nominated Upper House is established in parliament.
June	Cromwell reinstalled as Lord Protector.

1658

January	Second session of second Protectorate Parliament.
February	Second Protectorate Parliament dissolved.
September	Death of Oliver Cromwell. His son Richard appointed Lord Protector.

1659

January	Third Protectorate Parliament meets.
April	Third Protectorate Parliament dissolved.
May	Resignation of Richard Cromwell. End of the Protectorate. Rump Parliament recalled.
June	Booth's royalist rising in Cheshire crushed.
October	The Rump expelled by the army and a Committee of Safety appointed.
December	The Rump again recalled.

1660

January	General Monck marches south from Scotland.
February	Monck enters London and orders the reinstatement of those MPs expelled in Pride's Purge.
March	The Long Parliament dissolves itself and calls for new elections.
April	The Declaration of Breda by Charles II. The first session of the Convention Parliament declares in favour of rule by King, Lords and Commons.
May	Charles II restored and enters London.
December	The Convention Parliament dissolved.

1661

January	Thomas Venner's rising of Fifth Monarchists.
April	Charles II crowned in Westminster Abbey.
May	First session of the Cavalier Parliament. The bishops regain their seats in the House of Lords.

The Colonel . . . being in himself more persuaded that the people's freedom would be best maintained in a free republic, delivered from the shackles of their encroaching slaves the army.

(Memoirs of the Life of Colonel Hutchinson)

The Day they Killed the King

> . . . the lord in mercy lay it not as a sin to the charge of the kingdom, but in mercy do us good by the same.
>
> (Ralph Josselin, *Diary*, 4 February 1649)

They came for him at St James's soon after nine o'clock on a bitter cold January morning and brought him, guarded by two companies of infantry, across the park to Whitehall. He was taken to wait in the room which had once been his bedchamber, for the arrangements were still not complete and it was early afternoon before Colonel Hacker came to the door to give his last signal.

The scaffold had been erected against the wall of a now demolished brick extension to the north of Inigo Jones's Banqueting House and was accessible by a window on the staircase leading up to the first floor. The authorities had taken every possible precaution against any last-minute rescue attempt and 'the multitudes of people that came to be spectators' were kept at a safe distance by the 'divers companies of Foot and Horse' drawn up on every side. Seventeen-year-old Philip Henry standing in the crowd in the street before Whitehall gate, where the scaffold was erected, could see what was done, but was not close enough to hear anything. 'The Blow I saw given,' he recorded in his diary, 'and can truly say with a sad heart; at the instant whereof, I remember well, there was such a Groan by the Thousands then present, as I never heard before and desire I may never hear again.' Orders were immediately given for the soldiers to clear the streets and young Philip 'had much ado amongst the rest to escape home without hurt'.[1]

1

In spite of the shockingly unprecedented nature of the deed, public reaction to news of the King's execution was muted. The Dutch envoy, Adrian Pauw, reported that there had been no disturbance in London and 'all the shops were open in the usual way', but according to *The Kingdomes Weekly Intelligencer* 'it was a very wet day in and about the City of London by reason of the abundance of affliction that fell from many eyes'.[2] John Evelyn, then lodging at his father-in-law's house at Deptford, was struck with such horror over the villainy of the rebels that he could not bring himself to be present at 'that execrable wickedness' and stayed at home, keeping the day of the royal martyrdom as a fast. By contrast, Samuel Pepys, in 1649 still a pupil at St Paul's School, was later to remember with some embarrassment that he had been a great Roundhead as a boy and on the day the King was beheaded had said that, if he were to preach upon him, would have taken as his text: 'The memory of the wicked shall rot.'[3]

In the country at large the mood appears to have been one of rather nervous astonishment. 'There was such a consternation among the common people throughout the nation', commented a Puritan Yorkshireman, 'that one neighbour durst scarcely speak to another when they met in the streets, not from any abhorrence at the action, but in surprise at the rarity and infrequency of it.'[4] The Revd Ralph Josselin, vicar of East Colne in Essex, was no royalist, but he, too, had shed tears on hearing of the regicide and shared the general sense of unease. 'I was much troubled with the black providence of putting the King to death,' he wrote in his diary on 4 February, '. . . the lord in mercy lay it not as sin to the charge of the kingdom, but in mercy do us good by the same . . . The death of the king talked much of', he went on, 'very many men of the weaker sort of Christians in divers places passionate concerning it, but so ungroundedly that it would make any to bleed to observe it, the lord hath some great thing to do, fear and tremble at it oh England.'[5]

The cult of King Charles the Martyr began with the appearance, on the day of his burial, of *Eikon Basilike* (The Royal Image), an account of 'his sacred majesty in his solitude and sufferings',

2

purporting to have been written by himself but probably mostly the work of his chaplain, John Gauden. In spite of strenuous efforts to suppress it, it quickly became a best seller, while a brisk and profitable trade in relics had sprung up within minutes of the execution, so that soldiers selling chips of blood-stained wood from the scaffold and block, or admitting the curious to view the coffined corpse for a shilling or even half-a-crown, wished that 'we had two or three more Majesties to behead, if we could but make such use of them' – at least, according to one news sheet published on 7 February.[6]

Claims of miracle cures wrought by handkerchiefs dipped in the sacred blood proliferated in royalist circles, and Isabella, wife of Sir Roger Twysden of East Peckham in Kent, heard that, when the King was on the scaffold, 'a flight of wild ducks came and flew away, a drake first staying down and touching his bill on the block, as many said that was there by at the time and saw the soldiers strike and shoot at them, but hit none'.[7]

'The Fatal Blow is given,' thundered the royalist *Mercurius Pragmaticus*.

The Kingdom is translated to the Saints – Oh Horror! Blood! Death! Had you none else to wreak your cursed malice on but the sacred Person of the King? . . . Beware the building, for the Foundation is taken away, the winds begin to blow, and the waves to beat, the Restless Ark is toss'd; none but uncleane Beasts are entered into her, the Dove will not return, neither will the Olive Branch appear. The Axe is laid to the Root, even of the Royal Cedar, then what can the inferior Tree expect but to be crush'd and bruis'd in His fall, and afterwards hewn down and cast into the fire . . .[8]

But, in spite of these doomful prognostications, in 1649 a war-weary nation faced the prospect of life without the Royal Cedar, if not with any great enthusiasm, at least with a readiness to try the experiment of government by Puritan 'Saints'.

ONE

This Great Parliament

God hath called a Parliament, how long it will continue we are
not worthy to know, nor what it will bring forth . . .
>   (John Venn to Governor Winthrop, April 1640)

To the great majority of the nation Tuesday 3 November 1640
would have seemed a day like any other. It was a quiet time of
year for most people. The harvest was long since gathered and the
stubble gleaned. The Michaelmas fairs were over and the rents paid,
while the Christmas feast was still a long way off. But as their
neighbours were settling in for the coming winter, groups of
gentlemen had been leaving their homes in the counties and towns
all over England and Wales – from Cumberland, Carlisle and
Cockermouth in the north, Lincoln, Boston and Cambridge in the
east; from Dorset, Poole and Lyme Regis on the south coast; to
Cornwall, Bodmin and St Ives in the far south-west. These were the
'parliament men' on their way to Westminster, where the King had
called the fifth parliament of his reign. Relations between king and
parliament, never cordial, had become increasingly strained as time
went by, but although the recent elections had been more ill-
temperedly contested than usual, it seems unlikely that any of the
new members of the Commons riding up to London through the
autumn landscape could have foreseen the cataclysmic events which
lay ahead. On the contrary, there was a good deal of optimism.
'Great expectation there is of a happy Parliament where ye subject
may have a total redress of all grievances,' wrote one of them in his
diary, while another was hoping that 'by the blessing of God we
shall return with an Olive branch in our Mouths, and a full

Confirmation of the Privileges . . . which every Free born Englishman hath received with the Air he breatheth in'.[1]

No machinery existed for convoking parliament on a regular basis, and it remained an occasional affair, governed principally by the financial necessities of the Crown – its most important function, at least from the point of view of the sovereign, being to vote 'subsidies' (that is, taxation), to pay either for foreign adventures or for the defence of the realm in time of war. King Charles had famously contrived to manage without it for eleven years, and it was only his disastrous attempt to impose a version of the English prayer book on his Scottish subjects, resulting in the so-called Bishops' War, which had forced him to summon it again in the spring of 1640. This was the Short Parliament, lasting only three weeks – dissolution being also within the royal prerogative – but financial necessity had not gone away and fresh writs had therefore had to be issued to the sheriffs in September.

Elections tended to be rough-and-ready affairs, for there was as yet no recognised uniform electoral machinery, nothing resembling a modern party system and, of course, no question of anything resembling a secret ballot. In fact, unless there was a contest, the electorate was expected to do no more than 'acclaim' those candidates who had been preselected behind closed doors by the leaders of the local community. But this system, which was heavily influenced by considerations of kinship, patronage, local obligation and allegiance and had little to do with the exercise of free choice by the people, was beginning to change as the century progressed. Contested elections were, in fact, becoming more frequent as a more socially ambitious and politically aware gentry class began to compete for parliamentary seats, and consequently the electorate was more often being required to turn out and indicate its preference 'by voice, or by hands, or such other way, wherein it is easy to tell who has the majority'. It was only when the result was disputed that a poll or actual head count was called for, although this was intended more to weed out those unqualified to vote than to confirm the actual majority, and could be further complicated by a conviction on the part of some gentlemen that the status of those who had given their 'voyces' counted for more than numbers – not to mention the reluctance of such individuals to be included among the lower class of voter at the poll.[2]

The English counties (with the exception of Durham) each returned two members – the so-called Knights of the Shire – while towns or boroughs, again with certain exceptions, each elected two burgesses, generally regarded as being socially inferior to the county members. The bulk of the county electorate was, in theory at any rate, made up by the celebrated forty shilling freeholders – those having 'free tenement to the value of forty-shillings by the year at least, above all charges'. This qualification had been laid down in the mid-fifteenth century and was aimed specifically at restricting the franchise to the small independent yeoman farmer. Two hundred years later, however, inflation had made the financial requirement virtually meaningless, and in practice it appears that pretty well any cottager claiming free tenement of his patch of land could turn up at the hustings to give his voice if he felt so inclined. Not everyone did, of course. Voter apathy was not unknown, and one disgruntled candidate complained that, as long as men could plough and go to market, they did not seem to care who governed them.

In the towns the situation was rather more complicated. In some places, such as Great Yarmouth, Plymouth and Nottingham, the franchise was restricted to the civic authorities, the mayors, aldermen, bailiffs and other municipal officers, although this form of oligarchic government was often resented and resisted by the townspeople. Elsewhere the right to vote depended on a variety of factors – on being a freeman of the borough, a citizen with freedom to trade; on being a burgage tenant; or on paying scot and lot, that is, the poor and church rates. At the bottom of the pile came the felicitously named potwallopers, whose vote depended on being able to prove that they were self-supporting inhabitants of the borough who possessed a fireplace and boiled a pot there.[3]

When it came to the selection of parliamentary candidates, it was an accepted fact of political life that the executive would attempt to pack the Commons with its own officials and supporters (although it was noticeably unsuccessful in 1640); and in the towns and shires the influence of the local landed interests tended to be paramount. In 1604 the Earl of Suffolk, lord of the town of Saffron Walden, threatened his tenants that he would make the proudest of them repent if they did not give their free consent and voices to his good friend Sir Edward Denny; and in 1625 the aldermen of Thetford told Sir Robert Cotton that 'notwithstanding you are a stranger to us, yet upon the commendation of the right honorable, the Earl of Arundel, our most worthy lord, we have made choice of you to be a burgess of our borough of Thetford . . . Our election being so free and general that you had not one voice against you.'[4]

The system did not always work. Arundel was less successful in October 1640 when he wrote to the mayor and aldermen of King's Lynn desiring to nominate one of the borough's burgesses for a seat in the approaching parliament. The corporation replied that they had unanimously agreed 'to choose noe other burgesses to serve in Parliament, but only such as are resident and inhabitinge within the corporation', and went on to elect two candidates who later opposed the King. The City of York, too, picked two of their own aldermen, refusing to accept the nominations of the Lord Lieutenant.[5]

Those candidates who were obliged to fight for their seats, and it has been estimated that there were at least eighty-five and very likely more contested elections in 1640 ('there is great shuffling for burgesses for the parliament', wrote one observer that October) would have been obliged to undertake the tiresome and expensive business of canvassing the electorate for support – a process which led inevitably to accusations from the opposition that excessive amounts of beef, bag pudding, ale and tobacco were being lavished on the vulgar and factious. In the disputed election at Great Marlow, Peregrine Hoby was said to have 'unduly procured voyces by inviting to alehouses'. Sir Henry Slingsby, the successful candidate at Knaresborough, complained about the 'ill custom at these elections to bestow wine in all the town, which cost me £16 at the least, and many a man a broken pate', and in Hereford one William Morris spent over £150 at the election of the knights of the shire, his principal items being for 'wine and lodging at the Black Swan, the Angel and other taverns'.[6] But although there was no doubt an element of bribery and corruption and a fair amount of rowdyism – near riots in some places – there does not seem to be any real evidence of organised efforts to control the voting. If anything it was lack of organisation which appears to have characterised the elections, while the voters themselves were often characterised by a disappointing degree of volatility, not to say unreliability. This had a good deal to do with practical considerations. A poll might take up to three days to complete and few men could afford to take so much time from their labour, especially if they had to come from any distance. They might well turn up at the alehouse for a few hours to take advantage of the free drink and entertainment, but that was no guarantee they would stay on to be counted.

Four hundred and ninety-three members had been returned to Westminster in the October elections, and the 'restoring' of seven boroughs during the early months of the parliament brought their notional numbers up to just over five hundred. Typically they were country gentlemen of property and status. Most belonged to established county families and many were the sons of titled fathers. The law was also well represented – there were seventy-five professionally trained lawyers among the original members – as were commercial and financial interests. Mercers, clothiers, merchant tailors, general merchants and members of city guilds all sat in the Long Parliament. These categories were not necessarily exclusive. Nearly every landowner possessed at least a working knowledge of the law, acquired by a period spent as a student at one of the Inns of Court. Successful merchants invested their profits in land, while many a landowning family sought to increase its wealth by speculation in a commercial venture. Generally speaking, therefore, it seems that the parliament men could be said to represent a fair cross section of the landed gentry, and of the rising professional and mercantile middle class – men with much to lose, who were coming increasingly to dislike and distrust the King's government.

These, then, were the members of the Commons, generally known as the Lower House, who assembled at Westminster on that November Tuesday. Both Lords and Commons were accustomed to occupy accommodation granted to them by the Crown within the precincts of the ramshackle old Palace. The Lords met in the Parliament or White Chamber, which lay to the south of the Painted Chamber and roughly speaking on the site of the present House of Lords; while up until the Reformation the Commons' usual meeting places were either the Chapter House or the Refectory of Westminster Abbey. It was not until the reign of Edward VI that they were given a permanent home in the former collegiate chapel of St Stephen, whose choir-stall seating arrangements have influenced them ever since.

> The Lower House [wrote John Hooker, member for Exeter] is a place distinct from the others. It is more length than breadth. It is made like a theatre, having four rows of seats, one above another, round about the same. At the higher end, in the middle of the lower row, is a seat made for the Speaker, in which he always sitteth. Before is a table board at which sitteth the Clerk of the House, and thereupon layeth his books and writeth his records. Upon the lower row, on both sides the Speaker, sit such personages as be of the King's Privy Council, or of his chief officers; but as for any other, none claimeth nor can claim any place but sitteth as he cometh . . . Without this House [the main chamber] is one other [a lobby or vestibule] in which the under clerks do sit, as also such as be suitors and attendants to that House.[7]

Space in St Stephen's was strictly limited, so perhaps it was just as well that attendance was distinctly irregular – it has been estimated that the average daily number of members present during 1640–1 was probably below three hundred – and absenteeism was to become an increasingly serious problem. Understandably, gentlemen with estates to manage and merchants and lawyers with businesses and clients to attend to were reluctant to spend too much of their time crammed on to the hard, backless benches in St Stephen's. The House sat for six days a week, nominally from eight o'clock to eleven o'clock in the morning, the hours of the law courts, but as the months passed and the political situation became more threatening, more and more members began to find excuses for staying away. Nevertheless, during the first nine months of its existence, the Long Parliament secured the downfall, trial and execution of the Earl of Strafford, the King's most loyal and able servant; destroyed the prerogative courts of Star Chamber and High Commission; passed the Triennial Act, which ensured the calling of regular parliaments; abolished the controversial Ship Money tax; arrested and impeached the Archbishop of Canterbury and debated a measure – the so-called Root and Branch Bill – to do away with the episcopate. The Commons also ensured their own continued existence by means of an Act declaring that 'this present parliament' could not be dissolved except by its own consent. 'If this happens,' reported the Venetian ambassador, who had been watching the progress of events with increasing horror and incredulity, 'no further authority will remain to the king than to be the minister and executor of the will of his people.'[8]

This rapid and seemingly effortless dismantling of royal authority was due almost entirely to the skilled leadership of one man. John Pym, or King Pym as he came to be known, was now in his late fifties, a man of family and substance owning considerable estates in the West Country. A lucid and cogent speaker, with long experience and unrivalled knowledge of the arcane mysteries of parliamentary procedure, he used all his formidable intelligence and ruthless tenacity of purpose to promote the cause of political and religious reform. But for all that he was no republican, any more than his friends in the House of Lords, men such as the Earls of Bedford, Essex and Warwick, and the Lords Brooke and Saye and Sele. As a politician and parliamentarian, Pym sought for a third way, a

11

compromise, albeit on his own terms, whereby king and parliament could work together in partnership for the common good, but as events unfolded, the prospect of ever reaching such an ideal solution receded further and further into the distance.

By the late summer of 1641 the initial surge of energy and excitement which had combined to sweep away all the accumulated grievances of the past eleven years had begun to subside, and some ominous cracks were appearing in the unity of the Commons. Absenteeism, too, was now reaching alarming proportions. One, probably over-pessimistic, individual estimated that two hundred members, presumably under the impression that their task was done, had not bothered to return at all after the brief autumn recess. But John Pym knew that the task was far from done. He had no illusions as to the King's good faith, being well aware that, given the slightest opportunity, he would not hesitate to withdraw all the concessions extracted from him under duress. It was obvious that there could be no hope of any lasting settlement unless and until the Crown's prerogative powers were permanently curtailed. Oliver Cromwell, the member for Cambridge city, was already suggesting that parliament should appoint the reliable Earl of Essex commander of the southern militia – a first step towards ensuring parliamentary control of all the armed forces, and Pym was anxious to ensure that in future the king should be able to employ only those councillors and ministers as parliament 'may have cause to confide in'.

These were truly revolutionary measures, which would have to be carefully presented to an innately conservative establishment. Pym and his 'middle group' had therefore set to work preparing their so-called Grand Remonstrance for parliamentary approval. Although ostensibly addressed to the King, this was a thinly disguised piece of propaganda directed towards the nation at large and intended to undermine trust in the monarchy by recapitulating in minute detail every financial grievance, every last blunder, abuse and piece of tactlessness, every oppressive and/or illegal act perpetrated by the King's government during the years since his accession. It went on to remind the lieges of the great achievements of the present parliament and hinted at further, far-reaching reforms, especially in the matter of religion.

Since parliament was a council, its business, like that of the king's Privy Council, was not supposed to be made public. Indeed, it had been laid down in Elizabethan times that 'every person of the Parliament ought to keep secret and not to disclose the secrets and things done and spoken in the Parliament House to any manner of person, unless he be one of the same House, upon pain to be sequestered out of the House'.[9] Not surprisingly this was a rule more often broken than observed, and 'parliament matters' were pretty freely discussed in the taverns around Westminster and in the City. All the same, it was not until about 1640 that the speeches of leading members began to be published by order of the House, and some members began to print their own speeches without prior sanction. Finally, in July 1641, came formal recognition that the outside world did perhaps have a right to know something of what was happening inside St Stephen's Chapel, but only, it was insisted, through official channels, and individual members were actively discouraged from taking unauthorised notes of the proceedings. Fortunately some individual members, notably the lawyer and antiquarian Sir Simonds D'Ewes, who kept a journal, and Ralph Verney, who took notes surreptitiously jotted down in pencil on folded sheets of paper, were not discouraged, and largely thanks to them we have some idea of the flavour of the debate on the Grand Remonstrance which took place on 22 November 1641.

It was a lively occasion. A substantial number of members, led by Edward Hyde, Lucius Carey Viscount Falkland, John Colepepper and Sir Edward Dering, felt that the King had been pushed far enough and that no useful purpose could now be served by raking over old grievances. They were also suspicious of Pym's intentions, afraid that he was leading them too far into unknown territory and unimpressed by his assurances that if the King 'will join with us, we shall set him upon as great grounds of honour and greatness in that all the world shall not be able to move him'.[10] Edward Dering protested that when he had first heard of the Remonstrance he had thought that 'like faithful councillors we should hold up a glass to his majesty'. He had not dreamt that 'we should remonstrate downwards, tell stories to the people and talk of the king as of a third person'.[11] Others agreed with him, pointing out that it was unprecedented to be seen to remonstrate to the subjects and not to the king, while Pym retorted that it was time to speak plain English, 'lest posterity shall say that England was lost and no man durst speak truth'.[12] The debate dragged on all afternoon and into the evening, and it was past midnight when the House finally divided. The Grand Remonstrance was passed by a majority of eleven votes – 159 to 148. One disgruntled member likened it to the verdict of a starved jury, but another – it was Oliver Cromwell – was heard to say that, if it had been rejected, 'he would have sold all he had next morning, and never have seen England more'.

Eighty or so weary men stumbled out into the November darkness, but inside the chamber someone moved that the Remonstrance should now be printed. Edward Hyde, John Colepepper and 'divers others' protested, and Geoffrey Palmer, member for Stamford and a strong loyalist, stood up to demand that a protestation should be entered in his name and of those others who had voted against the Remonstrance. Pandemonium then broke out. Someone shouted 'take down the names'. There were cries of 'All! All!' as the King's supporters waved their hats in the air or took their swords out of their belts, holding them by the pommels and banging the scabbarded points on the ground, 'resolved that they would no longer stand to be baffled by such a rabble of inconsiderable persons, set on by a juggling Junto; but oppose their attempts by open Protestation'. In the general, dimly lit confusion, as the protesters were angrily shouted down by the majority, things might well have turned ugly. 'I thought we had all sat in the valley of the shadow of death,' wrote Philip Warwick, the member for New Radnor; 'for wee . . . had catcht at each others locks, and sheathed our swords in each others bowels, had not the sagacity and great calmnes of Mr Hambden by a short speech prevented it'.

This intervention by John Hampden, he of Ship Money fame, urging that nothing further should be done that night, restored some sort of order, and the House finally rose 'just when the clock struck two'.[13]

In fact, the Grand Remonstrance, finally presented to the King at the beginning of December, fell a little flat, as his majesty was able to ignore most of it as unconstitutional. What it did achieve was to draw the party lines in the Commons, effectively disposing of the polite fiction that the Great Council of the Realm was a single united body and any opposition no more than self-interested conspiracy. It was plain enough by this time that the rift between king and parliament had grown too wide to be bridged by peaceful means, and, significantly, that Christmas the opprobrious terms Cavalier and Roundhead were first being publicly bandied about, as City apprentices clashed with the royal officers in the streets of Westminster.

Meanwhile, the King was planning to launch a counter-attack against his tormentors in the Commons and on Monday 3 January ordered the Attorney General to bring charges of high treason against John Pym and his four closest associates, Arthur Haslerig, John Hampden, Denzil Holles and William Strode. The Commons, predictably, refused to surrender them, declaring the accusations to be an infamous libel and breach of privilege, 'thus casting shame on his Majesty's commands'. Next day, Tuesday 4 January, the five accused were present when the House assembled, although 'there was information that they should be taken away by force'. John Pym maintained an efficient intelligence network and at about three o'clock in the afternoon received the expected warning that 'his Majesty was coming from Whitehall to Westminster with a great company of armed men'. This was the signal for the five members to make themselves scarce. Having carefully baited the trap, it was no part of Pym's strategy to run the risk of arrest. There was one awkward moment when William Strode 'being a young man and unmarried could not be persuaded by his friends for a pretty while to go out but said that knowing himself to be innocent he would stay in the house though he sealed his innocency with his blood'.

15

There was no time for argument, and in the end Strode, still protesting, had to be hauled out by his cloak. A barge was waiting at the Watergate, and the Five Members were on their way downstream by the time the King arrived at Westminster Hall.[14]

There followed the famous scene when Charles, leaving his escort of about eighty armed men outside in the lobby, although they could be clearly seen through the open door, 'came upwards, towards the Chair, with his hat off'. Always meticulous in matters of courtesy, he bowed carefully to either side of the House as he went, the members, now also uncovered and standing, bowing in return. 'Mr Speaker, I must for a time make bold with your Chair,' said Charles, as the Speaker made way for him. He did not, in fact, sit down, but stood on the step, gazing out over the parliament men crowded on their benches. 'And after he had looked a great while,' wrote Ralph Verney, 'he told us he would not break our privileges, but treason had no privilege; he came for those five gentlemen, for he expected obedience yesterday, and not an answer. Then he called Mr Pym and Mr Holles by name, but no answer was made. Then he asked the Speaker if they were here, or where they were.' The Speaker, William Lenthall, a hitherto somewhat nondescript individual, fell on his knees and uttered the one sentence which has given him a place in the parliamentary hall of fame. He had neither eyes to see, nor tongue to speak, he told the King, but as this House was pleased to direct him, whose servant he was. 'Well, well, 'tis no matter,' answered Charles. 'I think my eyes are as good as another's.' He continued to look about him 'a pretty while' before finally accepting defeat – 'I see my birds have flown' – and went out of the House, which was by then in great disorder, many of the members crying aloud, 'so as he might hear them, Privilege! Privilege!'[15]

His credibility disastrously compromised by this public humiliation, and faced with violent demonstrations of hostility from the Londoners, the King lost his nerve, and on the night of 10 January 1642 the royal family made a sudden bolt to Hampton Court. Next day, Tuesday, the 11th, John Pym and the others, who had been hiding out in a safe house in the City, returned to

Westminster in triumph. As the cheering procession passed through Whitehall, under the windows of the deserted royal apartments, there were derisive cries of 'Where is the King and his Cavaliers?' Events now took on a momentum of their own. As Bulstrode Whitelocke, the member for Great Marlow, observed in July, 'it is strange to note how we have insensibly slid into this beginning of a civil war by one unexpected accident after another, as waves of the sea which have brought us thus far and we scarce know how . . . What the issue of it will be no man alive can tell. Probably few of us now here may live to see the end of it.'[16]

John Pym did not see the end of it. He died of cancer on 8 December 1643 and was buried in Westminster Abbey in the sorrowful presence of the parliament men he had led for the last three momentous years. Pym remains a shadowy figure inasmuch as he appears to have left no record of any life outside his public service which, according to the sermon preached at his funeral, had been 'his meat and drink, his work, his exercise, his recreation, his pleasure, his ambition, his all'.[17] Nevertheless, by his skilful and determined leadership he had successfully guided the Commons through unknown constitutional territory; had put in place the financial, military and political conditions necessary for winning the war, and, perhaps more than any other man, this unassuming West Country squire had laid the foundations of our modern parliamentary democracy. His work in parliament would now be carried on by men such as Henry Vane, the member for Hull, and the Solicitor General, Oliver St John, member for Totnes, an able lawyer and religious left-winger who was also the cousin, close friend and ally of Colonel, soon to become Lieutenant-General, Oliver Cromwell.

The House of Commons was now something of a shadow of that optimistic body which had assembled at Westminster in November 1640 prepared to redress all grievances and restore the privileges rightfully due to all freeborn Englishmen. The committed royalists, just over two hundred of them, had long since been 'disabled', and although their places would more or less be filled by the so-called recruiter elections of 1645 and 1646, absenteeism was still rife – sittings seldom seem to have exceeded two hundred members.

By the time the 'war without an enemy' approached its end, two distinct factions, conveniently labelled Presbyterian and Independent, were appearing in the ranks of the parliament men. Religious Presbyterians wanted to see bishops replaced by the system favoured by parliament's Scottish allies, where church government was in the hands of elected ministers (presbyters) and lay elders and strict uniformity of belief was enforced on a national basis. Politically they tended to the conservative right. Fearing breakdown of the accepted social order, they would have welcomed a settlement with the king, albeit on their terms. The Independents, on the other hand, believed in the freedom of individual congregations to choose their own form of worship unencumbered by either bishops or presbyters. Politically they tended to be hard-liners, insisting on prosecuting the war to its logical conclusion. Needless to say, it was not as simple or as clear cut as this. Religious Presbyterians were not necessarily political Presbyterians, any more than religious Independents were always political hard-liners. What is clear, though, is that, while the Presbyterians had a majority in Parliament, the Independents were strong in the army, that famous New Model which had risen out of the despondent confusion of the winter of 1644/5 and which was growing steadily more influential.

The royalist surrender at Stow-on-the-Wold in March 1646 marked the end of the fighting, and by the end of the summer even such stubborn royalist strongholds as Pendennis and Raglan Castles were in parliamentary hands, so that by the beginning of the following year parliament, increasingly nervous of the army's size and strength and the popularity of its victorious generals, was considering a programme of cut-price demobilisation. It was proposed to retain the cavalry, consisting of seven thousand horse and dragoons more or less intact, but to discharge some six thousand infantry and send the remainder off to Ireland, where the rebellion which had broken out in 1641 was still simmering, but the Presbyterian majority at Westminster were soon to discover that the formidable instrument it had created was not so easily disposed of. For one thing, soldiers who were owed up to nine months' back pay were not likely to go quietly.

On 25 May the Commons voted to disband the infantry regiments with no more than eight weeks' arrears of pay. A week later, on the evening of 2 June, Cornet George Joyce of General Fairfax's Lifeguard arrived at Holmby House in Northamptonshire, where the King was currently being held, at the head of a force of some five hundred troopers. His purpose, it quickly transpired, was to secure the person of his majesty and remove him from parliament's custody. When Charles asked what commission he had, Joyce, said to have been a tailor in civil life, at first tried to evade the question, but when the King persisted – 'have you nothing in writing from Sir Thomas Fairfax to do what you do?' – he turned in his saddle and silently indicated the businesslike ranks of troopers drawn up behind him. 'It is as fair a commission', said Charles, 'and as well written as I have seen a commission written in my life.'[18]

During the next eighteen months the army became increasingly politicised as its breach with Westminster grew wider, and both sides continued their efforts to find a solution to the seemingly insoluble problem of what to do about the King. It was the army which lost patience first – the brief but bloody Second Civil War in the summer of 1648, precipitated by Charles's underhand dealings with the Scots, proving the final straw. When, in the autumn, the Commons reopened negotiations with their slippery sovereign lord over the so-called Treaty of Newport, the Council of Officers was ready to act. On 20 November it presented the House with a Remonstrance demanding, among other things, 'that the king be brought to justice as the capital cause of all', and 'that a period be set to this parliament, and a provision [made] for new and more equal representatives of the people'. This, says Bulstrode Whitelocke, provoked 'a long and high debate' – some members 'inveighing sharply against the insolency of it', while some 'did not stick to justify it'. Most, though, were nervously silent, 'because it came from the army'.[19] In the end the debate was adjourned without a decision, and it was not until ten days later that the members finally summoned up enough courage to reject the Remonstrance by a majority of 125 votes to 58. By that time, though, it scarcely mattered, for the army was on the move. On 1 December it brought the King from his confinement on the Isle of Wight over to the mainland to begin his last journey to Windsor. At the same time the regiments were marching on the capital. On 2 December Fairfax and his officers took up their quarters in Whitehall, while the other ranks bedded down where they could – the infantry mostly in Whitehall, St James's and York House, the cavalry at the Mews, with some in Durham House and other conveniently empty mansions around Westminster, which was now seething with the military. Although they were under strict orders to 'demean themselves civilly and peaceably', there was no longer any doubt as to who was in charge, and the Londoners nervously awaited developments. 'The town was full of fears of the army,' noted Whitelocke in his *Memorials*.[20]

After a record all-night sitting – a motion calling for candles had been narrowly carried by a majority of 11 – the Commons, or those 214 members who had stayed the course, voted early on the morning of 5 December by a majority of 129 votes to 83 that the King's latest concessions were 'sufficient grounds for settling the peace of the kingdom', although Speaker Lenthall is said to have warned them that they were voting for their own destruction. So indeed it proved, and in a series of meetings held during that day a group of officers, led by Cromwell's son-in-law Henry Ireton, concluded that 'the measures taken by Parliament were contrary to the trust reposed in them', and that it was therefore the duty of the army to put a stop to such proceedings. After all, as they pointed out, they had engaged in the war not simply as mercenaries, 'but out of judgement and conscience, being convinced that the cause in which they were engaged was just, and that the good of the people was involved in it'.[21]

At seven o'clock on the morning of Wednesday 6 December the city-trained bands came marching down Whitehall to take up their usual positions as parliamentary guards, only to find the way barred by a thousand men of the New Model Army. By eight o'clock, as the parliament men began to assemble, Nathaniel Rich's regiment of horse and Thomas Pride's foot had been deployed within the precincts of the Palace of Westminster, while two more regiments patrolled the surrounding streets. Colonel Pride – he is variously described as having been a brewer or brewer's drayman – had drawn up a number of his men in the lobby of the House of Commons and the adjacent Court of Requests, while he himself was stationed on the stairs leading up to the Commons' chamber clutching 'a paper of names' listing all those members considered politically unreliable by the army and who were to be 'excluded or suspended the House'. Unfortunately the colonel knew very few of his prospective victims by sight and had to rely first on a helpful doorkeeper and later on Lord Grey of Groby to tell him who the members were. He then 'seized upon such of them as he was directed by his note, and sent them away with his soldiers, some to the queen's court and court of wards, and other places, by special order from the general and council of the army'.[22]

As the indignant members were hustled away, John Birch, member for Leominster, cried in vain to those who had been allowed to take their places 'whether they would suffer their members to be pulled out thus violently before their faces and yet sit still', while William Prynne, that well-known and irrepressible thorn in the flesh of past authority, protested angrily that 'he was a member of the House and was going into it to discharge his duty'. But when he attempted to 'thrust up a step or two', he was overpowered and dragged away, shouting that 'it was a high breach of the privileges of Parliament' and calling on the bystanders to bear witness that he was being forcibly removed by a superior power.[23]

The protesters and a number of others already marked down as targets by the Army Council were kept under guard in the nearby Queen's Court, and when the surviving members of the Commons despatched the Sergeant-at-Arms to demand their release the officer in charge replied that he could not act without orders. Two of the prisoners fortunate enough to have powerful friends were in fact released after a few hours, but those who enquired by what authority they were detained received the short answer 'by the power of the sword'.[24] It had been, as Bulstrode Whitelocke remarked, 'a sad and most disorderly day's work, and many were troubled, not only for their friends who were thus secured, but what to resolve upon in relation to themselves after this action'.[25]

The power of the sword remained much in evidence over the coming weeks. The imprisoned members were moved first to Mr Duke's alehouse adjoining Westminster Hall. The house, which was 'dark and low' and appropriately nicknamed 'Hell', offered only primitive accommodation, and the prisoners spent a cold and uncomfortable night in two upper rooms with nowhere to sleep other than on benches or the floor, so that they mostly passed the time walking up and down, talking and presumably discussing their predicament, or piously singing psalms. On the following day they were taken, still under guard, to two inns in the Strand, the Swan and the King's Head, where they continued to protest.[26] On 12 December Sir William Waller, himself once a military commander, drew up a formal Protestation from the King's Head, in which he complained 'that the present imprisonment and removal of our persons is a high violation of the rights and privileges of Parliament, and of the fundamental laws of the land, and a higher usurpation and exercise of an arbitrary and unlawful power than hath been heretofore pretended to, or attempted by this, or any King or other power whatsoever within this realm'.[27]

This did the detainees no immediate good, but with certain exceptions they were gradually released during the next few months. It is estimated that just over a hundred MPs, including the forty-five who had been arrested, had been forcibly excluded in what inevitably became known as Pride's Purge, but a considerably larger number had prudently removed themselves voluntarily from the arena. Around a hundred of these later returned, but it was a hard core or 'Rump' of no more than some seventy members who were left to address the momentous business of bringing the King to trial.

The legality of such an unprecedented action was, of course, doubtful to put it mildly, but the Rump got round the problem by declaring on 4 January 1649 'that the people are, under God, the original of all just power: that the House of Commons, being chosen by and representing the people, are the supreme power in the nation: that whatsoever is enacted or declared for law by the Commons in Parliament, hath the force of a law, and the people are concluded thereby, although the consent of King or Peers be not had thereto'.[28]

The purged or Rump Parliament – on paper it numbered 210 members, give or take a few, but average attendance appears never to have been more than 80 – was uniquely remarkable for the revolutionary energy it displayed during the early months of its existence. The execution of the King was followed by the abolition of the monarchy – 'to have the power thereof in any single person is unnecessary, burdensome and dangerous to the liberty, safety and public interests of the people'. The House of Lords (although not the hereditary peerage) was another casualty, being dismissed as 'useless and dangerous'. After all, it had never been commanded 'that the whole nation should be oppressed to maintain the lust and riot of a few drones'.[29] The passing of an Act declaring England to be a Commonwealth and Free State in May 1649 marked the end of this burst of destructive activity, but the Rump itself was to survive for another four years, although the relationship between parliament and the military grew increasingly uneasy.

Matters reached crisis point in the spring of 1653, when the Rump started to debate a bill providing for its own dissolution and for elections to be held on a new county franchise based on a property qualification of £200. Unfortunately a thick fog of mutual distrust and suspicion led the members to fear an army takeover and to try and take precautions against it. For its part the army suspected that the Commons intended merely to hold recruiter or by-elections to fill its vacant seats, while perpetuating the membership of the present House, which was considered both disappointingly conservative and unreliable by the radical sects powerful in the ranks – or, worse, that it might be contemplating some counter-stroke against its military overlords.

Exactly what was in the Bill for a New Representative remains uncertain, since the document was about to disappear in dramatic circumstances. What is certain is that the Lord General Oliver Cromwell feared, or was given to fear, the worst, so that on Wednesday 20 April, hearing that the measure was about to be passed, he made a sudden unheralded appearance in the Commons' chamber informally dressed in black with grey worsted stockings. According to the account of one eye-witness, who was sitting next to the Speaker, the member for Cambridge 'sat down as he used to do in an ordinary place' listening to the debate, but after a while he stood up, put off his hat, and at first spoke in commendation of the parliament 'for their pains and care of the public good'. But afterwards he changed his style, telling the members

of their injustice, delays of justice, self-interest and other faults . . . then he put on his hat, went out of his place, and walked up and down the stage or floor in the midst of the House . . . and chid them soundly, looking sometimes, and pointing particularly upon some persons . . . to whom he gave very sharp language, though he named them not, but by his gestures it was well known that he meant them. After this he said to Colonel Harrison (who was a Member of the House) 'Call them in', then Harrison went out, and presently brought in Lieutenant Colonel Worsley (who commanded the General's own regiment of foot), with five or six files of musketeers, about 20 or 30, with their muskets, then the General, pointing to the Speaker in his chair, said to Harrison, 'Fetch him down'; Harrison went to the Speaker, and spoke to him to come down, but the Speaker sat still and said nothing. 'Take him down', said the General; then Harrison went and pulled the Speaker by the gown, and he came down.[30]

The normally sober Chancery lawyer Bulstrode Whitelocke, who was also present, gives a more colourful account of Cromwell's behaviour. According to Whitelocke, 'he in a furious manner bid the Speaker leave his chair, told the house that they had sat long enough . . . that some of them were whoremasters . . . that others were drunkards, and some corrupt and unjust men, and scandalous to the profession of the Gospel, and that it was not fit they should sit as a Parliament any longer, and desired them to go away'. Whitelocke says that Harrison seized the Speaker by the arm to remove him from his seat and that, when some of the members rose up to answer Cromwell, he would suffer none to speak but himself, 'which he did with so much arrogance in himself and reproach to his fellow members that some of his privadoes were ashamed of it. But he and his officers and party would have it so, and among all the Parliament men, of whom many wore swords and would sometimes brag high, not one man offered to draw his sword against Cromwell, or to make the least resistance against him.'[31]

There then followed the famous episode of the Mace, that sacred symbol of the Speaker's office. According to Whitelocke, the General 'bid one of his soldiers to take away that Fool's Bauble the mace; and stayed himself to see all the members out of the House, himself the last of them, and then caused the doors of the House to be shut up. Thus', wrote Whitelocke sadly, 'was this Great Parliament which had done so great things, wholly at this time routed by those whom they had set up.'[32]

Edmund Ludlow, soldier, republican and member for Wiltshire, who was not himself present in the Commons on this momentous occasion, but heard all about it later from his friend Harrison, says that Cromwell had spoken with 'so much passion and discomposure of mind as if he had been distracted', stamping up and down and kicking the ground with his feet like a madman and shouting 'You are no Parliament! I say you are no Parliament! I will put an end to your sitting!' Finally, having ordered the soldiers to see the House cleared of all the members, the General snatched the dissolution bill out of the hands of the Clerk of the House, 'put it under his cloak, and having commanded the doors to be locked up, went away to Whitehall'.[33] Later that day, one of the members bolder than the rest found the courage to expostulate, saying: 'Sir, we have heard what you did at the House in the morning, and before many hours all England will hear it; but, sir, you are mistaken to think that the Parliament is dissolved; for no power under heaven can dissolve them but themselves; therefore take you notice of that.'[34]

In the world outside surprisingly little notice was taken of the upheavals in the Westminster village. Cromwell himself observed rather contemptuously that 'there was not so much as the barking of a dog, or any general or visible repining at it'. The Venetian ambassador, reporting the dissolution early in May, wrote: 'What has been most remarked is the slight emotion or rather the indifference with which this action was viewed by the populace.' Life, in short, went on, with the City trading, the courts sitting, and lawyers pleading after the usual manner.[35] An anonymous prankster stuck up a placard outside the locked and deserted St Stephen's which read: 'This House is to be lett; now unfurnished,' but perhaps it was Dorothy Osborne, writing from her Bedfordshire home to her lover, the diplomat William Temple, who made the aptest comment:

> Bless me, what will become of us all now? Is not this a strange turn? . . . If Mr Pym were alive again, I wonder what he would think of these proceedings, and whether this would appear as great a breach of the Privilege of Parliament as the demanding of the 5 members? But I shall talk treason by and by if I do not look to myself. [Dorothy's family were royalists.] 'Tis safer talking of the orange flower water you sent me.[36]

Certainly those parliament men who had been present at the demanding of the five members could scarcely have failed to contrast King Charles's careful courtesy in addressing the Speaker with Cromwell's brusque 'fetch him down' and the blatant display of military force to which they had been exposed. It was a different world now, one where the swordsmen would indeed determine the question.

TWO

The Case of the Army

... we were not a mere mercenary Army ... but called forth and conjured by the several declarations of Parliament to the defence of our own and the people's just rights and liberties.

(The Army's Declaration, 14 June 1647)

The Great Civil War ended as untidily as it had begun, leaving the country exhausted, bad-tempered and traumatised by the after-effects of a war in which it is estimated some 62,000 had died as a direct result of the fighting, plus a largely uncountable number of casualties, both military and civilian, from war-related accident and disease. People were also suffering from unprecedentedly high taxation, a series of cold winters and wet summers which had resulted in bad harvests, with consequent spiralling prices and food shortages, and a general breakdown of law and order. Not surprisingly, the Scottish Presbyterian minister Robert Baillie thought the land 'in a most pitiful condition ... Every shire, every city, many families divided in this quarrel, much blood and universal spoil made by both armies.' But if the nation yearned for peace, peace based on a lasting political settlement still looked a long way off. 'I hear all things are in England in a very great confusion still,' wrote a royalist exile in France. 'As the king at first called a Parliament he could not rule, and afterwards the parliament raised an army it could not rule, so the army had made agitators they cannot rule. What will in the end be the conclusion of this, God only knows.'[1]

The army and its future was fast becoming the burning issue of the day. In the spring of 1645 there were between 60,000 and 70,000 men in the pay of the parliament, of whom the so-called

New Model represented roughly a third. Formed from the remnants of the armies of the discredited Earls of Essex and Manchester and Sir William Waller and placed, together with Oliver Cromwell's Ironsides, under the unified command of Sir Thomas Fairfax, the New Model was to win all the decisive victories of 1645–6 but would also prove to be the biggest headache for its political masters.

Hugh Peter, chaplain to the artillery and a supporter of the Independent party, thought the army 'under a blessed conduct, their counsels godly and faithful'. On the other hand, Richard Baxter, also a chaplain, but of a more right-wing Presbyterian persuasion, was shocked by the growth of sectarianism among the ranks. 'I heard the plotting heads very hot upon that which intimated their intention to subvert both church and state,' he wrote. It was true that the majority of the common troopers, and many of the officers, were 'honest, sober, orthodox men, and others tractable, ready to hear the truth, and of upright intentions. But a few proud, self-conceited, hot-headed sectaries had got into the highest places . . . and by their very heat and activity bore down the rest.' The result was that Baxter found

> many honest men of weak judgements and little acquaintance with such matters, had been seduced into a disputing vein, and made it too much of their religion to talk for this opinion and for that. Sometimes for state-democracy, and sometimes for church-democracy; sometimes against forms of prayer, and sometimes against infant baptism; sometimes against set times of prayer, and against the tying of ourselves to any duty before the Spirit move us . . . But their most frequent and vehement disputes were for liberty of conscience, as they called it; that is, that the civil magistrate had nothing to do to determine anything in matters of religion by constraint or restraint, but every man might not only hold, but preach and do, in matters of religion what he pleased.[2]

Fairfax's men, the cavalry at least, were an élite corps, better armed and equipped than was usual – the New Model was the first army to wear the famous red coat – and paid fairly regularly. A dragoon, or mounted infantryman, received 1s 6d a day and a trooper in a cavalry regiment 2s, out of which they had to provide for their own keep and their horses' fodder. Officers were paid between 3s and £1 a day according to rank, although a proportion was always deducted to be paid at some future date, and the cavalry officer got an extra allowance for the upkeep of his horses. Right at the bottom of the pile, even in the New Model, came the private soldier, who got 8d a day, only a penny more than an agricultural worker's wage.

Not surprisingly, the infantrymen were always the hardest to recruit. Burdened with a 60lb load, often hungry – only a basic ration of cheese and hard biscuit could be carried in the field – frequently without shelter and consequently 'driven to lodge on the ground', cold, ragged and wet, not counting the risk of injury or death in action, these men experienced a life that was one of acute discomfort even by contemporary standards. Most were conscripts, drawn from the lowest ranks in society, 'men taken out of prison, tinkers, pedlars and vagrants that have no dwelling' (anyone worth £3 in land or £5 in goods was exempt) with little or no interest in the outcome of the conflict, and, once they had been given their shilling 'pressed money', liable to disappear over the horizon at the first opportunity unless continually watched and guarded. By contrast, the cavalry, with their advantages of better pay and social prestige, were likely to be sons of freeholders, yeomen or craftsmen, men such as Cromwell's famous 'plain russet-coated captain that knows what he fights for, and loves what he knows'. But although there was no doubt a solid core of committed believers in the cause, the New Model also contained quite a few cavaliers deserting from the defeated royalist armies.

Fairfax and his officers did their best to enforce discipline, and seem on the whole to have succeeded fairly well, but an increasingly resentful population could still find plenty to grumble about, and the practice of taking 'free quarter' came near the top of the list of civilian grievances. Since no other accommodation was generally available, innkeepers and private households were obliged to take in garrison troops as well as soldiers on the move and provide them with board and lodging. These uninvited and usually unwelcome guests were in theory supposed to pay for their keep, but since pay day tended to be an irregular occurrence, in practice the host had often to be content with a paper ticket or IOU, signed by the billeting officer, which might not be redeemed for months, if at all, and even then the set rates were far from generous at 4*d* a night for hay and 2*d* for grass pasture, 4*d* for a peck of oats, 8*d* a day for a trooper or horseman and 6*d* for a foot soldier, pioneer or waggoner. If a town or householder tried to resist, cold and hungry troops would not hesitate to take what they needed, and many families suffered the mortification of seeing their precious foodstores raided, their stocks of firewood comandeered and livestock rounded up and slaughtered. It was this sort of thing which had given rise to the activities of the Clubmen, so-called because they were mostly armed only with clubs or farm implements. These were a sort of Home Guard, especially active in the south and west, and formed of local people, exasperated by the depredations of the armies on both sides, who had banded together in an attempt to defend their homes and properties.

There were times when free quarter was not far removed from downright plunder – as late as 1649 Fairfax was getting complaints that some of his 'disorderly soldiers' were breaking into parks, chases and warrens 'and thence stealing all sorts of deer and conies, menacing the death of the keepers, and all such who anyways oppose them'. There was also the general sense of outrage attached to having one's private space violated by disagreeable strangers. 'My house is, and hath been full of soldiers this fortnight,' wrote one disgruntled individual in 1647, 'such uncivil drinkers and thirsty souls that a barrel of good beer trembles at the sight of them, and the whole house is nothing but a rendezvous of tobacco and spitting.'[3]

Even William Prynne, who had lost his ears for sedition under Charles I, suffered a frightening invasion by parliamentary troops, who roughed up his servants, broke his crockery, stole his money and, so Prynne remembered, 'roared, stamped, beat the tables with their swords and muskets like so many bedlams, swearing, cursing, blaspheming at every word'. And there were other nuisances associated with the rude, licentious and under-employed soldiery who were only too apt to leave behind them 'not a few great bellies and bastards on the inhabitants' and countries' charge'.[4]

But if the civilians had their genuine fears and grievances, so too did the military, and by the end of March 1647 a petition addressed to General Fairfax was circulating among the ranks. This was a moderate enough document, setting out the soldiers' demands – that 'a full and sufficient provision may be made by Ordinance of Parliament' indemnifying them from prosecution for any acts committed in time of war; that all their arrears of pay should be audited and settled before demobilisation; that there should be no compulsion on those who had volunteered for the army to serve outside the kingdom (that is, in Ireland), and no conscription of the cavalry to serve on foot; that such provision 'as may be agreeable to justice and equity' should be made for maimed ex-servicemen and the wives and children of the slain and, finally, that until disbandment the army should continue to be regularly paid 'so we may not for necessary food be beholden to the Parliament's Enemies, burthensome to their friends, or oppressive to the Country, whose preservation we have always endeavoured, and in whose happiness we should still rejoice'.[5]

Unfortunately, when news of the petition reached parliament, the Commons, or at least the Presbyterian majority, took serious umbrage and in an angry debate on the army on 29 March, which lasted very late into the night, they passed the so-called Declaration of Dislike (Denzil Holles, a leader of the Presbyterian party, is said to have scribbled it down on the spot) warning that all those who had any hand in it were to be looked upon 'as Enemies of the State and disturbers of the public peace', an insult which the army neither forgave nor forgot. Plans were now being made at Westminster for disbanding six cavalry regiments and all the foot unless their members agreed to go to Ireland, and even if they did, there was no guarantee that they would be allowed to stay together under their old commanders. 'You may see by this how the tyde turnes', wrote an anonymous correspondent in London to a friend in the army, 'and how soone all the soe lately much admired services of your Army are forgotten.'[6]

By this time feeling in the army was running high and the rank and file had begun to elect their own representatives, who became known as the Agitators or Agents, and in a paper entitled the *Apologie of the Common Souldiers of Sir Thomas Fairfaxes Army* they protested angrily that the Irish expedition was nothing more than a plot intended to 'ruine and break this Army in pieces' and 'a mere cloake for some who have lately tasted of Soveraignty, and being lifted beyond their ordinary Spheare of servants, seek to become Masters, and degenerate into Tyrants'.[7] In a second Apology, the private soldiers called on their officers to stand by them. 'We have been quiet and peaceable in obeying all orders and commands,' they declared, 'yet now we have just cause to tell you, if we be not relieved in these our grievances, we shall be forced to that, which we pray God to divert, and keep your and our hearts upright.'[8]

Faced with growing unrest among the military and its stubborn reluctance to volunteer for Ireland, at the end of May parliament, or, more accurately, the executive committee which met at Derby House, put together a conciliatory package which included an Indemnity Ordinance and went some way towards meeting the soldiers' other grievances. But the Declaration of Dislike was not withdrawn, nor were the plans for disbanding the army with no more than eight weeks' arrears of pay. It was at this point that Cornet Joyce made his celebrated descent on Holmby House, Thomas Fairfax and Oliver Cromwell came out openly on the side of the army, and the regiments began to muster in a general rendezvous on Kentford Heath near Newmarket.

On 5 June a document entitled *A Solemn Engagement of the Army*, probably the work of Henry Ireton, was promulgated, making it clear that, until its various demands had been fully satisfied, the New Model would

> not willingly disband nor divide, nor suffer ourselves to be disbanded or divided. And whereas we find many strange things suggested or suspected to our great prejudice, concerning dangerous principles, interests and designs in this Army (as to the over-throw of magistracy, the suppression or hindering of Presbytery, the establishment of Independent government, or upholding of a general licentiousness in religion under pretence of liberty of conscience, and many such things), we shall very shortly tender to the Parliament a vindication of the Army from all such scandals, to clear our principles in relation thereunto.[9]

In another statement, a *Representation* or *Declaration*, dated 14 June and also most likely Ireton's work, they went further, hoping that it would not seem strange or unseasonable to rational and honest men if, before disbanding, the soldiers should demand a say in the settling of their own and the kingdom's satisfaction and future security. 'Especially considering that we were not a mere mercenary army, hired to serve any arbitary power of a state, but called forth and conjured by the several declarations of Parliament to the defence of our own and the people's just rights and liberties.' The soldiers then proceeded to demand that parliament should be purged of those members who, for their delinquency, corruption or abuse of the state ought not to be there – especially, of course, those who had been prominent 'in the late unjust and high proceedings against the Army'. As well as this, the army wanted a fixed duration for all future parliaments, so that 'they shall not have the temptation or advantage of an unlimited power fixed in them during their own pleasure'; a secure provision for the continuance of future parliaments and a redistribution of seats in the Commons in order 'to render the Parliament a more equal representative of the whole'. They desired that the right and freedom of the people to petition parliament for the redress of grievances should be assured and some liberty granted to tender nonconformist consciences, always provided, of course, that such awkward individuals lived 'soberly, honestly, inoffensively towards others, and peacefully and faithfully towards the state'.[10]

By this time the senior officers were also taking steps to organise themselves and announced the formation of a new body, which came to be known as the General Council of the Army. This would consist of two commissioned officers and two soldiers elected by each regiment, plus the general officers, who were to meet together in council when summoned by the commander-in-chief. By this time, too, the army was on the move towards the capital. 'Our chief news here is of your Army', wrote a correspondent from London on 13 June, 'and I can assure you we have twenty stories in a day and scarce ever a true one; but your coming near London I promise you put the Parliament and City into a shrewd fright . . . it was much urged to raise forces against you, nay and they would have done it if they could have found any way how.'[11]

Parliament's alarm was understandable, for they were being confronted by an entirely new phenomenon – a military force with a clearly defined political programme and the will and the power to put its ideas into practice. The Commons had already made some further concessions, agreeing that full arrears would be paid on demobilisation. The infamous Declaration of Dislike had also been struck from the record, 'and a supplementary Ordinance of Indemnity covering all offences committed by soldiers while in the service of parliament' had been passed into law.

Unfortunately, like most concessions made under duress, these came too late to have the desired effect. The army now wanted blood and had drawn up formal articles of impeachment against Denzil Holles and ten other MPs whom they regarded as being leaders of the Presbyterian, anti-Independent faction in the Commons. By the end of June, with the New Model hovering menacingly no more than fifteen miles away and having failed to raise support in the City – the militia had refused to budge, 'not 10 men of some companies appeared' – Holles and the others found it prudent to leave town. Fairfax responded by withdrawing as far as Reading, although his friends in the capital warned him that this would be taken for weakness in some quarters and his more radical officers continued to press for an occupation, pointing out that 'the Army's removal to this distance from London hath given liberty and opportunity to an adverse party in that City to scandalise our persons and actions by pamphlets and otherwise, whereby they prejudice the spirits of many against us'.[12]

Disquiet among the regimental Agitators and their 'deep sense of the sad and heavy pressures, great distractions, continual fears, and eminent dangers under which this poor and bleeding Kingdom groans' increased steadily throughout the summer, as did a suspicion that the army commanders, or 'Grandees' as they became known, were growing altogether too friendly with the King, now comfortably ensconced at Hampton Court. The Grandees, notably the Lieutenant General Oliver Cromwell, were still hoping for a negotiated settlement with both king and parliament, but an attempted Presbyterian counter-revolutionary coup and an associated outbreak of mob violence forced the issue and by the first week of August the army had moved in and for the first time occupied the capital. 'After a long threatened storm to engage us in a new and bloody war . . . God hath so blest our endeavours in the preventing so wicked a design as to bring the wicked designers and contrivers upon their knees,' declared a triumphant newsletter from the army. 'In brief we may have what we desire . . . and be assured the crushing of this horrid design in the egg will have no little influence upon any part of the Kingdom where it was intended to have correspondence.'[13] Certainly the triumph of the military seemed complete, and their advance from Hounslow Heath, where the disciplined ranks could be seen to stretch for nearly a mile and a half, to Westminster and on through the City more resembled a victory parade than the occupation of defeated territory and Fairfax assured the Londoners that he and his men wished for nothing but 'the quiet and happy settlement of a firm and lasting peace'.

But peace was a long way off, and now cracks were appearing in the unity of the New Model, as the radical element within its ranks gathered strength and support from the London radicals, or Levellers, whose notions of constitutional reform went considerably further than anything the army commanders would be prepared to consider. They had not yet given up hope of persuading the King to accept terms offered to him that summer, which would have provided for biennial parliaments with parliamentary control of the armed forces and appointment of the great officers of state for the next ten years, a rational reform of the franchise, and a religious settlement which would allow all Protestants freedom to worship as they chose. In return the King and his family would be restored 'to a condition of safety, honour and freedom in this nation'. There would also be an Act of Oblivion extending to all royalists (with certain exceptions) and restoring to them the rights and privileges belonging to other subjects.[14]

These terms, set out in a document known as the *Heads of Proposals*, were surprisingly generous in the circumstances. They were too generous for the radical tendency who scented betrayal on the air and were openly accusing the Grandees of making an idol of the King. 'Why permit they so many of his deceitful clergy to continue about him?' demanded a pamphlet addressed to all the 'Souldiers of the Army' by the Free People of England. 'Why do themselves kneele and kisse and fawne upon him? Why have they received favours from him, and sent their wives and daughters to visit him, or to kiss his hand, or to be kissed of him? Oh shame of men! Oh sin against God!'[15]

The General Council of the Army was said to have become overgrown with Colonels, Lieutenant Colonels and Majors, but the officers most bitterly attacked in the pamphlet war were Cromwell and Henry Ireton.

Abroad they hold forth the white flag of accommodation and satisfaction, and of minding the same thing which ye mind, and to be flesh of your flesh and bone of your bone, and to invite you to their headquarters, where they hope either to work upon you as they have most lamentably done upon others, even to betray your trust, confound both your understandings and counsels, corrupt your judgements, and blast your actions . . . If ye do adventure to go thither, beware that ye be not frighted by the word *anarchy*, unto a love of *monarchy*, which is but the gilded name for *tyranny*; for anarchy had never been so much as once mentioned amongst you had it not been for that wicked end.

It was an old threadbare trick, the author – believed to be the Leveller and New Model veteran John Wildman – went on, of all those who, whenever the people insisted for their just freedoms, would immediately respond with accusations that 'Ye are for anarchy. Ye are against all government. Ye are sectaries, seditious persons, troublers both of church and state, and so not worthy to live in a commonwealth . . . Away with all such from Parliament-doors and Headquarters!'[16]

Wildman was also a co-author of *The Case of the Army Truly Stated*, which was presented to Fairfax on 18 October and complained bitterly of the delay in redressing the soldiers' grievances. 'We not only apprehend nothing to have been done effectually, either for the Army or the poor oppressed people of the nation, but we also conceive that there is little probability of any good without some more speedy and vigorous actings.' There was still 'no determinate period of time set' when parliament was to be dissolved and the House was still not purged of its delinquent members; nor had the honour of parliament been vindicated 'from the most horrid injustice of that declaration against the Army for petitioning'. The people had not yet been satisfied 'in point of accounts' for the vast sums of money disbursed by them. None of the public burdens or oppressions by arbitrary committees, injustice in the law, tithes, monopolies and restraint of free trade, inequalities of assessments or burdensome oaths had been removed or lightened. The rights of the people in their parliaments were not cleared and declared. 'So that we apprehend our own and the people's case, little (if in any measure) better since the Army last hazarded themselves for their own and the people's rights and freedoms.' The rights and liberties of the people ought to be secured before the king's business was determined, but now it seemed that their grievances 'are propounded to be considered after the restoring him to the regal power . . . and in like manner the security for the Army's arrears is proposed to be considered after the business of the king be determined'. Most important of all, it must be 'positively and resolvedly insisted upon' that a new parliament should meet once in every two years, 'that all the free-born at the age of twenty-one years and upwards be the electors' and that it 'may not be adjournable and dissolvable by the king, or any other except themselves'.[17] A week later came *The Agreement of the People* – restating the Levellers' manifesto for constitutional reform and demanding among other things a more equitable distribution of parliamentary seats, the sovereignty of the people exercised only by the representatives chosen by them, that is to say the House of Commons, freedom of conscience in religion, an end to conscription for military service and the equality of all citizens before the law.

The Army Council met on 28 October 1647 in what became the first of the famous Putney Debates, so called because they mostly took place in St Mary's church in what was then a rural village about four miles upstream from Westminster, and were attended both by the senior officers and by the Agitators with two of their civilian advisers, John Wildman and Maximilian Petty. Fairfax being absent with a convenient illness, the Lieutenant General Cromwell took the chair, announcing that, since the meeting was for public business, those who had anything to say concerning it might have liberty to speak.

Trooper Edward Sexby, one of the original Agitators, promptly took up the invitation, declaring that 'the cause of our misery [is] upon two things. We sought to satisfy all men . . . but in going [about] to do it we have dissatisfied all men. We have labour'd to please a King, and I think, except we go about to cut all our throats, we shall not please him; and we have gone to support an house which will prove rotten studs, I mean the Parliament which consists of a Company of rotten Members.' And he went on to inform both Cromwell and the Commissary General Ireton that their credits and reputation had been 'much blasted upon these two considerations . . . I desire that you will consider those things that shall be offer'd to you', he went on; 'and, if you see any thing of reason, you will join with us that the Kingdom may be eas'd, and our fellow soldiers may be quieted in spirit. These things I have represented as my thoughts. I desire your pardon.'[18]

The Debates, which lasted for some ten days, examined in detail the various propositions and demands set out in *The Case of the Army* and *The Agreement of the People*, but they are best remembered for the celebrated exchange which took place on Friday 29 October between Colonel Thomas Rainborough and Henry Ireton on the subject of manhood suffrage. 'I think', said Rainborough, 'that the poorest he that is in England hath a life to live as the greatest he; and therefore truly, Sir, I think it's clear, that every man that is to live under a Government ought first by his own consent to put himself under that Government.'

This was too much for Ireton. 'Give me leave to tell you', he retorted, 'that if you make this the rule I think you must fly for refuge to an absolute natural Right, and you must deny all civil Right . . . For my part I think it is no right at all. I think that no person hath a right to an interest or share in the disposing or determining of the affairs of the Kingdom . . . that hath not a permanent fixed interest in this Kingdom.'[19]

The argument raged to and fro, Ireton sticking to the absolute need of a property qualification for voting. It was 'the most fundamental Constitution of this Kingdom, which if you do not allow, you allow none at all'. Take that away and you would 'plainly go to take away all property and interest that any man hath, either in land by inheritance, or in estate by possession, or any thing else'. Rainborough was not impressed. He had heard nothing at all that could convince him why any man born in England ought not to have his voice in the election of burgesses and could find nothing in the law of God which said 'that a Lord shall choose twenty Burgesses and a Gentleman but two, or a poor man shall choose none'. And what about all those men who had fought for the parliament and in their zeal and affection for the cause had spent their estates? Was such a man now to be told that because he was no longer worth 40s a year he had no interest to entitle him to vote? Rainborough, in short, refused to budge from his stated belief that 'every man born in England cannot, ought not, neither by the law of God nor the law of nature, to be exempted from the choice of those who are to make laws for him to live under, and for him, for aught I know, to lose his life under'. Ireton retorted by raising the bogey of communism. 'Let every man consider with himself that he do not go that way to take away all property . . . which if you take away, you take away all,' and then, by implication, anarchy would rule.[20]

The civilians then chipped in, Maximilian Petty to point out the obvious anomaly of the forty-shilling freehold as a qualification to vote, for, after all, a man might have a lease worth £100 a year, or a lease for three lives and have no voice; while John Wildman, exasperated by all the pettifogging arguments about property and precedents, tried to bring the debate back to what he considered the essential point at issue, that 'every person in England hath as clear a right to elect his representative as the greatest person in England', and that no one could justly be bound by law who had not given his consent that such persons should make laws for him.[21]

Wildman spoke passionately of the fight for freedom, but it was left to Trooper Sexby to speak up for those who had actually done the business in the blood and spilled guts of the battlefield, lost limbs themselves or seen their comrades die messily and painfully in front of them. 'There are many thousands of us soldiers that have ventur'd our lives,' he said; 'we have had little propriety in the Kingdom as to our estates, yet we have had a birthright. But it seems now except a man hath a fix't estate in this Kingdom, he hath no right in this Kingdom. I wonder we were so much deceived . . . I shall tell you in a word my resolution. I am resolved to give up my birthright to none.' He was rewarded with a sharp set-down from the Commissary General. 'For my part,' declared the man of property Henry Ireton, 'rather than I will make a disturbance to a good Constitution of a Kingdom wherein I may live in godliness, and honesty, and peace and quietness, I will part with a great deal of my birthright.' Colonel Rainborough came valiantly to Sexby's support, remarking sardonically that he could see it was impossible to have liberty unless all property was taken away. If that were laid down for a rule, then it must be so. 'But', he went on, 'I would fain know what the soldier hath fought for all this while? He hath fought to enslave himself, to give power to men of riches, men of estates . . . We do find in all presses that go forth none must be pressed [conscripted] that are freehold men. When these gentlemen fall out among themselves they shall press the poor scrubs to come and kill [one another for] them.'[22]

A compromise of sorts was finally arrived at. Even the most vociferous advocates of universal manhood suffrage (no mention, naturally, of womanhood) agreed that exceptions should be made of servants, apprentices living in their masters' houses and beggars, while defenders of the status quo were prepared reluctantly to recommend giving the vote to all those who had fought for parliament prior to the decisive battle of Naseby or who had voluntarily contributed to the war effort. By the time the meeting at Putney broke up at the beginning of November, it had also been recommended that future parliaments should be elected biennially and sit for six months. In the intervals the country would be governed by a council of state. The whole vexed question of the future of the monarchy had been carefully skated over, leaving a tacit assumption that the king would remain on his throne, albeit with his powers drastically reduced. Unsurprisingly this did not satisfy the Agitators, and Trooper Sexby was soon on his feet again, quoting fluently from the Scriptures.

We find in the word of God 'I would heal Babylon, but she would not be healed'. I think that we have gone about to heal Babylon when she would not. We have gone about to wash a Blackamoor, to wash him white, which he will not. I think we are going about to set up a power which God will destroy. We are going about to set up the power of Kings, some part of it, which God will destroy; and which will be but as a burdensome stone that whosoever shall fall upon it; it will destroy him.[23]

The Agitators were now calling for another general rendezvous of the whole army at which they were hoping to get their own original demands accepted by acclamation and then to impose it on parliament. But the generals, dismayed by the spread of dangerous democratic notions and unrest among the ranks, had had enough, and on 8 November Cromwell proposed and carried a motion that the Council's meetings should be suspended and the representative officers and Agitators be sent back to their regiments. It was high time, he felt for the army 'to conform to those things that are within their sphere'. There had been much that was useful in *The Case of the Army Truly Stated* and 'to be condescended to', but he was not inclined to go any further, believing that the demand for universal suffrage would 'tend very much to anarchy'. The military must now be content with requiring that parliament should be properly constituted, and leave it to parliament to decide what was fit for the kingdom.[24]

Of course this was not the end of the matter, and the Levellers continued to spread their word within the army, scattering a snowstorm of inflammatory pamphlets warning the men not to trust their officers who had dissolved the Council rather than allow any more free debate and who were now attempting to frighten them with warnings about distempers and mutinies. There were some 'distempers' that autumn, and some angry protest meetings were convened in a couple of City taverns to muster civilian support for the army radicals. But in the end the only potentially serious trouble took place on 15 November at Corkbush Field outside Ware in Hertfordshire, when two disaffected regiments paraded, uninvited, with copies of *The Agreement of the People* stuck in their hats and the slogan 'England's Freedom and Soldiers' Rights' written on the outside. The mutiny, if such it was, was quickly suppressed, and the army leaders experienced no further trouble in getting an agreement from the other officers to the conclusions reached by the General Council at Putney, Fairfax having declared that he would resign his command if discipline were not restored.

The beginning of 1648 finally saw a drastic reduction of army numbers. No fewer than twenty thousand men were demobilised in January and February, mostly from the provincial forces and garrisons, but the generals took the opportunity of weeding out as many dissident elements as possible, leaving the New Model reduced in strength but with the bulk of its original regiments intact. This restructured, less costly and hopefully more politically reliable force was soon to be employed in fighting the Second Civil War, but by the early spring of 1649 trouble was again spreading through the ranks.

In the months leading up to Pride's Purge the army's hostility had been principally directed against the corrupt and delinquent parliament, but now that its officers could be seen enjoying some of the fruits of political power, rank and file resentment began to be turned in their direction. In March eight troopers from different regiments registered a protest against new rules laid down by the Council of Officers forbidding private meetings and unauthorised petitions to parliament. They denounced the newly constituted Council of State and asserted the soldiers' democratic right to bring their grievances before parliament without their officers' permission. After all, the strength of the officer depended on the arm of the soldier and was it not 'the soldier that endureth the heat and burden of the day, and performeth that work whereof the officers beareth the glory and the name'?

The Council of Officers, which had now replaced the old General Council of the Army (the elected regimental representatives no longer being admitted), was not impressed by this blatant challenge to its authority. The troopers were court martialled and five of them sentenced to ride the wooden horse. The 'horse' in question consisted of a couple of boards nailed together so as to form a sharp ridge with four posts forming the legs. Sometimes this was mounted on a movable stand and provided with a rough representation of a head and tail. The culprit was forced to sit on the ridge for up to an hour facing the 'tail', with his hands tied and with one, two or three muskets tied to his legs. On this occasion the troopers were also ordered to have their swords broken over their heads and to be cashiered from the army.[25]

The officers suspected rightly that 'divers persons not of the army' – that is, the Levellers – were endeavouring to seduce and divide the soldiers, and on 28 March four leaders of the movement, John Lilburne, William Walwyn, Richard Overton and Thomas Prince, were committed to the Tower on charges of treason. Not that this seems to have cramped their style unduly, and throughout April Lilburne and Overton in particular continued to do their best to persuade the army to mutiny and bring about a Leveller takeover. But although unrest was widespread and growing alarmingly throughout the ranks, the predominant grievances remained the old ones: fear of being forced to enlist for Ireland – always regarded as the soldier's graveyard – and arrears of pay, about which very little had even now been done. Significantly, disaffection was almost entirely confined to the cavalry regiments, for rising prices meant that mounted troops, with their additional expenses, were now finding themselves out of pocket even when regularly paid.

Real trouble first erupted in London on 24 April, when thirty men in Colonel Whalley's regiment seized their colours and refused to leave their quarters until they had received the fortnight's pay they claimed was due to them. A sympathetic crowd gathered, and the situation was looking dangerous when Fairfax and Cromwell appeared on the scene, 'furiously breathing forth nothing but death to them all' and refusing to hear their grievances until they had been carried to Whitehall under guard. On 26 April fifteen culprits were tried by court martial and six, regarded as ringleaders, were sentenced to death. In the end, however, five were pardoned and only one singled out to serve as an example to the others. This unfortunate, 23-year-old Trooper Roger Lockyer, faced a firing squad of six musketeers in St Paul's churchyard and quickly became a popular martyr. His funeral procession was followed by thousands of his fellow Londoners, so that it was said he had more mourners than the late king.[26]

There were other short-lived, sporadic outbreaks of disobedience at Banbury and Northampton, but the best-known and probably most serious episode came to a climax at the Oxfordshire village of Burford on 15 May. When four troops of Scrope's regiment of horse, stationed at Salisbury, were informed that they had been chosen to go to Ireland, they told their officers that they chose not to go and, taking their regimental colours, marched off to rendezvous with men of Ireton's regiment and then headed north, hoping to join up with troops from Harrison's horse stationed in Buckinghamshire. Their journey took them through the little market towns of Marlborough, Wantage, Bampton and Faringdon, finally reaching Burford on the evening of 14 May. It was here, after midnight, that Fairfax and Cromwell caught up with them and immediately went in to the attack. The mutineers, taken by surprise and roused from sleep, put up very little resistance, and after a brief but desperate little skirmish at the Crown Inn, where Sheep Street joins the High Street in the centre of the town, it was all over. Of the 900 or so mutineers, 340 were taken prisoner and locked up in the parish church, the rest escaping on foot in the darkness and general confusion.

The following day saw some affecting scenes of tearful contrition as the prisoners melted 'into a noble and Christian sorrow' and begged Fairfax to extend the bowels of his tender compassion towards them. This, of course, was just what Fairfax and Cromwell wanted to hear, and it was agreed to limit extreme retribution to four of the ringleaders – two cornets and two corporals – though one of them, Cornet Denne, was reprieved at the last minute. The others were shot against the west wall of the churchyard, their comrades having been drawn up on the leads of the church to witness the execution. According to the royalist newsletter *Mercurius Pragmaticus*, the other three, whose names were Thompson, Church and Perkins, carried the business 'most gallantly, and looking death in the face with a world of Magnanimity; which Saint-like dispatch being over, King Oliver went into the Church and sang a Psalm of mercy to their fellows'.

Burford effectively marked the end of the army Leveller alliance. As *Mercurius Pragmaticus* remarked, 'the Proverb saith, A Dog hath his day, and so hath the Independent; for Brother-Leveller hath had his good-night as well as Sir John Presbyter, and must be forced, like him, to live upon the mercy of the ruling faction'.[27] Certainly the Leveller defeat came as an immense relief to the army leaders, for it meant that there would be no further resurgence of unwelcome democratic notions in the ranks. The prompt action taken by both Fairfax and Cromwell in suppressing the Burford mutiny had had a good deal to do with this, but so had Fairfax's renewed promises that no one would be forced to serve in Ireland and that the soldiers' grievances would be redressed – indeed parliament was working to implement the requirements of *The Agreement of the People*. Justices of the Peace had been charged with doling out relief to maimed veterans, war widows and orphans, and, perhaps most important from the soldiers' point of view, arrangements were finally being made to secure the payment of their arrears against the value of Crown lands and the confiscated estates of defeated royalists.

Cromwell was now at last free to concentrate on Ireland, and for the next three years the army was too busy defeating the Irish, the Scots and, on 2 September 1651, Charles II and his ragbag of Scots and English at the 'crowning mercy' of Worcester, to have much time and energy left over for playing politics. All the same, it was undoubtedly the army, the 'power of the sword', which from the 1645–6 campaigns onwards had provided driving force behind the revolutionary movement, just as it was the army which in the end, ironically enough, was to destroy it when, on 1 January 1660, George Monck led his Coldstreamers across the Tweed on the first stage of his long march to the capital to restore the civil power in the shape of the purged parliament.

THREE

Levellers, Diggers and Ranters

> . . . the first time that ever the Church of England was reduced to
> a Chamber and a Conventicle . . . The parish churches filled with
> sectaries of all sorts, Blasphemous & Ignorant Mechanics
> usurping the Pulpits everywhere.
>
> (John Evelyn, *Diary*, 3 August 1656)

After the debacle at Burford the Leveller movement lost its
influence in the army and began to lose its momentum as a
political force. John Lilburne was already deeply disillusioned.
'We were before ruled by King, Lords and Commons,' he wrote
in March 1649; 'now by a General, a Court Martial, and House
of Commons: and we pray you what is the difference?'[1] Free-
Born John was not, however, ready to give up the fight and on
26 February had presented the Commons with a petition bearing
the provocative title of *England's New Chains Discovered*.
'Where is that liberty so much pretended, so deerly purchased?'
it enquired.

> If we look upon what this House hath done since it voted itself
> the Supreme Authority and dis-burthened themselves of the power
> of the Lords. First we find a high Court of Justice erected, for
> Tryal of Criminal causes; whereby that great and strong hold of
> our preservation, the way of tryal by 12 sworn men of the
> neighbourhood is infringed . . . Then the stopping of our mouths
> from Printing is carefully provided for . . . in searching, fining,
> imprisoning, and other waies corporally punishing all that any
> waies be guilty of unlicensed Printing.

The list of complaints continued: new and increased fees imposed in lawsuits, an Act for the impressing of seamen, a member of parliament censured for 'declaring his judgement in a point of Religion'. And lastly:

> for compleating this new kind of liberty, a Councel of State is hastily erected for Guardians thereof, who to that end are possessed with power to order and dispose all the forces appertaining to England by Sea or Land, to dispose of the publike Treasure, to command any person whatsoever before them, to give oath for the discovering of Truth, to imprison any that shall disobey their commands, and such as they shall judge contumatious. What now is become of that liberty that no man's person shall be attached or imprisoned, or otherwise dis-eased of his Free-hold . . . but by lawful judgement of his equals?[2]

A month later Lilburne was back with *England's New Chains*, part II.

> If our hearts were not over-charged with the sense of the present miseries and approaching dangers of the Nation, your small regard to our late serious Apprehensions would have kept us silent; but the misery, danger and bondage threatened is so great, imminent and apparent, that whilst we have breath, and are not violently restrained, we cannot but speak, and even cry aloud, until you hear us, or God be pleased otherwaies to relieve us.[3]

As *New Chains*, part II, contained a fierce and comprehensive attack on the army Grandees, it was perhaps not surprising that its publication resulted in the arrest, in a series of dawn raids, of Lilburne, Thomas Prince, William Walwyn and Richard Overton; or that, after their preliminary examination, Oliver Cromwell was heard to thump his fist on the table and tell the President of the Council that he had no other way to deal with them, but to break them in pieces, for 'if you do not break them, they will break you!'

In spite of a determined effort to suppress it, *England's New Chains* circulated widely in the capital and surrounding districts and provoked a flood of petitions for the prisoners' release, from their supporters. Many of these were women and five hundred 'lusty lasses of the levelling party' or 'the bonny Besses in the sea-green dresses' – green being the colour associated with the Levellers – laid siege to the House of Commons for three days. On the second day the Sergeant-at-Arms was sent out to tell them that 'the Matter they petitioned about was of a higher concernment than they understood . . . and therefore desired them to go home, and look after their own business, and meddle with their huswifery'. This provoked a minor riot, as the women's tongues 'pelted hail-shot against the Members as they passed to and fro, whilst the Souldiers threw in squibs under their Coats'. One of the members was mobbed by angry women, who 'rounded him in a Ring' and refused to let him go until he swore he was for the liberties of the people; another, who rashly suggested they should stay at home and wash dishes, was told they scarcely had any dishes left, and were hardly sure of keeping those they had. Someone else remarked that it was strange for women to petition. 'It was strange that you cut off the king's head', came the reply, 'yet I suppose you will justify it.' Eventually, on 25 April, twenty ladies of the 'sea-green order' were admitted to the lobby with their petition, which is said to have borne ten thousand signatures. It was not a very edifying occasion, the soldiers on guard throwing squibs and cocking their pistols in a threatening manner as they pushed and jostled the petitioners down the stairs.[4]

But the ladies of the sea-green order were not easily discouraged, and on 5 May they published a dignified reply to the Commons, which had treated them so rudely.

Since we are assured of our creation in the image of God, and of an interest in Christ equal unto men . . . we cannot but wonder and grieve that we should appear so despicable in your eyes as to be thought unworthy to petition or represent our grievances to this honourable House. Have we not an equal interest with the men of this nation in those liberties and securities contained in the Petition of Right, and other the good laws of the land? Are any of our lives, limbs, liberties or goods to be taken from us more than from men, but by due process of law and conviction of twelve sworn men of the neighbourhood? And can you imagine us to be so sottish and stupid as not to perceive, or not to be sensible when daily those strong defences of our peace and welfare are broken down and trod underfoot by force and arbitrary power? Would you have us keep at home in our houses, when men of such faithfulness and integrity as the four prisoners, our friends, in the Tower, are fetched out of their beds and forced from their houses by soldiers, to the affrighting and undoing of themselves, their wives, children and families? . . . Let it be accounted folly, presumption, madness, or whatsoever in us, whilst we have life and breath we will never leave them nor forsake them . . . And therefore again we entreat you to review our last petition in behalf of our friends above mentioned, and not to slight the things therein contained because they are presented unto you by the weak hand of women, it being a usual thing with God, by weak means to work mighty effects.[5]

The Levellers' faith in the jury system was to be vindicated on this occasion, for when John Lilburne came to trial in September 1649 'twelve sworn men of the neighbourhood' acquitted him of all the charges against him – a verdict which was greeted with such a shout of joy from the crowded court 'as is believed was never heard in Guildhall'. But while Free-Born John himself remained a popular hero – bonfires were lit and medals struck to celebrate his acquittal, and when he and the others were eventually released on 8 November a great feast was held at the King's Head tavern in Fish Street – the Levellers were now definitely in decline and John, with a wife and young family to support, took to the trade of soap-boiling. 'The wild levelling representative is at an end since John Lilburne turned off the trade of state-mending to take up that of soap-boiling,' reported the news-sheet *Mercurius Pragmaticus*. Not quite at an end, for controversy, persecution, exile and captivity were to follow him to his death in 1657.

The Levellers had been essentially an urban movement of artisans, small tradesmen and merchants who had supported the parliamentary cause, and reflected their general sense of disillusion and betrayal. 'Is this the men my husband hath stood for, and adventured his life, as he hath done, and trusted the Parliament in their necessities, above six years past, with above £1,000 and is yet unpaid?' cried Mary Prince when the soldiers arrested her husband and ransacked her house.[6] In this she was echoing Elizabeth Lilburne, who, in an earlier clash with authority, had turned on *her* husband exclaiming, 'I told thee often enough long since, that thou would serve the Parliament, and venture thy life so long for them, till they would hang thee for thy pains, and give thee Tyburn for thy recompense.'[7]

Although believing firmly in liberty of individual conscience, in their concentration on democratic constitutional reform the Levellers were essentially a secular movement, but the revolutionary year 1649 was to throw up a variety of more or less bizarre sects reflecting the general confusion of 'a world turned upside down'. One of the more optimistic and short-lived of these, the so-called Diggers, or True Levellers as they preferred to call themselves, attempted to establish what would now be described as a commune at St George's Hill in Surrey. According to information laid before the Council of State by Henry Sanders of Walton-on-Thames on 16 April, one William Everard, 'who termeth himself a prophet', together with four other men, arrived at St George's Hill and began to dig and sow the ground with parsnips, carrots and beans. The next day they were there again, 'being increased in their number' and soon there were thirty or forty of them, reported Henry Sanders indignantly, firing the heath, ploughing up the land and sowing corn.

They invite all to come in and help them, and promise them meat, drink and clothes. They do threaten to pull down and level all park pales . . . and intend to plant there very shortly. They give out, they will be four or five thousand within 10 days and threaten the neighbouring people there that they will make them all come up to the hills and work, and forewarn them suffering their cattle to come near the plantation, if they do they will cut their legs off.[8]

The Council of State forwarded Sanders's complaint to General Fairfax, for 'although the pretence of their being there by them avowed may seem very ridiculous, yet that conflux of people may be a beginning whence things of a greater and more dangerous consequence may grow to a disturbance of the peace and quiet of the Commonwealth'.[9] Two troops of horse under Captain John Gladman were therefore despatched to investigate, and Gladman reported back on 19 April that he thought the whole thing had been greatly exaggerated.

I cannot hear that there hath been above twenty of them together since they first undertook the business [he wrote]. Sir, I intend to go with two or three men to St George's hill this day, and persuade these people to leave this imployment if I can, and if then I see no more danger than now I do, I shall march back again to London tomorrow . . . Indeed this business is not worth the writing nor yet taking nottis of: I wonder the Council of State should be so abused with informations.[10]

The leaders of the Diggers, William Everard and Gerrard Winstanley, now came to London themselves for an interview with Fairfax to justify their activities, but refused to remove their hats in his presence, it being against their principles to recognise any distinctions of rank. Everard made an excitable speech declaring that he was of the race of the Jews, that all the liberties of the people had been lost by the coming of William the Conqueror, and ever since the English had lived under a tyranny and oppression worse than the Israelites under Pharaoh, but now the time of deliverance was at hand and God would bring his people out of slavery and restore them to their freedoms in enjoying the fruits of the earth. He had, he said, recently been vouchsafed a vision which bade him arise and dig and plough the earth, and the Diggers' intent was now to restore the creation to its former condition. 'And that as God had promised to make the barren Ground fruitful, so now what they did was to renew the ancient Community of the fruits of the Earth and to distribute the benefits thereof to the poor and needy.' They did not mean to interfere with any man's property or to break down any enclosures, but only to occupy ground which was common land and untilled.

Everard was happily convinced that soon 'all men should willingly come in, and give up their Lands and Estates, and willingly submit to this Community. And for those that will come in and work, they shall have meat, drink and clothes, which is all that is necessary for the life of man; and that for money there was not any need of it, nor of any clothes other than to cover their nakedness.' The Diggers would not defend themselves by arms, but were content to submit to authority 'and wait till the promised opportunity be offered which they conceive to be near at hand. And that as their forefathers lived in Tents, so it would be suitable to their condition now to live in the same.'[11]

Having satisfied himself that they were harmless, Fairfax, who had other more urgent matters on his mind just then, seems to have regarded his eccentric visitors with some sympathy. Others were less charitable, the press poking fun at their ambitions to restore the earth to its first condition on hermits' fare of parsnips and beans, and generally dismissing them as 'a distracted crack-brained people' who 'would have the world believe they have dreamed dreams, seen visions, heard strange voices and have dictates beyond man's teaching'.[12] But if the outside world was content to have a cheap laugh at the Diggers' expense and then forget about them, their neighbours in the St George's Hill area took them very seriously and were openly and violently hostile. Time and again their newly sown crops were trampled under foot, their tools broken and they themselves attacked by the local farmers and landowners, who saw them as dangerous invaders, but the Diggers refused to admit defeat, returning time and again throughout the summer and announcing their intention of cutting and selling the wood on the common, which they maintained belonged to the poor along with the land.

William Everard seems to have faded from the scene by this time, and leadership of the little group was taken over by Gerrard Winstanley, a less-colourful but equally determined character. Meanwhile, the persecution continued unabated. Winstanley was twice arrested and fined for trespass, and his four cows seized. 'They took away the cows which were my livelihood', he complained, 'and beat them with their clubs, that the cows' heads and sides did swell, which grieved tender hearts to see: and yet these cows never were upon George Hill . . . and yet the poor beasts must suffer because they gave milk to feed me.'[13]

At the end of the year Winstanley addressed another appeal to the Lord General Fairfax and his Council of War, protesting about reports that

> we that are called Diggers are a riotous people, and that we will not be ruled by the Justices, and that we hold a man's house by violence from him, and that we have 4 guns in it, to secure ourselves, and that we are drunkards and Cavaliers waiting an opportunity to help to bring in the Prince, and such like. Truly Sir, these are all untrue reports . . . We are peaceable men, and walk in the light of righteousness to the utmost of our power. Our enemies have sent divers times to beat us, and to pull down our houses, yet we never gave them bad language, nor resisted again, but took all their abuses patiently, waiting upon God till he make their hearts quiet.

The Diggers asked no more than freedom to work, and to enjoy the benefit of their labours, 'for here is waste land enough to spare to supply all our wants'. Indeed, they believed they had every right to claim this freedom in the common land, a right bought by their blood and money, for had not parliament, in effect, said 'give us your taxes, free quarter, and adventure your lives with us to cast out the oppressor Charles and we will make you a free people'? This they considered to have been a bargain made and confirmed on their part by performance, but now the victory had been won England could never be a free Commonwealth 'unless all the poor Commoners have a free use and benefit of the land'. Winstanley ended with a plea that 'you will rule in love as Moses and Joshua did the Children of Israel before any kingly power came in, and that the Parliament will be as the Elders of Israel, chosen freely by the people to advise for and assist both you and us'.[14]

It was a plea which fell on deaf ears, and by the spring of 1650 the Diggers' brave but doomed experiment was over. The little colony on St George's Hill had finally been wiped out, and attempts to establish other communes in the Midlands and Home Counties also ended in failure. Winstanley was a prolific producer of pamphlets and Utopian ideals, but he was no match for the tough, suspicious freeholders of Walton, Weybridge and Cobham, to whom the Diggers represented an alien threat to their way of life and who were profoundly unimpressed by the Diggers' Song:

> You noble Diggers all, stand up now, stand up now,
>   You noble Diggers all, stand up now,
> The waste land to maintain, seeing Cavaliers by name
> Your digging does disdain, and persons all defame
>   Stand up now, stand up now.[15]

And a good deal more in similar vein.

The general mood of disappointment and disaffection continued to find expression in various forms of religious radicalism, the most extreme being the so-called Ranters, who first came into prominence in 1649 and flourished briefly in the early 1650s. Since man's puny attempts by sword and spade had failed to accomplish the desired 'levelling' of the people, the Ranters maintained that the revolution would shortly be completed by the mighty Leveller, the eternal God the Lord of Hosts, who was coming, 'yea even at the doores to

Levell to some purpose, to Levell with a witnesse, to Levell the Hills with the Valleys, and to lay the Mountains low'.[16]

The Ranters had their roots in the medieval heresy of the Free Spirit and the twelfth-century Joachim of Flore, who foretold the Age of the Spirit, in which the sons of God would enjoy perfect spiritual liberty. Their belief in the concept of 'the indwelling spirit', that God existed only in material and living creatures, 'Man and Beast, Fish and Fowle, and every green thing, from the highest Cedar to the Ivey on the wall; and that God is the life and being of them all', led to the happy conviction that for the sons of God no moral law applied, no act could be considered sinful.

> They taught as the Familists [wrote that serious Puritan Richard Baxter] that God regardeth not the actions of the outward man, but of the heart, and to the pure all things are pure (even things forbidden). And so, as allowed by God, they spake most hideous words of blasphemy; and many of them committed whoredom commonly, insomuch that a matron of great note for godliness and sobriety, being perverted by them, turned so shameless a whore that she was carted in the streets of London.[17]

This sort of behaviour, together with their rejection of all forms of organised religious observance, not surprisingly brought the Ranters rapidly into conflict with the authorities, and accusations of blasphemy, drunkenness, sexual promiscuity, singing filthy songs, and men and women dancing together stark naked became common. They were also said to dismiss the sacred Bible as 'but a mere Romance . . . only invented by the Wits of Former Ages, to keep People in subjection' and to have declared that 'the Devil could do no evil at all, if God did not give him a power to do it'. Tales were told of Ranters at dinner, and one taking a piece of beef in his hand and tearing it apart, saying to another, 'This is the flesh of Christ, take and eat', while the other, throwing a cup of ale into the chimney corner, said, 'There is the blood of Christ'. And, so this story went on, 'having some discourse of God it was proved that one of them said, that he could go into the house of Office, and make a God every morning, by easing his body'. There was also the story told of a certain journeyman shoemaker, who, when he heard any mention of God, 'used to laugh, and in a disdainful manner say that he believed money, good clothes, good meat and drink, tobacco and merry company to be Gods: but he was little beholding to any of these: for his God allowed him but eightpence or tenpence a day, and that he made him work for'.[18]

Since most of the surviving information about the Ranters comes from their enemies, it is not easy to be sure just how much they practised what they preached. One of their leaders, Jacob Bauthumley, wrote that 'men should not sin because grace abounds; but yet if they do sin, that shall turn to the praise of God, as well as when they do well'. Another, Laurence Clarkson, while drawing the line at murder, believed 'God made all things good, so nothing evil but as man judged it; for I apprehended there was no such thing as theft, cheat or a lie, but as man made it so'.[19]

Politically the Ranters, who looked forward to an imminent golden age of brotherhood and social justice, stood well to the left of the Levellers and Diggers, as their chief prophet Abiezer Coppe made clear in his *Fiery Flying Roll: A Word from the Lord to all the Great Ones of the Earth*, which appeared in 1650 and contained a virulent, if somewhat incoherent, denunciation of the rich and great.

The plague of God is in your purses, barns, houses, horses, murrain will take your hogs . . . blasting, mildew, locusts, caterpillars, yea, fire your houses and goods, take your corn and fruit, the moth your garments and the rot your sheep, did you not see my hand, this last year, stretched out? . . . Your gold and silver, though you can't see it, is cankered, the rust of them is a witness against you, and suddainly, suddainly, suddainly, because of the Eternal God, myself, it's the dreadful day of Judgement . . . Howl, howl, ye nobles, howl honourable, howl ye rich men for the miseries that are coming upon you.[20]

The government's reaction to this sort of thing was predictable, and in June 1650 a parliamentary committee was set up to enquire into the activities of the Ranters. A bill to deal with their Atheistical, Blasphemous and Execrable Opinions was debated and passed into law on 9 August, as a result of which the leading Ranters all landed in gaol. Their books, containing those 'horrid Blasphemies, and damnable and detestable opinions', were publicly burnt – Jacob Bauthumley, a militant cobbler from Leicester, was bored through the tongue for one of his literary productions. Their meetings were raided and broken up and every effort was made to wipe out all trace of them – so successfully, in fact, that a controversy has since arisen over whether they ever existed as an organised force at all. Certainly they had ceased to exist as any kind of organisation by the end of 1651, although some survived to be absorbed into the early Quaker movement.

The Ranters, like the Levellers, had been mostly town-dwellers, attracting support from among the very poorest and most wretched in society, even the criminal element, 'rogues, thieves, whores and cut-purses' who were, they held, every bit as good as the great ones of the earth. The Fifth Monarchy Men, by contrast, drew their support mainly from respectable craftsmen in the cloth trade and soldiers in the New Model Army, one of their leaders being the formidable Colonel, later Major General, Thomas Harrison, he who was to pull the Speaker from his chair at the expulsion of the Rump in 1653.

In common with other so-called millenarian sects, the Fifth Monarchists were confidently expecting the imminence of the Second Coming. Their name refers to an interpretation of King Nebuchadnezzar's dream described in the Old Testament Book of Daniel, foretelling that four kingdoms or ages – they listed Assyria, Persia, Greece and Rome – would be succeeded by a fifth, when Christ and his saints (among whom they naturally numbered themselves) would rule on earth for a thousand years of blessedness. The Fifth Monarchists saw the execution of King Charles – Thomas Harrison had always been an unrepentant and enthusiastic regicide

– as a necessary preliminary to this happy state of affairs. Consequently they supported the Commonwealth and, for a time, were able to wield a good deal of political influence.

Another group which had sought inspiration in the Scriptures were the Muggletonians – so-called from their founder and chief prophet Ludovick Muggleton, a London tailor – who believed, among other things, in the doctrine of the Two Seeds, that mankind was divided between the descendants of Cain, who were automatically damned, and the righteous sons of Abel, who were to be saved. Muggleton and his co-prophet John Reeve also declared themselves to be the two witnesses mentioned in the Book of Revelations sent to seal the elect and the reprobate with the eternal seals of life and death. They added, helpfully, that if any of the elect desired to speak with them, they were to be heard of 'in Great Trinity Lane, at a Chandler's shop, against one Mr Millis, a Brown Baker, near the lower end of Bow Lane'.[21]

Other sects flourishing around this time included the Family of Love, an offshoot of the Anabaptists, the Seekers or Waiters, who seem to have had much in common with the Quakers, and the Socinians, who rejected the doctrine of the Trinity and often the divinity of Christ. More familiar and more durable were the Baptists and the Quakers. The Baptists, who presently divided into the General, who believed in toleration and salvation for all, and the Particular, who followed the Calvinist creed of predestination, and who were also known inevitably as the Dippers, rejected the practice of infant baptism, holding that the only scriptural form was the baptism by total immersion of adult believers who chose or were chosen by their congregations. Although regarded with deep hostility in some quarters as a threat to the discipline of a national church, the Baptists gained support among a number of thoughtful Christians, notably Colonel John Hutchinson, the Governor of Nottingham Castle, and his wife Lucy, who both developed doubts as to the validity of infant baptism. The Colonel, having 'diligently searched the Scriptures . . . could find in them no ground at all for that practice', nor, wrote his wife in her Memoirs of her husband's life, could any of the religious authorities he consulted defend it with any satisfactory reason 'but the tradition of the church from the primitive times'.[22] The Society of Friends or Quakers, founded in the 1650s by George Fox, a weaver's son from Fenny Drayton in Leicestershire, rejected any professional ministry or structured form of worship in 'steeple houses', as they called churches, preferring instead to wait for the revelation of God to an individual through an inner light. Since they also disrupted church services, refused to swear oaths, pay tithes or to observe any of the usual polite forms of address in social contacts, they were, not surprisingly, unpopular. In July 1656 the diarist John Evelyn had the curiosity to visit some Quakers in prison at Ipswich. 'A new fanatic sect of dangerous principles,' he observed. 'They show no respect to any man, magistrate or other and seem a melancholy proud sort of people and exceedingly ignorant: one of these was said to have fasted 20 days, but another endeavouring to do the like perish'd the 10th, when he would have eaten but could not.'[23]

All these various assorted sects probably represented less than 10 per cent of the population, but they attracted a disproportionate amount of attention and hostility. The Puritans – a generic term applied to all those Protestants favouring greater purity in religion – might now be in power, but so far they had been more successful in destroying the established fabric of the church than in unifying the nation.

By the end of the Civil War parliament had abolished the episcopate and, with it, what remained of the administrative machinery of the Anglican church. Getting rid of the bishops had not been difficult. Already deeply unpopular, even among more moderate laymen, for their perceived tendencies towards popery during the pre-war period, in October 1646 they had surrendered before the onslaught of a victorious House of Commons almost without a fight. Replacing them with a Presbyterian system organised on Scottish lines was to prove a good deal more problematic.

England's conversion to Presbyterianism had been the price exacted by the Scots for their urgently needed military assistance in the conduct of the war; and in January 1645 parliament passed ordinances substituting a Presbyterian Directory of Worship for the Book of Common Prayer, the use of which was now forbidden 'in any Church, Chapel, or Public place of worship, or in any Private place or Family within the Kingdom of England or Dominion of Wales'. Any minister failing to 'pursue and observe' the Directory would in future be liable to a fine of 40s, while anyone continuing to use the Prayer Book would be fined £5 for a first offence, £10 for a second, 'and for the third offence shall suffer one whole years imprisonment'.[24]

In June 1646 a start had finally been made on the countrywide reform of religion along Presbyterian lines, but progress was slow and patchy. All members of parliament had already been required to subscribe to a Solemn League and Covenant pledging themselves to endeavour to preserve the Church of Scotland and to reform religion in England and Ireland 'in doctrine, worship, discipline, and government, according to the Word of God and the example of the best Reformed Churches'. They were also to endeavour to bring the Churches of God in the three kingdoms to the nearest conjunction and uniformity in religion, and 'in like manner, without respect of persons, endeavour the extirpation of Popery, Prelacy . . . superstition, heresy, schism, profaneness, and whatsoever shall be found to be contrary to sound doctrine and the power of godliness'.[25] This statement of intent was adopted by the Commons in September 1643, albeit in the teeth of strong opposition from the Independent party, and a body known as the Westminster Assembly, consisting of Learned and Godly Divines plus representatives from both Houses of parliament and a number of Scottish commissioners, was established in June of that year to settle the future government of the church. But English contempt for and suspicion of all things Scottish was deeply ingrained, and they were especially suspicious of a theocratic Presbyterian system which would vest so much untrammelled power in the hands of the clergy. 'As yet a presbytrie to this people is conceived to be a strange monster,' lamented the Scot Robert Baillie.

61

There was, though, a solid core of support for at least a modified form of Presbyterianism in the City of London and among the middle and gentry classes, who were frightened and repelled by the growth of the sects, and saw the rigid disciplinary structure of ministers or presbyters and lay elders, organised in local *classes*, provincial assemblies and national synods as their best defence against the dangerous democratic notions spread by those who openly declared that 'they were all taught of God, and needed not that any one should teach them'.

The conservatives were especially concerned by the growth of lay preaching, by the fact that any man or, worse, woman who felt an inner call, 'even if not gifted with a black coat, a university dialect and the external advantages of Arts and Sciences', now apparently felt free to harangue their fellow citizens with their own version of the Word of God. The Presbyterian pamphleteer Thomas Edwards was particularly revolted by this manifestation of religious freedom. 'Among all the confusion and disorder in Church matters both of opinions and practices, and particularly of all sorts of mechanics taking upon them to preach and baptise, as smiths, tailors, shoemakers, pedlars, weavers, etc. there are also some women-preachers in our times, who keep constant lectures, preaching weekly to many men and women.' Many dangerous and false doctrines were being disseminated in this way, thought Edwards, for 'many of the sectaries of our times, anabaptists, libertines, Independents, are not only against government in the Church, all authoritative power of classes, synods, but against civil government too'. They might call for democracy, 'yet in pleading for it they have laid down such positions as are not consistent with any civil government at all, but what necessarily would bring any Commonwealth into a chaos and confusion'.[26] John Evelyn, although a staunch Anglican, would have agreed. Evelyn records that he was 'surprized' one December day in 1653 to see 'a Tradesman a Mechanic' step up to the pulpit of his parish church, but was yet resolved to stay and see what the man would make of it. Evelyn was not impressed – a lot of 'truculent anabaptistical stuff' inferring that, when God called for shedding of blood, the Saints were called upon to destroy temporal governments.[27] Anabaptists – literally 'rebaptisers' – were especially suspect for their habit of 'dipping' or totally immersing adult believers, men and women, with all its associated suggestive possibilities of nudity and sexuality.

The battle between the Presbyterians and Independents, fought out both in parliament and by the pamphlets which flowed from the pens of men like Thomas Edwards and the Levellers William Walwyn and Richard Overton, continued throughout the second half of the 1640s. But the Presbyterians still commanded a majority in the Commons. They did their best to enforce attendance at the newly established Presbyterian state church and to ban unlicensed preachers, and in May 1648 passed an Ordinance, which imposed prison sentences on any dissenters convicted of denying the orthodox Calvinist doctrine of predestination or of advocating anabaptism. Nevertheless, the settlement which finally emerged proved, to the disappointment of the Scots, to be a typically English compromise. While accepting the basic Presbyterian confession of faith, parliament set definite limits to the powers of ministers and elders, for there could be no question of allowing the nobility, gentry and Commons to become subordinate to rule by clergy. Parliament, in short, was reserving to itself that supremacy in church affairs once exercised by the sovereign. Even this did not please the majority of the nation. As one cynic remarked, 'he that lives but a short time shall surely see a Presbyter as fat as ever was a Bishop', and many people resented the loss of the familiar liturgy in the Elizabethan Prayer Book. Especially they resented state interference with the observance of those traditional rites of passage, baptism, marriage and burial.

When Ralph Verney's wife, Mary, came over from their exile in France in the winter of 1646 to try and get the sequestration order on his estate lifted, she was already in the early months of pregnancy, and the business took her so long that she had to face the prospect of giving birth in this strange new England of committees and church elders. Ralph had wanted her to try and find a minister who would come to her lodgings and perform the christening ceremony in the old way, for godparents had become a thing of the past and nowadays the father was expected to bring the child to church and 'answer for it' himself. 'Truly one lives like a heathen in this place,' Mary complained, and to those accustomed to the Anglican rite the new Presbyterian-type service, with its total absence of ceremonial and heavy emphasis on preaching, seemed alien, 'and in such a tone that most people do nothing but laugh at it'. Then again, anyone wishing to receive communion had first to be examined by the elders, who, it was said, were liable to ask the most blush-making questions. In the end Ralph thought it better not to worry too much about the christening. It would not do to risk offending the authorities, and 'so it be done with common ordinary water', he wrote, 'and that these words "I baptise thee in the name of the Father and of the Son, and of the Holy Ghost" be used with the water, I know the child is well baptised. All the rest is but a matter of form and ceremony.' But he urged his wife to take the sacrament as soon as she could, if not in church, then privately at home, 'for you know not how soon you may lye in'.[28]

Strict Presbyterian insistence on admitting to the Lord's Supper only those considered worthy by the elders had given rise to so much un-Christian ill-feeling in some parishes that the ministers were refusing to give communion at all, and it was only after great heart-searching that Ralph Josselin at East Colne had decided to 'celebrate the ordinance', as he put it. 'We all sat round and near the table,' he wrote, 'the bread was broken not cut in blessing it, the lord poured out a spirit of mourning over Christ crucified on me and most of the company, and my soul eyed him more than ever, and God was sweet to me in the work.'[29]

Christenings could take place at home, providing a sympathetic clergyman was prepared to cooperate, but funerals obviously presented a more serious problem. However, when John Evelyn's mother-in-law died of 'a Scarlet feaver' in the autumn of 1652, Evelyn records that he was able to arrange her interment at Deptford, 'with all decent Ceremonie, and according to the Church

Office, which I obtained might be permitted, after it had not been used in that Church of 7 years before, to the great satisfaction of that innumerable multitude who were there'.[30]

It was the ordinance of 1653, replacing church weddings with a basic civil ceremony, which met with the greatest resistance. After due notice had been given on 'three several Lords-days', the couple must now go before a Justice of the Peace and two 'credible witnesses'. The man to be married, taking his bride by the hand, was then ' plainly and distinctly' to declare: 'I, A.B., do here in the presence of God the searcher of all hearts, take thee C.D., for my wedded Wife; and do also in the presence of God, and before these witnesses, promise to be unto thee a loving and faithful Husband.' The woman then made a similar declaration, although she had to promise to be 'a loving faithful and obedient Wife.' The presiding justice would then pronounce them to be from thenceforth husband and wife, and as from 29 September 1653, no other marriage within the Commonwealth of England would be 'held or accompted a Marriage according to the Laws of England'. All eventualities had been provided for. In the case of dumb persons the justice (who received a fee of 12*d* for his services) was allowed to dispense with the spoken declarations, 'and with joining of hands in case of persons that have not hands'.[31]

Very few couples felt properly married by this bleak little ritual. When, in order 'to conform to the order of those that were then in power', Anne Murray and Sir James Halkett appeared before Justice Elkonhead at Woolwich in March 1656, the proceedings, according to Anne's memoirs, were even briefer.

> The Justice [she remembered] performed what was usual for him at that time, which was only holding the Directory in his hand, asked Sir James if he intended to marry me. He answered 'Yes'; and asked if I intended to marry him, I said 'Yes'. 'Then', says he, 'I pronounce you man and wife'. So calling for a glass of sack, he drank and wished much happiness to us, and we left him, having given his clerk money, who gave in parchment the day and witnesses and attested by the Justice that he had married us.

But Anne and her new husband took care also to be married by 'Mr Gaile, who was chaplain to the Countess of Devonshire', the ceremony taking place privately in the presence only of Anne's brother and sister. 'If it [the marriage] had not been done more solemnly afterwards by a minister, I should not have believed it lawfully done,' wrote Anne.[32] Many people shared her scruples, and it came to be said that barely one marriage in a hundred was made according to the Act. Indeed, some ultra-cautious couples were known to have gone through three ceremonies – once before a Justice of the Peace, once according to the Directory of Worship and once by an Anglican priest.

The Directory of Worship remained unpopular, and by no means every parish priest bothered to acquire a copy. Many of them, indeed, throughout the country, continued to conduct services loosely but still recognisably based on the Book of Common Prayer. The Presbyterian *classis* system – that is, the linking of numbers of neighbouring parishes into groups or *classes* controlled by local ministers and elders of local congregations, in turn responsible to provincial assemblies – also failed to catch the public imagination and was certainly not universally adopted. Apart from London, only the counties of Essex, Hampshire, Lancashire, Shropshire, Suffolk, Surrey, possibly Warwickshire and parts of Yorkshire appear to have achieved anything like a complete classical organisation.

The military coup of 1649 effectively deprived the Presbyterian movement of its backing from central government, so that, although Presbyterianism continued, in theory at least, to be the official state church throughout the period of the Interregnum, in practice it fell into a steady decline. The army and the Independents, who remained adamantly opposed to a compulsory system of belief, now introduced a degree of toleration for the so-called gathered churches – that is, the independent congregations who elected their own ministers, disciplined their own members and worshipped as they saw fit. In September 1650 the Rump Parliament passed an Act repealing those former statutes which imposed penalties for not attending church, but made it clear this did not mean that 'profane or licentious persons' could neglect the performance of their religious duties. On the contrary, it was now enacted

> that all and every person and persons within this Commonwealth and the Territories thereof, shall (having no reasonable excuse for their absence) upon every Lord's Day, Days of public Thanksgiving and Humiliation, diligently resort to some public place where the Service and Worship of God is exercised, or shall be present at some other place in the practice of some Religious Duty, either of Prayer, Preaching, Reading or Expounding the Scriptures, or conferring upon the same.[33]

The great majority of the Independent congregations were Calvinist in doctrine and so could coexist quite comfortably with the more moderate Presbyterians. Some Baptists, too, were included and even some of the more peaceable sects. But there were definite limits to this consideration for 'tender consciences'. Blasphemy was definitely out, as was any rejection of the Trinity or the divinity of Christ, nor was there any place in the Commonwealth's new broad church for either the Roman Catholics or the Episcopalian Anglicans.

There had been something of a resurgence of Catholicism during the 1630s, owing largely to the influence of the Catholic Queen Henrietta and the King's perceived interest in and sympathy for Catholicism, and it has been estimated that by 1640 the number of English Catholics had risen to approximately sixty thousand. This was still a small enough percentage of a total population of between four and five million, with its power base confined to London and the Court, but one regarded with disproportionate alarm and suspicion by the Protestant majority, especially after the Catholic Irish rebellion of 1641.

When war came, by no means all Catholics were active supporters of the royalist cause – by no means all of them trusted the King not to throw them to the parliamentary wolves any time it seemed to his advantage. Those who did declare for him, either from conviction or from other external pressures, were subjected to grievous financial penalties by the victorious republicans. The two best-known victims – the wealthy Marquesses of Worcester and Winchester – were both ruined. Winchester, who had spent £600,000 in the king's cause, saw his great house at Basing looted and destroyed and all his estates confiscated – and many another, lesser, family found itself being doubly penalised, once for being papist and again for being royalist.

A convicted papist was subject to confiscation of two-thirds of his property, unless he agreed to take the explicitly anti-Catholic Oath of Abjuration. A papist who had also been a known supporter of the King, either financially or militarily – that is, a delinquent – might or might not be gaoled, depending on how dangerous he was considered to be, but would certainly suffer confiscation of all his goods and real estate, unless he swore allegiance to the new Republic and paid his fine, or composition, for delinquency, usually amounting to one or two years' income. Quite a number of Catholics did take both these oaths, and it is hard to blame them. Those few resolute souls who insisted on remaining true to either their religion or their royalism, or both, did indeed face ruin. Some were able to find an escape route by employing a lawyer and a body of non-Catholic trustees, who bought up a confiscated estate and then leased it back to its dispossessed owner at a peppercorn rent, leaving him with a heavy burden of debt but at least a glimmer of hope that he would eventually be able to redeem his property. The lawyer John Rushworth, who combined a career in the service of the Republic with that of historian, also maintained a profitable side-line acting as agent and facilitator in a number of these transactions. A few irreconcilables either sought refuge abroad or lived precariously at home on the charity of friends and relations. A few others began to form undercover resistance groups or took to highway robbery in the northern hills and moors.

The future of English Catholicism looked bleak, and certainly the terms presented to the King by parliament in 1646 made it plain that the Presbyterian majority aimed at its final extinction, but the King's execution and the army's victory three years later were to bring the embattled Catholics an unexpected measure of relief. Since they were not explicitly excluded from the ordinance of 1650, removing the old penalities for not attending the parish church, and since all the former apparatus for enforcing the recusancy laws had been swept away, Catholics now found themselves largely unmolested. Not that Mass had suddenly become legal, of course – practising Catholics were still obliged to resort to undercover services in private houses or, for the more privileged, the chapels of foreign embassies, and could still be subjected to the fines for popery if detected – but the degree of tolerance now being extended to the dissenting sects emboldened a group of Catholic secular clergy to try to reach a form of accommodation with the new regime. This group, which came to be known as the Blackloists after their leader Thomas White alias Blacklo, put forward a scheme which would, in effect, have allowed the English Catholics to operate as a self-governing entity with its own hierarchy independent of Rome, in exchange for taking an oath of allegiance designed by parliament, any Catholic refusing it to be banished. Not surprisingly, this optimistic scheme failed to find favour with either Rome or parliament and the Catholics had to resign themselves to remaining a disadvantaged minority, whose degree of disadvantage continued to vary according to the prevailing political climate.

Hardest hit and most visible casualty of the new dispensation was the Anglican church, the state religion for nearly a century, but now to all appearances obliterated, its liturgy proscribed, its hierarchy destroyed, its courts dismantled, its property confiscated. In February 1651 the Commons debated a motion that 'all Cathedral churches, where there are other churches or chapels sufficient for the people to meet in for the worship of God . . . be pulled down and sold, and be employed for a stock for the use of the poor'. Fortunately for posterity, the cathedrals escaped the fate of the monasteries, although several of them suffered some structural damage during the Civil War – Lichfield lost its central spire as a result of artillery bombardment – while others suffered various degrees of desecration and abuse. The portico of St Paul's was let out to shopkeepers and the body of the church became a cavalry stables, one visitor recording indignantly that the carved work on the portico had been 'broken down with axes and hammers, and the whole sacred edifice made not only a den of thieves, but a stable for unclean beasts'. At Exeter a brick wall was built in the middle of the cathedral, dividing it into two, and the bishop's palace was taken over by a bakery. In Peterborough, Gloucester and Wells, the townspeople petitioned to take over their cathedrals to be enjoyed by them for 'the preaching of the word, education of children and other public uses', and others again functioned as barracks and prisons.[34]

But by far the most serious damage inflicted on both great cathedrals and humbler parish churches up and down the land was the deliberate and systematic destruction of 'all crucifixes, crosses, and all images and pictures of any one or more persons of the Trinity, or of the Virgin Mary, and all other images and pictures of saints'. This had begun even before the outbreak of the war. Ralph Josselin noted in his diary for Michaelmas 1641 that 'upon an Order of the House of Commons . . . we took down all images and pictures and such like glasses', and everywhere the railed off altars insisted on by Archbishop Laud were being torn down and replaced by a simple communion table in the body of the church. Once the fighting began, of course, there was plenty of casual damage and looting of anything that looked valuable carried out by the soldiers on both sides, but the parliamentary troops, 'who thought they saw popery in every picture and piece of painted glass', had the cast-iron justification of doing the Lord's work as they set about their task of destruction. At Peterborough, in April 1643, they pulled down the organ and tore up all the service books they found in the choir, before going on to burn the altar rails and smash 'a stately screen . . . well wrought, painted and gilt' which had stood behind the communion table. To the special sorrow of one eye-witness to this 'more than Gothish barbarity of those ignorant people, who took upon them the glorious name of Reformers', the stained glass for which the cathedral was famous was also destroyed.

'Notwithstanding all the art and curiosity of workmanship these windows did afford, yet nothing of all this could oblige the reforming rabble, but they deface and break them all in pieces.'[35]

There was a similar story at Canterbury, when

the soldiers entering the church and choir, giant-like began a fight with God himself, overthrew the communion table, tore the velvet cloth from before it, defaced the goodly screen, or tabernacle work, violated the monuments of the dead, spoiled the organs, brake down the ancient rails and seats, with the brazen eagle that did support the Bible, forced open the cupboards of the singing-men, rent some of their surplices, gowns and bibles, and carried away others, mangled all our service books, and books of Common Prayer, bestrewing the whole pavement with the leaves thereof.

And, according to the report of Dr Paske, the subdean, worse was to follow, when, finding a statue of Christ 'in the frontispiece of the South-gate, they discharged against it forty shot at the least, triumphing much when they did hit it in the head or face'.[36]

Nor was it by any means always soldiers who were the wreckers, as Bishop Hall of Norwich found in his cathedral in 1643.

It is no other than tragical to relate the carriage of that furious sacrilege whereof our eyes and ears were the sad witnesses, under the authority and presence of [Alderman] Lindsey, Toft the sheriff and Greenwood [he wrote]. Lord, what work was here, what clattering of glasses, what beating down of walls, what tearing up of monuments, what pulling down of seats, what wresting out of irons and brass from the windows and graves . . . What tooting and piping upon the destroyed organ-pipes, and what a hideous triumph on the market day before all the country, when, in a kind of sacrilegious and profane procession, all the organ-pipes, vestments, both copes and surplices, together with the leaden cross which had been newly sawn down from over the Green yard pulpit, and the service books and singing books that could be had,

71

were carried to the fire in the public market place . . . Near the public cross all these monuments of idolatry must be sacrificed to the fire; not without much ostentation of a zealous joy, in discharging ordnance, to the cost of some who professed how much they had longed to see that day.[37]

Also in 1643, a Commons committee headed by Sir Robert Harley was authorised to order the demolition of all those monuments of idolatry and superstition in London and Westminster as crosses, crucifixes and images inside and outside churches. That famous City landmark, the Cross in Cheapside, was an early casualty, as was the altar in the Henry VII Chapel in Westminster Abbey, where Edward VI, ironically England's first Protestant monarch, was buried. Similar acts of desecration continued throughout the 1640s, as headless statues, whitewashed walls and plain glass windows still bear witness in parish churches up and down the land.

The government employed a number of official 'visitors' to oversee the extirpation of any remaining relics of popery, and William Dowsing of Laxfield in Suffolk cut a swathe of destruction through East Anglia. At Gorleston near Great Yarmouth he triumphantly recorded that

in the chancel, as it is called, we took up twenty brazen superstitious inscriptions . . . broke twelve apostles, carved in wood, and cherubims, and a lamb with a cross . . . broke in pieces the rails, and broke down twenty-two popish pictures of angels and saints. We did deface the font and a cross on the font . . . Ordered Moses with his rod and Aaron with his mitre to be taken down. Ordered eighteen angels off the roof and cherubims to be taken down . . . The organ I brake; and we brake seven popish pictures in the chancel window.[38]

Another official iconoclast, Richard Culmer, is credited with the personal destruction in Canterbury Cathedral of 'the great high prized most idolatrous window' in the chapel of Thomas Becket. 'The labourers not acting as was desired, Mr Culmer said, "If we neglect this opportunity, we may repent it"; and thereupon threw off his cloak, and took a whole pike in his hand, and went up a ladder fifty-six steps high, and did full execution upon the idolatrous monuments there.' It is almost possible to hear the crash of falling masonry and broken glass, but by no means all the onlookers applauded. Some, indeed, 'wished he might break his neck', while others were heard to say 'it should cost blood'. But Richard Culmer finished the work unscathed and, according to his son's account written fourteen years after the event, remained in very good health.[39]

It was not only the church fabric which suffered. As early as December 1640 parliament had set up a Committee for Scandalous Ministers, later supplemented and largely superseded by the Plundered Ministers' Committee. The purpose of these bodies was to remove all those members of the clergy regarded as disaffected or hostile to the new regime and to compensate those learned, religious and Puritan sympathisers who had suffered under the previous dispensation, but in practice it seems that most of the work of sequestration was carried out by local county committees.

It is estimated that approximately three thousand Anglican priests – that is, about a third of the total number – were deprived of their livings or subjected to some form of harassment, mostly on the grounds of having royalist sympathies, although there were also accusations of drunkenness, neglect and other forms of scandalous living, for continuing to conduct marriage ceremonies in the old manner, for churching women in a 'popish' manner, using the forbidden liturgy in the Prayer Book or insisting that the people received communion kneeling at the altar rails. The severity of this purge of the Anglican ministry seems to have largely depended on local circumstances and was strongest in London, East Anglia, Kent, Essex, Yorkshire, Cheshire and the East Midlands – anywhere, in fact, where parliamentarian Puritan influence was most active on the county committees. It was no doubt a time for the settling of old scores, and yet it appears to have been rare for parishioners to denounce their parson to the authorities, so much so that the Earl of Manchester felt obliged to issue a set of directions to the committees in his Eastern Association, urging them to encourage the people to come forward with their accusations. 'Because it is found by sad experience, that parishioners are not forward to complain of their ministers, although they be very scandalous, but having this price and power in their hands, yet want hearts to make use thereof, too many being enemies to that blessed reformation so much by the Parliament desired.' The answer, it was felt, was to make use of informers, and the committees were therefore instructed to call before them 'some well-affected men within every hundred, who, having no private engagements, but intending to further the public reformation may be required and encouraged by you to inquire after the doctrines, lives and conversations of all ministers and schoolmasters, and to give you information both what can be deposed, and who can depose the same'.[40]

Not all the deprived ministers went quietly and not all parishioners were prepared to submit to be being deprived of their pastor. At Soham in Cambridgeshire there was a riot as a result of the intrusion of a parliamentary nominee in place of the regular incumbent, and there are several instances of petitions being presented on behalf of clergymen summarily ejected on the evidence only of 'some few sectaries savouring independency'.[41] Later, in March 1654, a commission of mainly so-called Triers, consisting of Presbyterian, Independent and Baptist ministers, was appointed to examine and approve, or otherwise, clergy nominated by the lay patrons of church livings.

Although the deprived ministers undoubtedly suffered for their beliefs and their royalism, some were able to remain within the ranks of beneficed clergy. Four hundred of them were subsequently appointed to another living and about two hundred pluralists managed to keep one of their parishes, while others again kept their heads down and, with the support of their parishioners, were able to cling on in the face of official hostility. Some, who had been closely connected with royalty, joined the other expatriates eking out a poverty-stricken existence in France or the Low Countries or struggled on at home as best they could. In March 1656 John Evelyn reported that a collection was being taken up 'for persecuted and sequestered ministers of the Church of England, whereof divers are in prison'.

In spite of everything, it was still possible to find places where the priest was prepared to defy the law and conduct services according the Anglican rite. Certainly there was at least one church in the capital itself where 'the ruling powers' appear to have connived at the use of the liturgy, and in April 1656 John Evelyn was able to go with his family to celebrate the feast of Easter after the familiar fashion. But later that year there was a general tightening-up of discipline, and a proclamation was issued forbidding any Anglican minister either to preach, administer the sacraments or teach school on pain of imprisonment or exile, causing John Evelyn to lament that the Church of England 'was reduced to a chamber and conventicle; so sharp was the persecution. The parish churches', he went on, 'were filled with sectaries of all sorts, blasphemous and ignorant mechanics usurping the pulpits everywhere.' However, Dr Wild, one-time chaplain to Archbishop Laud, preached in a private house in Fleet Street, where, Evelyn could record, 'we had a great meeting of zealous Christians, who were generally much more devout and religious than in our greatest prosperity'.[42] Nevertheless, the diarist found it prudent to continue to attend his parish church, making it clear that the only reason he did so 'while these usurpers possessed the pulpits was that I might not be suspected for a papist, and that, though the minister was Presbyterianly affected, yet he was as I understood duly ordained, and preached sound doctrine after their way, and was besides an humble, harmless and peaceable man'.[43]

While the Church of England suffered, another group received a semi-official blessing when, in the mid-1650s, the Jews, excluded from England since the late thirteenth century, were again able to live and trade under the protection of Oliver Cromwell.

Their position was not yet legalised, nor was their presence universally approved, although Puritan interest in biblical studies – especially the Old Testament – had encouraged a belief that the chosen people should once again be welcomed among the Saints. Was it not prophesied that the coming of Christ's kingdom on earth would be preceded by the conversion of the Jews? Other considerations, not so publicly admitted, were of a more practical variety and may have weighed more heavily with Cromwell and his spymaster, John Thurloe, who could appreciate their usefulness as 'able and general intelligencers' whose intercourse with the continent could be very valuable to a government always conscious of its inveterate enemies abroad. There was also the matter of commercial and financial advantage to be taken into account. The returning Jews, Marranos from Spain and Portugal, were therefore able to purchase a burial ground at Mile End and allowed to worship without interference at their synagogue in Creechurch Lane, despite some strong opposition from the Council of State and those city merchants who did not welcome competition.

FOUR

His Highness the Lord Protector

Although England has had Lord Protectors before, she never made them so absolute as this . . . He [Cromwell] lacks nothing of royalty but the name . . .

(Lorenzo Paulucci, December 1653)

In mid-seventeenth-century England the great majority, something like 80 per cent of people of all classes, still lived on and by the land. Outside London the only towns of any consequence were Bristol, Exeter, Norwich, York and Newcastle with a total population of less than 100,000. London, though, was in a class of its own, already well on its way to becoming the largest and most important European capital city. By 1650 the population has been estimated at slightly over 400,000 and growing, just as the built-up area was fast increasing in spite of official attempts to control it. The town, which had, of course, long since burst the boundaries of its medieval city walls, now extended from Stepney in the east to Westminster, a distance of more than five miles, and on the south bank of the Thames from Lambeth and Southwark out to Rotherhithe. North of the river the outlying villages of Clerkenwell and Islington were already being swallowed up by the urban sprawl, and enterprising landlords had begun to develop the area between Holborn and the Strand to accommodate the better class of tenant. Further west the former royal hunting grounds of Hyde Park had been opened for public recreation. Piccadilly, or the 'way to Reading', had not yet been paved, and wild bugloss, whose root mixed with oil was said to cure green wounds, grew along the dry ditch banks, but by 1630 some modest properties were being built there and soon the fields round St James's would also be attracting the attention of developers.

London represented the political, commercial and cultural heart of the country. It was the seat of government, containing the Parliament House, the law courts, the foreign embassies, the principal fortress of the Tower containing the royal mint and armoury. It was a great sea port handling nearly all overseas trade and, perhaps most important of all, the financial centre. When the King fled to Hampton Court at the beginning of 1642, abandoning the capital with its vital wealth and resources, he had to all intents and purposes lost the war before it began. He had, of course, already lost the support of the Londoners through his usual mixture of bad luck and bad judgement, culminating in that disastrous attempt to arrest the Five Members, and it was the menacing attitude of the crowds thronging Whitehall which had panicked him into flight.

The London crowd was always a force to be reckoned with, especially in the highly charged atmosphere immediately preceding the outbreak of war, and although it could usually be manipulated in favour of the parliamentary cause, this was not always the case. There were peace protests, demonstrations and counter-demonstrations in Westminster in 1643, when the war was going badly, and on 9 August a mob of women had swarmed into Palace Yard, hammering on the door of the Commons chamber, yelling 'Give us those traitors that were against peace!' and 'Give us that dog Pym!'[1] When the militia men on guard tried to disperse them by firing powder, the women responded with stones and brickbats, so that in the end a troop of horse had to be called in to restore order, and there was another episode during the stand-off between the Commons and the army in 1647.

Like any great city, London provided a fertile seed-bed for the germination of new and subversive ideas – especially at a time when so many long-accepted truisms were being questioned – and attracted a wide variety of ideological theorists, from serious-minded social reformers like the Levellers to wild men who rejected the notion that men could sin or who believed themselves to have been vouchsafed divine revelations. But there was also that hard core of sober citizens, the businessmen, the small traders, shopkeepers and artisans, men 'that never lived beyond the view of the smoke of their own chimnies', who wanted nothing more than a return to normal peacetime ways, relieved of the heavy burden of taxation and bureaucracy which the war had brought. The excise duty, first introduced by John Pym in 1643 and imposed on a wide variety of commodities in everyday use, including food and drink, beer, cider and even meat, was particularly unpopular. It was supposed to be paid by the manufacturers, but they naturally passed it on to the consumer, using it as an excuse for putting up prices. This led to riots in the winter of 1646/7, culminating in a strike by the butchers and the burning-down of the Excise Office together with its records. The 'mechanick citizens' hated the tax gatherers and feared both the sects and the army, but more than anything they dreaded the prospect of more violence and plunder, the loss and destruction of precious, hard-won property. Presbyterianism was strong in the City, and these were its supporters, to whom it seemed to offer their best protection against anarchy, the military and the Independents. They were even prepared to have the King back, provided he would agree to take the Covenant.

It was fear that parliament was giving way to the demands of the army by agreeing to take control of the militia out of City, that is, Presbyterian, hands which provoked a serious disturbance in the summer of 1647, when a mob invaded the Commons 'in a most rude and tumultuous way', demanding that the ordinance for change of the militia of London be repealed. According to Bulstrode Whitelocke, 'the apprentices and many other rude boys and mean fellows among them, came into the House of Commons, and kept the door open, and their hats on, and called out as they stood, *Vote, vote . . .*', and, having successfully intimidated the Speaker and the Clerk of the House, 'in this arrogant posture stood till the votes passed in that way . . . Here', thought Whitelocke, 'we may observe an instance of the highest insolence in the rabble and of popular madness that can be met with in any other story.'[2] The members were also forced to demand that the King, who was then in the hands of the army, should be brought to London. 'They that imprisoned us', wrote one of those present, 'beat and cry out at the door and would not permit us to divide, the votes being doubtful.'[3] After this outrage a number of MPs fled to the protection of the army and ambitious plans for a counter-revolutionary *putsch* which had been maturing between the Presbyterian pressure group in parliament and the Common Council of the City collapsed in a general failure of nerve. The King stayed in captivity and the army marched peacefully into town.

Although the Londoners had been spared any direct experience of the unpleasantness of warfare, they remained geographically in the political front line. After General Cromwell's dramatic 'dissolution' of the Rump in the spring of 1653, the Venetian ambassador remarked that the people 'for the most part seem pleased and especially satisfied by a step which gives hope of relief and better management in everything. To judge from present appearances,' he went on, 'it is probable that parliament will be utterly abolished rather than renewed and that all affairs, both domestic and foreign, will be subject to a council consisting of a few persons appointed by the military . . . In short, as I have often said, the army will always be paramount and will finally dispose of everything.'[4]

But while the Lord General and his officers conferred behind closed doors over the future shape of the government of the republic, intense excitement was being generated among the London sects – especially the Fifth Monarchy men – who believed that at long last power was about to be delivered into the hands of the Saints, that is, themselves, in preparation for the Second Coming, and 'that the question is not so much now who is Independent, Anabaptist, seeker etc. as who is for C[hris]t and who is for Crom[well] but the day of God will put an end to these things'.[5] The Saints might be confidently expecting the imminent prospect of rule by King Jesus, but the Venetian ambassador was beginning to hear rumours of the possibility of rule by a rather more mundane figure.

'The general belief ', he wrote early in June, 'is that for the future he [Cromwell] will not content himself with a private station, especially as by posters put up in the streets and by the voice of some of the preachers he has been proclaimed worthy of the crown, under pretence that a monarchical form of government is indispensable for the welfare and quiet of England.'[6]

Some of the military men, notably the Fifth Monarchist General Harrison, were in favour of government by a supreme Council of seventy members, along the lines of the ancient Jewish Sanhedrin. In the end, however, a new Council of State consisting of eight army officers and four civilians was set up to deal with day-to-day matters of administration and met for the first time at the end of April, but some form of legislative body would obviously be necessary. Cromwell and the army were not about to risk holding elections which would be all too likely to return another hostile assembly at Westminster, so it was agreed that a nominated parliament consisting of 140 reliably God-fearing individuals, recommended by the Independent or gathered church congregations, should be summoned to present themselves at Westminster on the fourth day of July.

The new Representative, as it was originally known, duly came together in the Council Chamber at Whitehall to be addressed by Cromwell, who stood bare-headed and surrounded by as many of his officers as could squeeze themselves in behind him. It was a hot day and the atmosphere in the crowded room quickly became uncomfortable, nor did the Lord General's speech do anything to bring down the temperature. In the course of a long, impassioned diatribe he told his audience: 'Truly you are called by God to rule with Him, and for Him. And you are called to be faithful with the Saints, who have been somewhat instrumental to your call . . . I confess I never looked to see such a day as this – it may be nor you neither – when Jesus Christ should be so owned as He is, at this day, and in this work . . . this may be the door to usher in the things that God has promised.'[7]

It all sounded hopeful, and when the Representative's members gathered in St Stephen's chapel at eight o'clock on the following morning they proceeded to dedicate the whole day to prayer and humiliation, their devotions being led by a dozen or so of their own number, among them Arthur Squibb, a Fifth Monarchist representing Middlesex, and Samuel Moyer, a radical Congregationalist, one of seven London members. While the Long Parliament had not infrequently spent whole days in prayer, it had been in the habit of calling on some well-known clergymen to lead the members. The new assembly, however, true to its sectarian principles, which held that any man feeling the call was entitled to preach and pray publicly, preferred to rely on its own members to perform this office.

Having elected a Speaker, appointed a Clerk and Sergeant-at-Arms and even retrieved the mace, that sacred bauble so unceremoniously removed by Cromwell, the Representative now published a Declaration, announcing itself to be the Parliament of the Commonwealth of England. It promised to be 'as tender of the lives, estates, liberties, just rights and properties of all others as we are of ourselves and our posterities', and ended with the pious aspiration 'that in peace and joy we may all wait, expect and long for his glorious coming, who is King of Kings, and Lord of Lords, our hope and righteousness'.[8]

Although known officially as the Nominated or Little Parliament – the Venetian ambassador believed that the Representative's new title was intended to 'render its acts more authentic and prevent murmuring among the people, who are attached to the term "parliament"' – the assembly was to become known to history as Barebone's Parliament, an indelible label derived from one of its members, who rejoiced in the unfortunate and eye-catching name of Praise-God Barebone. Barebone himself was a Londoner, probably of Huguenot stock – his name originally being Barbon or Barbone. He was a man of some substance, a leather-seller, admitted freeman of the Leathersellers' Company in 1623 and a liveryman in 1634. A religious radical and lay preacher, he ministered to a congregation which worshipped at his warehouse, the Lock and Key in Fleet Street, and became a member of several parliamentary committees, but appears to have taken little or no part in debates. Inevitably, though, the parliament which has immortalised his name was to become a target for denigration and ridicule in royalist circles – 'Pettifoggers, Innkeepers, Millwrights, Stockingmongers and such a rabble as never had hopes to be of a Grand Jury' – and Clarendon was to call them 'a pack of weak, senseless fellows', the major part of them consisting 'of inferior persons, of no quality, or name, artificers of the meanest trades, known only by their gifts in praying and preaching'.[9]

This was both unfair and untrue, for at least a third of the membership came from the sort of landed gentry families typical of previous parliaments. There were a few former Rumpers and others who between them possessed a wide range of solid legal, administrative and financial experience. Of the 140 members, 45, possibly more, had had a university education and/or been trained at one of the Inns of Court, and although there were about 30 members classed as merchants and professional men, none of them could in any sense be described as 'artificers of the meanest trades'. Nor, for that matter, was there a preponderance of religious zealots in Barebone's Parliament. Only about a dozen members were actual Fifth Monarchy Men and the other radicals appear to have been mainly Baptists by persuasion.

The new Representative or parliament set about its task with commendable diligence, meeting at eight o'clock every morning except Sundays and appointing no fewer than ten standing committees, which were reported to sit daily and take great pains 'to dispatch business, and make things ready for the House'. They had an ambitious programme before them, including setting up new machinery for the probate of wills and registering births, marriages and deaths, which had fallen into abeyance with the abolition of the old Church courts (it was Barebone's Parliament which first legalised civil marriage before a Justice of the Peace). They also proposed reform of the debtors' law and the revenue, with abolition of the hated excise. Measures were passed for the relief of poor prisoners and lunatics. Ways of simplifying the legal system to make it intelligible to litigants as well as lawyers were discussed and abolition of the Court of Chancery, notorious for its inefficiency and 'faculty of bleeding the People in the Purse-vein', was proposed and agreed, although unfortunately no one could agree about what should replace it.

All this was sensible enough and generally uncontroversial, but friction was not long in appearing between the moderate majority and the radical faction, which, although small, was highly organised, meeting regularly to discuss tactics in the London house of Arthur Squibb. Outside the chamber loud demands for a far more thoroughgoing spring-clean of both law and religion, in preparation for the millennium, than had so far been attempted were being made by fanatical preachers such as Christopher Feake, who wanted all law abrogated in favour of the Mosaic code, and by pamphleteers such as John Rogers. In a publication resoundingly entitled *Doomesday drawing nigh, with Thunder and Lightening to Lawyers* he declared the people were crying out 'for justice upon the usurping proud lawyers, for their lying, perjury and treachery' and went on to proclaim that the citizens of the Commonwealth of England had work to do 'about the Lawes and Tithes, to strip the whore both of her outward scarlet array, and to rend the flesh off her bones, by throwing down the standing of Lawyers and Priests'.[10]

The final breakdown of relations between moderates and radicals came to a head over the question of tithes. This method of financing the clergy by the payment of a tenth of annual income to the church had long been bitterly unpopular, especially among the sectaries who wanted to see an independent ministry supported voluntarily by their congregations and to abolish the system of lay patronage. This was too much for the moderates, some of whom not only had livings in their gift but also benefited from the impropriation of tithes, and who were in any case becoming increasingly alarmed by the zealotry of the Saints, often unfortunately their social inferiors. They could see a general attack on property, the magistracy, parochial ministry, in short, red revolution looming on the horizon, and on 12 December, therefore, they arrived early at the House, perhaps counting on most of the radicals being absent at their Monday prayer meeting at Blackfriars, and proceeded to dissolve themselves, since they no longer felt able to prevent 'the confusion and despoliation of the nation'. While the moderates, led by the Speaker, Francis Rous, who as a Presbyterian was strongly in favour of a properly maintained preaching ministry, trooped off to Whitehall to hand in their resignation, a group of some thirty radical members sat tight and were presently visited by a detachment of musketeers, who enquired what they thought they were doing. Getting the predictable reply that they were seeking the Lord, the colonel in charge is said to have remarked sourly: 'Come out of this place then, for to my knowledge the Lord has not been here these twelve years past.'[11] The army had been losing its enthusiasm for the Saints just recently, since they started showing signs of interfering in military matters and suggesting a reduction in the soldiers' pay.

Bitterly disappointed at parliament's abject failure to prepare the country for the reign of King Jesus, the millenarian preachers raged in impotent defiance from the pulpits of St Anne's, Blackfriars, Allhallows the Great in Upper Thames Street, and Christ Church, Newgate Street. Christopher Feake and Vavasor Powell attacked Cromwell as 'the dissemblingest perjured villain in the world', and Feake went so far as to identify the Lord General with the 'Little Horn' of the ten horned beast featured in the Book of Daniel which would make war with the saints and prevail against them, 'until the Ancient of days came . . . and the time came that the saints possessed the kingdom'.[12] Vavasor Powell, having decided that Charles I was the 'king of the north' in Daniel 11, went on to apply verse 21 to Cromwell: 'And in his estate shall stand up a vile person, to whom they shall not give the honour of the kingdom: but he shall come in peaceably, and obtain the kingdom by flatteries.' Powell also attacked those army Grandees who supported Cromwell. 'Have our army men all apostasised from their principles? What is become of all their declarations, protestations and professions? Are they choked with parks, lands and manors? Let us go home and pray, and say, Lord, wilt thou have Oliver Cromwell or Jesus Christ to reign over us?' Powell believed that the Saints might now face persecution and be prevented from meeting at their Blackfriars headquarters, 'but then', he announced fiercely, 'we can meet at another, and if we be driven from thence, we will meet at private houses, and if we cannot have liberty there, we will into the fields, and if we be driven thence, we will into corners, for we will never give over!'[13]

Feake and Powell were arrested and cautioned on 21 December but released three days later, and, for all the noise they were making, it seems that the Fifth Monarchy Men had had their day. Indeed, the disappearance of Barebone and his parliament was greeted with about as much public apathy as that of the Rump eight months previously. The lawyers, it is true, allowed themselves a little quiet celebration, but the ordinary citizens, grumbling about their taxes and increasingly disillusioned with parliaments of all descriptions, remained unmoved. 'A very general belief prevails that there is now an end of parliaments', wrote the Venetian ambassador, 'and that everything will be directed by a single council.' Lorenzo Paulucci had already observed that 'the Londoners think they have gained little by the present form of government. A large part of the people', he went on, 'is now obliged to live on the profits they obtained of yore from the nobility and gentry, as luxuries are at present practically abolished, wealth having fallen into the hands of people unused to possess it and who are more inclined to hoard than to spend, so that the tradesmen here and all over England sigh for the old state of affairs.'[14]

Paulucci may have been exaggerating, but there is no doubt that the Londoners, especially those engaged in luxury trades, had always relied heavily on the money to be made when the King and his court were in town for the winter season. Now, though, it appeared that there was to be a court at Whitehall again, albeit a rather different kind of court, for on 16 December Oliver Cromwell, wearing a plain black suit and cloak and escorted by the Lord Mayor and all the aldermen and sheriffs, processed through streets lined with soldiers to Westminster Hall to be publicly installed as

Lord Protector of the Commonwealth of England, Scotland and Ireland. Seated on what had once been a royal throne, he listened bareheaded as his new powers and responsibilities, as set out in the Instrument of Government – the nearest thing to a written constitution which the country had ever had – were read out to him. He then signed the Instrument and swore to abide by its articles.

> Thus [reported the Venetian ambassador] by universal consent and in the most solemn and conspicuous manner he found himself created Protector of the whole kingdom. He then covered and the military officers and other functionaries, hat in hand, did him homage, in the obsequious and respectful form observed towards the late kings. He was presented with the seals and the Lord Mayor gave him the state sword. He returned both to their bearers in token of his authority. All the officials then accompanied him back, bareheaded, amid salutes of musketry from the troops, to Whitehall, where he is expected to reside with his wife and where he will exercise sovereign authority . . .'[15]

He was now empowered, together with his council, to declare war or make peace. He could confer dignities, levy taxes and do whatever he thought best for the common good. It had been expressly stipulated in the Instrument that he should summon parliament once in every three years, with the power to prolong or dissolve it at his pleasure, but this article, thought Paulucci, might not be so readily carried into effect. 'Although England has had Protectors before', he concluded, 'she never made them so absolute as this.' Cromwell, the brilliant military commander and comparatively modest landowner from the English shires – he described himself as being 'by birth a gentleman living neither in any considerable height not yet in obscurity' – had now become, in effect, 'king in all but name'.

As was customary on the day of a king's accession, the occasion was marked by bell ringing and bonfires – the Inner Temple spending the princely sum of 8s 10d on their bonfire – and three days later Cromwell, by order of his Council, was officially proclaimed Lord Protector in cities and towns throughout the land. Early in February his new Highness made his first state visit to the City, riding in 'a costly coach accompanied by Gen. Lambert of the army and Admiral Monck of the navy. The march', wrote Paulucci, 'was preceeded and closed by a great number of gentlemen and his privy councillors in a long string of coaches and six, which drove thus through the faubourg to the city gates, whither the heralds, in rich attire had gone before to announce his approach by sound of trumpet.' The Protector was received at Temple Bar by the Lord Mayor and aldermen 'in their state gowns, with gold chains and jewels', and with all the ceremony previously accorded to royalty. But, says Paulucci, 'although the entire population of London came forth to view the pageant, not the faintest sound of applause was heard, nor were any blessings invoked on the head of his Highness, very different from what happened when the kings similarly appeared in public'.[16]

The procession now made its way to Grocers' Hall in Coneyhope Lane, off the Poultry, where a 'sumptuous banquet' had been prepared, the company being 'saluted by all the Tower guns in the middle of it'. At the conclusion of the feast the guest of honour was presented with a gift, 'some say of 20,000*l*. sterling while others report it as a service of gilt plate', and in return his Highness exercised his new sovereign prerogative by knighting the Lord Mayor, Thomas Vyner. At seven in the evening the Protector set off back to Whitehall

in the same pomp, with the addition of 300 lighted torches and all outward signs of respect and honour, but with very scanty marks of goodwill from the people in general, who, on the contrary, greeted him with a rancour which increases daily because he has arrogated to himself despotic authority and the actual sovereignty of these realms under the mask of humility and the public service. He lacks nothing of royalty but the name [concluded Paulucci], as his power is certainly greater than that of the late kings.[17]

The Venetian was able to add in his next despatch, that, on his way home from the city banquet,

> his Highness not only missed the popular applause which he expected but received proof of a very different sentiment. A large stone was suddenly flung at him from a window, though fortunately it fell a short distance from his coach without hurting anyone. Efforts were made instantly to discover the author of this daring act, but owing to the confusion caused by the crowd and the darkness of the night it was impossible to find out any particulars.[18]

Lorenzo Paulucci was of the opinion that 'obedience and submission were never so manifest in the English as at present, the fear of coercion under which they labour increasing with the remembrance of the tragical events of the civil wars'. Their spirits, he felt, were 'so crushed that although they consider themselves oppressed, dissatisfied and deluded, they dare not rebel and only murmur under their breath'.[19] Although foreign observers were agreed on the general sullen indifference of the populace, whether the Londoners were really as crushed as Paulucci believed seems open to some doubt. According to a report in the news-sheet *Mercurius Politicus*, 'an ordinary fellow' in the street, seeing the heralds, with the sergeants-at-arms, members of the Council, the Lord Mayor and aldermen gathered at Temple Bar about to proclaim the Protector to the sound of trumpets, had asked one of the cavalry troopers in attendance what was going on. 'Proclaiming His Highness Lord Protector Cromwell,' was the reply. 'He protects none but such rogues as thou art,' retorted the citizen, and when the soldier made to strike him, pulled him off his horse and dealt him some hearty blows, while the other onlookers laughed and shouted encouragement, apparently unconcerned by the presence of the great and good.[20]

Apart from the Fifth Monarchy Men, who continued to breathe fire and brimstone against the new regime, critics of the Protectorate included men such as Edmund Ludlow, soldier, regicide and staunch Commonwealth man who felt deeply the apparent betrayal of the ideals of the revolution, of 'that which we fought for, that the nation might be governed by its own consent', and John Hutchinson, another soldier, devout Puritan and convinced parliamentarian, whose wife observed bitterly how 'Cromwell and his army grew wanton with their power'. 'His court was full of sin and vanity', she went on, and 'true religion was now almost lost . . . to the sad grief of Colonel Hutchinson and all true-hearted Christians and Englishmen'.[21]

The Venetian ambassador had heard reports of 'prophecies foretelling a change of rule ere long' – prophecies which might be corroborated by 'certain events savouring of prodigy. Just before the late king's death', he went on,

> the tide in the Thames protracted its ebb and flow for two hours longer than usual and this has been observed again. Also a part of St Paul's famous cathedral here has fallen, killing several persons, and finally . . . many credible witnesses declare that they have seen the ghost of the beheaded King Charles in the former royal palace, who afterwards vanished. Whether this is true or not [concluded Paulucci], the conviction certainly gains ground that it is impossible for this kingdom to remain long quiet without the sceptre of its legitimate king.[22]

But in spite of a certain amount of grumbling among the citizenry, and the misgivings of the Independents and Commonwealth men, the bulk of the population seem to have been prepared to accept the recent turn of events philosophically enough. The most irrepressible of the Fifth Monarchists had now been imprisoned in Windsor Castle, having fallen foul of a new ordinance making it a treasonable offence to write, teach or preach that the Protector's authority was tyrannical, usurped or unlawful, and by the spring of 1654 preparations to provide his Highness with accommodation suitable to his quasi-royal status were well under way.

The new court naturally required a palace, and it was decided that the old royal residences of St James's, Whitehall, Somerset House, Greenwich, Windsor and Hampton Court together with their various parks and appurtenances should now be vested 'in the present Lord Protector and succeeding Lord Protectors, for the maintenance of his and their state and dignity'. Unfortunately, however, back in 1649 it had been decreed that all Crown property – manors, castles, houses, parks and lands – should be surveyed, valued and sold for the benefit of the new Commonwealth.[23] The then Council of State had decided to exempt those properties which were now to be put at the disposal of the Protector, but under a subsequent Act of Parliament some of them had been either partially sold off or leased and had now to be retrieved – a process which was to prove both complicated and expensive.

Hampton Court, which had been earmarked as the Protector's country residence, had passed entirely into private hands, and negotiations with the new owners of the estate, which began in February 1654, were barely completed by April, when his Highness proposed to move in. The cost, involving additional compensation paid to a number of individuals who had bought leases from the original purchaser, who appears to have been a Mr Edmund Blackwell or Backwell, a goldsmith and jeweller of London, had been considerable, and as well as this, there had been a problem with squatters, several enterprising residents of Kingston-on-Thames having been fencing off some of the meadows belonging to the palace.[24]

There was a squatter problem, too, at Whitehall, where a number of old retainers and their dependants were still clinging on in nooks and corners of the palace complex. When John Claypole, Cromwell's son-in-law and newly appointed Master of the Horse, arrived to take over in the stables, it was discovered that the widow and children of John Sanderson, who had been waterman to James I and Charles I, several aged former grooms of the late king, the widow of Charles I's sumpterman and her three small children, plus five other widows of former royal servants, were all living in makeshift lodgings over the stables in the dunghill yard. The problem of what to do with these sad relics of a past age seems to have been difficult to resolve, as it was more than a year before the stables were finally cleared of their unauthorised tenants – one of the last to go being 92-year-old Henry Zinzan, who had been an equerry to James I and who was not evicted until February 1656. He did, though, succeed in extracting a pension of 20s a week from the authorities.[25]

Since Oliver's return from Ireland in 1650, the Cromwell family had been living in the so-called Cockpit lodgings, that part of the Whitehall village adjacent to the cockpit and overlooking St James's park. Now they were about to move into the former royal apartments, and on 14 April it was announced that 'his Highness the Lord Protector, with his Lady and family, this day dined at Whitehall, whither his Highness and family are removed, and did this day lie there, and do there continue'. It had also been decreed that part at least of the Cromwells' new quarters were to be redecorated 'according to the instructions of her Highness the Lady Cromwell'.

Her Highness the Lady Cromwell, born Elizabeth Bourchier, had been Oliver's wife for over thirty years and had borne him two surviving sons and four daughters. She seems to have been a blameless wife, mother and housewife, thrifty, unassuming and devoted to her husband and family – domestic virtues which attracted much unkind mockery from the Protector's enemies, who accused her, among other things, of meanness, lack of dignity and having no taste in dress. She does not appear to have made any contribution to the grandeur of her new surroundings – on the contrary, she is said to have divided up some of the state rooms with partitions, presumably in an attempt to make them into cosier and no doubt warmer living quarters.

The Council, however, was determined to surround the Protector with the sort of royal state necessary to impress the outside world, and Cromwell was soon receiving foreign ambassadors in the Banqueting Hall designed by Inigo Jones, under the ceiling painted by Rubens, and through which Charles I had walked to the scaffold, with all the elaborate ceremony of former days – an irony which the ambassadors concerned did not fail to appreciate. Now that Whitehall and Hampton Court were having to be refurbished and brought back into use, it was a pity that so much of King Charles's incomparable art collection had been hastily sold off – much of it at knock-down prices to foreign buyers – in the years immediately following his execution. Some items, however, had survived, most notably Titian's *Herodias with the Head of John the Baptist*, the Raphael cartoons of The Acts of the Apostles and Andrea Mantegna's masterpiece *The Triumph of Julius Caesar*, which remains in the long gallery of Hampton Court today.[26]

Equally necessary to palace comfort and splendour were the tapestries, or arras hangings, most of them produced by Flemish weavers at the Mortlake factory in Surrey and usually illustrating classical or biblical themes such as *The History of Vulcan, Mars and Venus, The Story of King Hezekiah, The Siege of Jerusalem* and a ten-piece set dealing with the story of Abraham. The Abraham tapestry, which had originally been acquired by Henry VIII, was valued at £8,260 and, like the *Triumph of Caesar*, can still be seen at Hampton Court. Some of these tapestries had to be bought back from private collectors. In October 1654 the government paid £350 to redeem the six-piece set of Vulcan, Mars and Venus, and later that month £168 6s 0d went on a job lot of hangings portraying Cupid and Venus, Elijah the Prophet and the Story of Jacob, together with twenty Turkey carpets, fifteen of damask and one of taffeta.[27] The work of restoration continued through the early 1650s, so that when John Evelyn ventured to visit Whitehall in February of 1656, after many years' absence, he found it 'very glorious and well furnish'd'.

All the royal family's personal possessions and household goods which could be salvaged, from a crimson velvet bed with a canopy of cloth of gold and silver down to candlesticks and kitchen utensils, were now placed at the disposal of the Lord Protector, but not everything was second hand. Two services of plate for the Protector and his lady to the value of £3,000 were ordered from Sir Thomas Vyner, goldsmith and Lord Mayor of London, and a new Great Seal was struck, showing Oliver riding in triumph across a background scene of London with the Thames and the bridge, while on the other side appeared newly approved arms of the Protectorate, which at first glance bore a startling resemblance to the old royal arms, surmounted as they were by a kingly crown, while on a small shield in the centre the Cromwell family arms of a lion rampant had been worked into a design incorporating the cross of St George, the harp of Ireland and the saltire cross of St Andrew.

As well as their regal accommodation, the new first family would obviously need a household staff modelled on the royal pattern, with a Lord Chamberlain, a Comptroller, Master of Ceremonies, Gentlemen of the Privy Chamber, Grooms of the Bedchamber, plus chaplains, physicians and surgeons, a life guard and all the other miscellaneous extras and hangers-on normally associated with royalty, not to mention a whole separate establishment below stairs of kitchens, larders, butteries, bakehouse, pantry, beer and wine cellars, spicery, scullery, slaughterhouse and woodyard. Eating arrangements, or 'tables for diet', for the Protectoral court had been reported in the press as providing for: a Table for His Highness, a Table for the Protectress, a Table for Chaplains and Strangers, a Table for the Steward and Gentlemen, a Table for the Gentlewomen and so on down to the Inferiors or Sub-servants.[28] Out of doors there were the stables with their clerks and keepers, coachmen, grooms, postilions and footmen. There was the Master of the Barges with his watermen; the Office of Works with its complement of carpenters, masons and joiners, plus gardeners, falconers, huntsmen, gate-keepers, clock-winders and porters. Lucy Hutchinson remarked nastily that, with the possible exception of Oliver himself, all this 'principality' suited the rest of the Cromwell family no better than 'scarlet on the ape', and it is hardly surprising that the Fifth Monarchy men should have continued to regard the Lord Protector as being 'the perfidious betrayer of the cause of the godly, and the chief obstacle to the inauguration of the reign of King Jesus and his saints'.[29]

Daily life at the Protector's court bore little outward resemblance to that of his immediate predecessor, though Charles, himself a stickler for order and propriety, had been as intolerant as any Puritan of anything which could be characterised as 'goings-on'. But while Oliver's court – described by a contemporary as being strictly regulated, 'here no drunkard, nor whoremonger, nor any guilty of bribery was to be found' – certainly never became the glamorous sophisticated cultural centre presided over by Charles and his mercurial French consort, it was no joyless wasteland. Even his enemies conceded that Oliver was a great lover of music who 'entertained the most skilful in that science in his pay and family', and the organ from Magdalen College chapel was transferred to Hampton Court for his special delight. The abolition of the cathedral choirs and church music in general had, of course, seriously limited the career opportunities for both singers and musicians, but there were still some openings in the households of the well-to-do, while the Protector employed John Hingston as his Master of the Music at a salary of £100 a year, together with seven other instrumentalists and singers, plus two boys to be 'brought up to music'.[30]

It is not likely that the ordinary Londoner was greatly interested in the growing splendour of the Lord Protector's home life. Nehemiah Wallington, master turner and devoutly religious Puritan of the parish of St Leonard's, Eastcheap, was more concerned, in the summer of 1654, with the anxious business of seeking a new apprentice. Nehemiah, always nervous and socially diffident, had to interview four candidates before he finally succeeded in finding a suitable applicant, and the whole thing, he recorded, did 'so vex and terrify' his mind that he knew not what to do.[31] Poor Nehemiah, never a very successful businessman, was always worried about money – on one occasion, having had to find 12s to pay a creditor, he thought he had scraped the barrel only to discover another 13s or 14s distributed about his pockets and in various drawers in his workshop and chamber. Like many of his fellows, his income had been seriously affected by the upheavals of war and politics, and after the army occupied London in 1647 he wrote in one of his numerous notebooks, 'then my trading in my shop failed me very much'. Between 1647 and 1649 his half-yearly takings fell by over £100, 'and that', he reflected mournfully, 'was very small gain'.[32]

Nehemiah was unusual, if not unique, in that as a comparatively humble artisan he produced a voluminous written record of his daily and spiritual life, plus notes on sermons, psalms, histories, lists of books he had read, of sins that troubled him and God's mercies to his soul and body. Out of fifty meticulously numbered and catalogued notebooks, only six appear to have survived, but these do at least give us some tantalising glimpses of a sensitive, introspective individual, often a prey to what would no doubt today be recognised as clinical depression. He makes New Year resolutions and fines himself 2*d* for failing to keep them. A painfully honest man, who destroys a false coin which had found its way into his money box – 'my conscience did begin to chide me and said I had a thief in my box, a brass shilling which will canker all the rest' – and a good family man who takes his widowed sister-in-law and her children into his home, he still constantly torments himself about his sins – 'about two o'clock I did awake and I could not but think what a base, filthy, vile heart I have, my conscience hagging me for my sins of omission yesterday . . .'.[33]

A master turner was a skilled craftsman, turning out stools, chair legs, wooden bowls, shovels, scoops, bushel measures, washing tubs and suchlike useful domestic objects, but although their guild was an ancient one, the Turners ranked low in the pecking order of London crafts and were prevented from expanding into the more profitable areas of household furniture by the powerful Joiners and Carpenters, so that even if Nehemiah had been a better businessman, he was unlikely ever to have become rich. Certainly he seems to have had very little idea of book-keeping. When burglars broke in one Sunday morning while the family were in church he could only guess at his losses. 'They had taken out, as I think, about three pounds and a box . . . with, as I think, about twenty shillings in it.' He was, in fact, grateful that the thieves had not broken into his chamber and taken 'that little plate and some other money that was there'. Typically, he began to wonder how he had gained the money, 'whether I have not robbed others by lying and deceit', and whether perhaps this was God's way to wean him from the world.[34]

Nehemiah and his wife, Grace, had many occasions to question the Almighty's purposes, as one after another their children sickened and died – Elizabeth, followed by John, little Nehemiah and finally Samuel, all before reaching their third birthdays. Grace, who seems to have been the stronger character, faced her losses with extraordinary patience, giving each child as freely back again unto God as she had received it from him. Nehemiah, on the other hand, was prostrated with grief on every occasion, temporarily at least forgetting his 'purposes, promises and covenants' with God and refusing all comfort from men. One child, Sarah, did survive, but even she had several narrow escapes, including smallpox at the age of three and on another occasion nearly falling into the fire, a constant hazard for small children playing around open grates. Fortunately, the Lord seems to have been keeping a special eye on Sarah, for in the summer of 1631 at about six in the evening, she wandered away from the shop door, where she had been playing with a neighbour's child and got as far as the road into East Smithfield before she fell down and bumped her forehead. A passer-by picked her up, and thinking she must have come from the Wapping direction, would have taken her there had not another passer-by recognised the little girl and brought her home. Meanwhile, faced with every parent's nightmare, Nehemiah had begun a frantic fruitless search for his daughter, only learning of her rescue when he returned, exhausted, some hours later. This, at least, was a clear sign of God's providence, 'for it might have been that we should have seen [Sarah] no more . . . and then what strange distractful thoughts should we have had, and how could we eat or have slept that night with thinking what is become of our poor child'.[35]

Nehemiah Wallington had taken no part in the Civil War and had at first been reluctant to condemn the King, but, as a Puritan who saw the political situation in moral terms, a struggle against Antichrist as represented by papists, prelates and similar malignants, his sympathies naturally lay on the side of the parliamentary cause, though he never regarded the war itself with any enthusiasm – 'a sad business, the Lord of his mercy help us'.[36] He took an informed interest in the great events going on around him, being an avid buyer of news-sheets and 'diurnals', but his own public activities were confined to the ward, where he served as constable in 1638 and 1639, and as a grand juryman in the 1640s and 1650s, and the parish as one of its ruling elders.

Nehemiah was no sectarian, believing the modified form of Presbyterianism approved by parliament in 1645 to be most conducive 'to the preservation of religion and the worship of Almighty God' and the best defence against 'a most dangerous inundation of horrid blasphemies, damnable heresies, and abominable profaneness daily increasing over the whole kingdom'.[37] He was, though, only too well aware of the shortcomings of the system, and in the spring of 1650 lamented the 'profaning of the Lord's day, drunkenness, whoredom, the swearing and blasphemies, the error and schisms, and neither the sword of magistracy nor ministry pulled out against them', not to mention 'the covetousness, the oppression, the cruelty and unmercifulness to the poor'.[38] Predictably, he feared the vengeance of the Lord 'on such a nation . . . in these declining times', but there's no doubt that he would have approved the government's efforts to suppress the evils associated with the stage and its players.

Both King Charles and his wife had been keen theatre-goers, and the court masque, that curious amalgam of pageant, pantomime and propaganda vehicle, scripted by leading poets and brilliantly staged by Inigo Jones, had reached its apotheosis in the 1620s and 1630s. The King and Queen themselves would take part, and on one occasion the Queen took a leading part in a pastoral play entitled *The Shepheard's Paradise*. The Puritan faction, not surprisingly, disapproved strongly and vocally, and in 1633 William Prynne, barrister of Lincoln's Inn and Puritan polemicist, had published his notorious *Histrio Mastix: The Players Scourge, or, Actors Tragedie*, a comprehensive and uncompromising denunciation of the evils of all stage plays, players and play-going. Prynne foresaw God's wrath being provoked if players were allowed to perform in defiance of the Scriptures, as happened every time one of them appeared dressed as a woman; while the plays themselves, with their obscenities and adulterous representations, the posturing of the actors and the ravishing music which accompanied them, would naturally give rise to every kind of wicked lust in the audience. Added to which, attendance at the theatre only encouraged habits of waste, idleness and vanity, corrupted the young and impressionable, provided opportunities for crime from whoredom to theft and, since plays were normally performed on Sunday afternoons, the crowds of undesirables they attracted caused traffic jams and sometimes even interrupted church services. Prynne also attacked dancing, another favourite royal diversion, as 'heathenish, carnal, worldly, sensual and misbeseeming Christians'. He got into serious trouble with the authorities for his reference to 'women actors notorious whores', which was interpreted as an attack on the Queen, and dramatists, notably Ben Jonson, retaliated by ridicule. Jonson's caricature of Ananias Wholesome, a fanatical Anabaptist, in *The Alchemist* was so successful that Ananias became a general nickname for any Puritan, and in *Bartholomew Fair* Zeal-of-the-Land Busy is portrayed as a fool and a hypocrite who sees the mark of the Beast everywhere and a basket of gingerbread men as a 'flasket of idols'.

The stage had always been a precarious profession, and actors were regarded with suspicion by civic authorities wherever they appeared. This was especially true of London, where the City fathers held opinions very similar to those of William Prynne, and was the reason that playhouses were generally to be found outside the City limits. Actors depended heavily on royal or aristocratic patronage and protection – an Act of 1572 declared that common players not belonging to any baron of the realm or other honourable personage of greater degree, who were found wandering abroad without a licence from at least two Justices of the Peace, 'shall be taken adjudged and deemed Rogues, Vagabonds and Sturdy Beggars' – so that, when this protection effectively disappeared with the Civil War, so too did most of the players.

Not quite all of them, however. In September 1642 parliament had issued an ordinance closing the theatres on the grounds that public sports and stage plays had no place in time of war and calamity. But the habit of theatre-going was by now too firmly entrenched and too popular to be easily stamped out, and the order was often ignored. In 1643 three theatres, the Cockpit, the Red Bull and the Fortune, were still open, a defiance which caused parliament to issue another edict in the autumn of 1647 'for the better suppression of the said Stage Playes, Interludes and common Players'. In future all common players were to be regarded as rogues and punishable as such, 'whether they were wandering or no and notwithstanding any License whatsoever from the King or any person or persons to that purpose'. Rather more to the point, the civic authorities of the City of London and Westminster and of the counties of Middlesex and Surrey were now authorised and required to pull down and demolish 'all Stage Galleries, Seats, Boxes . . . which shall be erected and used for the acting or playing, or seeing acted or played such Stage Playes, Interludes and Plays aforesaid, within . . . their respective jurisdictions'. As a final sting in the tail, it was further ordained 'that every person or persons which shall be present and a Spectator at any such Stage Play, or Interlude hereby prohibited, shall for every time he shall be so present, forfeit and pay the sum of five shillings to the use of the poor of the Parish where the said person or persons shall at that time dwell or sojourn'.[39]

But even a series of raids by the military on the remaining theatres did not succeed in finally extinguishing the evil. One playhouse, the Red Bull in Clerkenwell, remained open and continued somehow to present various dramatic entertainments. When it became too difficult to perform full-length plays, Interludes and 'drolls', short comic pieces, were given instead. While ordinary citizens continued to enjoy one of their favourite amusements as and when they could in makeshift surroundings, the 'better sort' were able to organise performances in private houses – Holland House out at Kensington was a favourite location – and a large number of plays were printed during the period 1640–60.

Although the theatre continued to be proscribed, under the patronage of the music-loving Protector opera was considered acceptable, especially if it could be shown to convey some moral message. The first English opera, William Davenant's *The Siege of Rhodes*, was privately produced with a small cast of singers in the autumn of 1656, followed by *The Cruelty of the Spaniards in Peru*, staged at the Cockpit in Drury Lane, although John Evelyn, who went to see a new opera after the Italian way in May 1659, considered it to be 'much inferior to the Italian composure and magnificence'. There was even some attempt to revive the court masque at the wedding of the Protector's third daughter in November 1657, when *Two Songs at the Marriage of the Lord Fauconberg and the Lady Mary Cromwell* by Andrew Marvell was performed.

Other traditional amusements such as bear-baiting and cock-fighting were also banned by the authorities for the same reasons that they attracted crowds of undesirable elements who would lead their foolish and unwary fellow citizens into habits of idleness or worse, and most probably pick their pockets at the same time. The great Bartholomew's Fair held in Smithfield every August, with its booths selling everything from singing birds to mousetraps, its freak shows, fortune-tellers, dancing and drinking, quacks and prostitutes, was, however, tolerated throughout the Commonwealth period – it did, after all, encourage trade and provide an outlet for the high spirits of the young and unruly.

Earnest Presbyterians continued to bewail the numbers of those who profaned the Sabbath by tavern-haunting, selling their wares, sleeping in church or otherwise backsliding, and Nehemiah Wallington continued gloomily to foresee the judgement of God on London's sins, which included idolatry and superstition, profaning the name of God himself 'with the perfect language of hellish swearers in every child's mouth', plus fornication, murders, drunkenness, contempt of the Gospel, 'silencing and stopping the mouths of God's prophets and servants, and other gross secret sins'.[40] The majority of Londoners, however, continued to live their lives as best they could, raising their families, earning their livings, fighting the unending battle against poverty, disease, overcrowding and squalor in a town which, apart from Inigo Jones's upmarket development on the Earl of Bedford's estate round Covent Garden, had changed very little in outward appearance since the days of the Tudors.

Despite its growth, London was still a small place by modern standards, a place of recognisable neighbourhoods where people knew one another and where it was still possible to walk from one end to the other in a morning. At its heart was still the ancient City, the twenty-six wards ruled by the Lord Mayor and Common Council of Aldermen, who, with other members of the mercantile aristocracy, lived in princely splendour in tall, handsome houses in the fashionable areas of Lothbury and Bishopsgate. But in the courts and alleys behind the fine houses and sumptuous shops of Goldsmiths' Row at the western end of Cheapside and the galleries of the Royal Exchange in Cornhill, or further out in the new suburbs of St Giles, Clerkenwell, Cripplegate and Shoreditch, Deptford, Rotherhithe and Southwark, lurked the rat-infested slums and the hundreds of small factories and workshops – the tanners and metal-workers, silversmiths, cabinet-makers, joiners and turners like Nehemiah Wallington, shoemakers, butchers, coopers, soap-boilers, chandlers, brewers and dyers – all adding to the constant noise, the stink and pollution of the seething, overcrowded city where, in the unending struggle for survival, most people had rather more urgent things to do than worry about their sins.

FIVE

The Major-Generals

The Arraignment Conviction and Imprisonment of CHRISTMAS
. . . And how he broke out of Prison in the Holidays . . . With
divers other Witty Passages. Printed by Simon Minc'd Pie, for
Cissely Plum Porridge.

(Anonymous pamphlet)

To a casual eye the landscape of republican England would
appear to have changed little since the days of the Tudors and
beyond. Thousands of acres, from Cannock Chase in Staffordshire
to Sussex and Hampshire were still covered by dense woodland. The
Midlands and the northern moors were as yet unscarred by the
blight of the Industrial Revolution, most of Lancashire was still
morass or 'moss' and in the remoter parts of Wales and the Lake
District the wolf was not yet finally extinct. In the east the Great
Fen, stretching for nearly seventy miles from Cambridge to Lincoln
and from King's Lynn to Peterborough, was a region apart, where
the inhabitants, 'people of brutish uncivilised tempers' according to
the Elizabethan historian and topographer William Camden, lived
out their strange, amphibious lives much as they had done in the
days of Hereward the Wake. England was still mostly farmed on the
old medieval open-field system, with the land divided into half-acre
strips separated by narrow, unploughed paths known as balks, while
the sheep, on whose backs grew so much of the nation's wealth,
wandered in huge flocks over the Cotswolds, the South Downs,
Romney Marsh and the rich pasture lands of the Midland counties.

A closer look would have revealed some changes. Forward-
looking farmers and landowners were experimenting with new
ways, separating their land from the common fields, fencing them in

and cultivating them individually, either themselves or with hired labour. New crops, such as potatoes and turnips, were being tried; new methods of sowing and ploughing discussed; lucerne, clover and sainfoin suggested as possible solutions to the problem of providing winter fodder for cattle. Over to the east, the Dutch engineer Cornelius Vermuyden had made a start on draining the Fen country, and already visible were the first signs of the industrial age which would soon transform England for ever. Lead, tin, copper and iron ore had been mined since Roman times, and by the end of the sixteenth century iron smelting in Sussex had decimated the Wealden forest. Birmingham, a busy little Puritan town, made swords for the New Model Army, and there was a thriving cottage industry in South Staffordshire producing nails and pins. Further north, in Derbyshire, parts of Lancashire, Durham and Northumberland, coal mining was becoming increasingly important and coal was fast replacing wood as a domestic fuel. It was transported south from the Tyne by sea, and the Newcastle Company of Hostmen, which claimed the monopoly of its transport and shipping, grew rich and powerful.

The scars left by the war were all too painfully visible, especially to those whose property had suffered. The most spectacular examples of this were probably the Marquess of Winchester's great fortified mansion at Basing, of which only the foundations now remain, the Bankes family's Corfe Castle, 'slighted' after a long siege in the spring of 1646, and the Earl of Derby's Lathom. There were other, less well-known, country houses on both sides of the political divide destroyed in the fighting – among them the parliamentarian Harleys' Brampton Bryan, the royalist Arundells' Wardour Castle and Sir John Winter's Whitecross at Lydney in Gloucestershire. Towns in the war zone had also suffered damage – for instance, Faringdon, 'a good market town turned into ashes and rubbage', Taunton, 'here a poor forsaken chimney and there a little fragment of a wall', and Banbury, 'where there was scarce the one half standing to gaze on the ruins of the other'. There was serious damage, too, at Exeter, Lichfield, Lincoln, York, Chester, Hereford

and Worcester; Bridgnorth in Shropshire was virtually destroyed in 1646, and John Evelyn, passing through Colchester in 1656, called it 'a faire Towne but now wretchedly demolished . . . especially the suburbs all burnt'.

By the 1650s, though, reconstruction had already begun. As early as January 1648 a parliamentary committee had been established 'to examine and consider how, and in what Manner, such Churches, Towns or Houses, as have been burnt, demolished or spoiled since these Wars, may be repaired'. This body came to be known more succinctly as the Committee for Burning and was soon busy dealing with a flood of petitions for assistance from victims of war damage. In some cases, regarded as especially deserving, nationwide appeals were organised, but it was clear that charity alone was not going to solve so large a problem, and parliament turned to forfeited estates in Ireland as a possible source of relief. Some places were authorised to help themselves to money and materials from the sequestered estates of royalist 'delinquents', but progress was inevitably slow. Communities regarded as pro-royalist found themselves being pushed to the back of the queue for grants, and civic authorities generally preferred to rebuild town halls, churches and court houses at the expense of individual householders, who were not infrequently reduced to camping in 'outhouses, barnes and other desolate places' – a family from Gloucester took up residence in a pigeon house. As conditions began to return to normal it became a common practice for the homeless to move back to their former neighbourhoods and put up rough shelters from whatever materials they could salvage. Although intended as a temporary expedient, such makeshift dwellings were often occupied for several years, and with improvements became more or less permanent. This caused problems with the authorities, who had no desire to see these shanty towns grow up on their boundaries, and efforts, usually it seems unsuccessful, were made to have them demolished. The building of unplanned cottages was not the only unfortunate social legacy left by the war. A number of schools and almshouses, even if not damaged or destroyed themselves, suffered serious loss of income if the property which formed their endowment was destroyed and consequently the rents from it lost. Progress in reconstruction, too, was often hampered by disputes between landlords and lessees over who should be responsible for the costs involved. A modest town house, for example, might be built for less than £100, but that was still a very large sum for a man in a small way of business. Gradually, though, progress was made, and it should be remembered that, although many innocent men, women and children found themselves caught up in a conflict not of their making and lost homes, possessions and livelihoods, not to mention their lives, as a result, war damage had directly affected only a relatively small percentage of the total population.[1]

What did affect the total population, both directly and indirectly, was the form of government imposed upon them, which must sometimes have seemed to change as often as the seasons. As the Revd Ralph Josselin of Earls Colne remarked in his diary for 22 January 1654, 'this yeare brought forth notable revolucions at home, in dissolving parliaments and declaring Cromwell protector'. Josselin took an informed interest in current affairs but remained more immediately concerned with the state of his soul – 'the lord keepe mee, in soule and body without spott . . . for in thy grace and strength is my strength and tower' – and the state of the weather, which in February 'was for divers dayes winterly, cold winds with frost and snow'.[2]

In London that spring, the Protector and his council were occupied with tidying up the unfinished business left by Barebone's aborted parliament. Among other things, they did away with the so-called Engagement, introduced by the Rump back in 1650, requiring every adult male to 'engage obedience' to the government of the day. It also introduced some modest reforms intended to make access to Chancery cheaper and simpler. But the most important matter facing the administration was that of church reform, or rather of church organisation, and here again it moved with caution. Tithes and lay patronage both remained untouched, but the system by which ministers were appointed or dismissed and to what extent the state should be able to control their teaching and preaching had now to be regulated. On 20 March, therefore, an ordinance was issued for the setting-up of a Commission for Approbation of Public Preachers. This body, which became known as the Triers, consisted of twenty-three ministers representing the three main strands of religious opinion – Independent, Presbyterian and Baptist – and ten laymen, all of them naturally of 'known ability and godliness', and was authorised to 'examine, judge and approve' any candidate who had been presented to a benefice by a lay patron and confirm his appointment. Later that year another Commission, for the Ejection of Scandalous Ministers – the Ejectors – which replaced the old Committee for Scandalous Ministers, was created, with the power to remove 'all ignorant, scandalous, insufficient or negligent clergymen and schoolmasters'. Also, of course, any who could be proved to 'hold, teach or maintain' any Popish opinions, or 'such blasphemous and atheistical' opinions as came within the meaning of the 1650 Blasphemy Act, or, indeed, who could be shown to be guilty of any conduct unsuitable to a clergyman or schoolmaster. This was far-reaching and included activities such as fornication, common haunting of taverns or alehouses, profane cursing or swearing, frequent quarrelling or fighting, frequent playing at cards or dice, public reading of the Common Prayer Book, scoffing at strict professors of religion and godliness, encouraging and countenancing Whitsun ales, maypoles, morris dancing, stage plays or suchlike licentious practices, preaching or otherwise publishing their disaffection to the present government. Anyone found guilty of any of the above and removed by the 'Ejectors' would then be replaced by another incumbent approved by the 'Triers'.[3]

This turned out to be a rather more easy-going system than at first appears, for no set doctrine or form of worship had been ordained from above, and while it handed considerable power to any congregation, who would now be able to get rid of an unpopular pastor by informing against him, fairly or unfairly, to the authorities, it also meant that in other places the familiar Church of England service with its Prayer Book was able to survive more or less intact with the unofficial consent of parson and people – especially in places where the local squire was of the conservative persuasion. The Revd Richard Baxter, minister and preacher of the gospel at Kidderminster in the West Midlands and himself a man of very moderate left-wing tendencies, describes how such an individual could influence the situation in his neighbourhood. One gentleman, Sir Ralph Clare, he wrote,

> which lived amongst us, did more to hinder my greater successes than a multitude of others could have done. Though he was an old man of great courtship and civility, and very temperate as to diet, apparel and sports, and seldom would swear any louder than 'by his troth' etc., and showed me much personal reverence and respect (beyond my desert), and we conversed together with love and familiarity. Yet having no relish of this preciseness and extemporary praying and making so much ado for heaven, nor liking that which went beyond the pace of saying the Common Prayer . . . his coming but once a day to church on the Lord's days, and his abstaining from the sacrament, etc., as if we kept not sufficiently to the old way, and because we used not the Common Prayer Book . . . did cause a great part of the parish to follow him and do as he did, when else our success and concord would have been much more happy than it was.

Nevertheless, the Revd Baxter considered that 'God did so wonderfully bless the labours of his unanimous faithful ministers that had it not been for the faction of the prelatists on one side that drew men off, and factions of the giddy and turbulent sectaries on the other side . . . England had been like in a quarter of an age to have become a land of saints and a pattern of holiness to all the world . . .', and he lamented all those fair opportunities which had been 'lost and trodden underfoot'.[4]

The first Protectorate parliament met on 3 September 1654 and proved a serious disappointment to the executive by refusing to rubber-stamp the Instrument of Government and even going so far as to question its legality. Alarmed, the executive reacted quickly, and on Tuesday 12 September Guybon Goddard, one of the burgesses returned for the borough of King's Lynn, heard a report that 'the Parliament House was dissolved; that, for certain, the Council of State and Council of War had sat together all the Sabbath day before and had then contrived this dissolution'. All the same, Goddard decided to go and satisfy himself of the truth of this disturbing news, 'and to take my share of what I should see or learn there. Going by water to Westminster,' he went on, 'I was told that the Parliament doors were locked up and guarded with soldiers.' Still determined 'not to take things merely upon trust', he made for the Parliament stairs and, sure enough, encountered a guard of soldiers who told him there was no passage that way, 'that the House was locked up and command given to give no admittance to any; that if I were a member, I might go into the Painted Chamber, where the Protector would presently be'.

Goddard joined the crowd of members milling about in the Court of Requests and the Painted Chamber, and presently the Protector arrived, attended by his officers and life guard. He then made a long speech 'wherein he did not forbear to tell us that he did expect and hope for better fruit and effect of our meeting . . . than he had yet found . . . That having received his office from God and the people, he was resolved never to part with it, until God and the people should take it from him.' His Highness then announced that all those who wanted to continue sitting must sign a formal recognition of their support for his authority. This 'recognition', written on a long piece of parchment, declared that the signatories would 'freely promise and engage' to be true and faithful to the Lord Protector and the Commonwealth of England, Scotland and Ireland, and would not 'propose or consent to alter the government as it is settled in a sole person and the Parliament'.[5]

With the exception of an irreconcilable minority of republicans, the members reluctantly accepted Cromwell's ultimatum, but this did not prevent them from continuing to debate the detail of the Instrument of Government over the ensuing months. They were also making difficulties over finance and the size of the army until finally, on 22 January 1655, the Protector lost patience and dissolved the session, telling the parliament men, once more assembled in the Painted Chamber, 'that it is not for the profit of these nations, nor for common and public good, for you to continue here any longer'. But the summary dismissal of yet another unsatisfactory parliament did little to solve the problems now besetting the Lord Protector. He was well aware that his position depended heavily, if not entirely, on the support of the army; that, as one member of the late parliament had remarked, his authority was no more than 'the length of his own sword'.

At the end of 1654 there were approximately 53,000 men under arms in the British Isles – about 23,000 in Ireland, nearly 19,000 in Scotland and the remaining 11,000 in England. Of those, some 3,000 were stationed in London, with the rest dispersed in provincial garrisons, mostly situated on the coast and the Welsh and Scottish borders. Some army officers had seriously disapproved of the establishment of the Protectorate and had either been dismissed or resigned their commissions as a result, and Cromwell knew that he could not take the loyalty of some of his remaining generals for granted. He was still regarded with an awesome respect and affection in the ranks, but unfortunately even respect and affection came at a price, and the cost of maintaining the army was becoming harder and harder to meet. At the beginning of 1655 the government was still demanding £90,000 a month from the taxpayers by direct assessment, in addition to the much-resented excise duty, but even this unprecedentedly high rate of taxation was not enough to cover expenditure, and soon the Protectorate was facing a serious and growing financial crisis.

An obvious solution to the problem would have been to reduce the size of the army by at least a third, as parliament had tried to insist, but faced with an uncooperative House of Commons, the entrenched hostility of the republicans and the Fifth Monarchists and unsettling rumours of royalist insurgency, even possible assassination plots, Cromwell and the military were in no mood to start dismantling their vital power base. An attempted rising in the West Country that spring, although easily suppressed, did nothing to reassure them, and the Venetian ambassador reported that steps were being taken to forbid public gatherings 'from fear lest these should serve as a pretext for meetings and plots'. With the approach of Easter, an occasion when 'the young apprentices of London are allowed great liberties', Paulucci added that his Highness had ordered 'three large companies of horse to march through the city, and bodies of mounted men were kept moving in every part of it, to observe and control and to bring to naught any evil designs'.[6]

Nevertheless, a sense of general unease persisted. Ralph Josselin was having troubled dreams about Cavaliers up in arms and seeing 'the horse marching down a long street'; and, in a despatch dated 28 March, Paulucci wrote that, on receiving a report that the exiled king had left Germany with the intention of descending on one of England's ports, the Protector had at once given orders for increased security everywhere.

In this city [he went on], they have intensified their watchfulness, as shown by the doubling of the guards and the numerous arrests and examinations of malcontents. One night recently the Protector suddenly had all the horses seized that were found in different places . . . Those which belonged to their lawful owners . . . were released the next morning, but a good number remained in the hands of the military, and upon these they immediately mounted foot soldiers, who will serve as dragoons.

Again, early in April, Paulucci wrote, 'constant watchfulness is observed everywhere and the bodies of troops in various parts of the country are reinforced with orders to prevent any gathering of the people, great or small'.[7]

None of this, however, was doing anything to solve the growing financial crisis, and during the spring arrangements were being made to recruit a new mounted militia to replace some of the regular cavalry, always the most expensive to maintain. This new reserve force, many of them old soldiers, consisting of volunteers 'well mounted for service and armed with one good sword and case of pistols', would be on call at forty-eight hours' notice to march anywhere in the country, ready to put down civil unrest or repel foreign invasion. They were to receive, in theory at least, a retainer of £8 a year, and the standard rate of pay when on active service. Organised into troops by counties, they numbered 6,500 men with a notional wage bill of around £64,000 to be paid for by a so-called decimation tax levied on the royalist community. In fact, the size of the regular army does not seem to have been much reduced, although some rates of pay were cut, cavalry from 2*s* 6*d* to 2*s* 3*d*, infantry from 10*d* to 9*d*.

It soon appeared that the formation of the new militia was only the first step in a ground-breaking scheme intended not only to ensure the security of the regime, but also forcibly to improve the general moral tone of the population – something which the Protector regarded as a matter of urgency – and in August a group of senior officers was appointed to take command in the twelve regional associations into which England would now be divided. They were given the rank of major-general – in effect military governor – and their rule, unsurprisingly, proved a deeply unpopular and short-lived experiment. Although they were to work with the civil power, their authority was final and all-embracing. Apart from suppressing 'all tumults, insurrections, rebellion, and other unlawful assemblies', they were also to make sure that all papists and known royalists in their districts were disarmed. The highways were to be made safe, and robbers, footpads and highwaymen arrested and prosecuted according to the law. No horse races, cockfights, bear baiting or stage plays were to be allowed, on the ground that rebellion was more easily hatched under cover of such gatherings. The major-generals were, by their 'constant carriage and conversation', expected 'to encourage and promote godliness and virtue and discourage and discountenance all profaneness and ungodliness'. They were to deal severely with the idle and dissolute, but take steps to improve the lot of the deserving poor. They were also to 'endeavour – with the other justices of the peace and other ministers and officers who are entrusted with the care of those things – that the laws against drunkenness, profaneness, blaspheming, and taking of the name of God in vain by swearing, cursing, and suchlike wickedness and abominations, be put in more effectual execution than they have been hitherto'. Any justices and local officials found to be 'remiss and unfit for their trusts' were to be reported to the Protector and his Council, who would take the necessary action against them.[8]

There is no doubt that a serious tightening-up of national discipline was now under way. Press censorship, abolished by parliament at the beginning of the war but reinstated in 1647, was reinforced in October by an Order of the Protector and Council against printing unlicensed and scandalous books and pamphlets, and for regulating of printing. No person, it reminded the citizenry, was 'to presume to publish in print any matter of public news, or intelligence, without leave and approbation of the Secretary of State'.[9]

In the end, it was November before the major-generals were finally sent forth on their reforming mission. Lucy Hutchinson, always a staunch republican as well as an unreconstructed social snob, described them as 'a company of silly, mean fellows . . . who ruled according to their wills, by no law but what seemed good in their own eyes, imprisoning men and obstructing the course of justice'.[10] This was unfair, for the major-generals seem to have done their best to work with the magistrates, sheriffs and town corporations in their districts. It is true, though, that an element of class consciousness told against them. The Swedish ambassador commented on the ill will created among the people, 'the common folk being irritated at being ruled and commanded by those of their own class, and people of good birth despising the latter in their minds'.[11] Of the sixteen individuals eventually chosen for their thankless task, only nine can be identified as coming from pre-war landed families, while most of the remaining seven seem to have risen from more lowly origins. John Barkstead and Thomas Kelsey had been tradesmen in London; Charles Worsley, in charge of the north-west, was the son of a Manchester businessman; James Berry, whose territory included Herefordshire, Shropshire and Worcestershire, had worked as a clerk in an iron works before the war; and Tobias Bridge was said to have been a common dragooner.[12] It is also true that they had mostly done well out of the war – as many as thirteen of them are known to have been able to buy estates confiscated either from the Crown, the church or individual royalists, which probably did not help to endear them to their contemporaries.

The promotion of godliness and virtue had always been at the heart of Puritanism, and the authorities had always cherished the vision of 'an ordered and godly commonwealth', to be created by force if necessary. They had certainly made every effort to impress their views on the unregenerate and frequently ungrateful majority in a stream of Acts, Ordinances and exhortations issued over the past decade. Perhaps one of the more optimistic of these was the Act for suppressing the detestable sins of Incest, Adultery and Fornication passed in March 1650, making incest and adultery criminal offences punishable by death, 'as well the man as the woman', unless the man could show that he had not known his partner was married, or if the woman's husband had been 'continually remaining beyond the seas by the space of three years, or shall by common fame be reputed to be dead'. The lesser crime of fornication attracted a prison sentence of three months for a first offence, while anyone convicted of keeping a common brothel or bawdy house was to be publicly whipped and set in the pillory to be branded on the forehead with the letter 'B' before being committed to hard labour in prison or house of correction for three years. Any subsequent offence for either of these crimes would be treated as a felony.[13] In fact, it seems that only in three cases can it be definitely established that the death penalty for adultery was actually carried out. In 1654 Nicholas Tyrett was bound over to appear at the next Assizes 'to answer for being accused to live incontinently with Joan, wife of Henry Marks, and in the meantime to be of good

Oliver Cromwell, after Samuel Cooper. *(© Wallace Collection/Bridgeman Art Library)*

Elizabeth Cromwell, wife of Oliver Cromwell, by Peter Lely. *(The Cromwell Museum, Huntingdon)*

John Pym. *(Mary Evans Picture Library)*

St Mary's Church, Putney. *(Guildhall Library, Corporation of London)*

Cromwell dissolves the Rump Parliament, 1653. *(© Hulton-Deutsch Collection/Corbis)*

King James I in the Houses of Parliament. *(British Museum/Bridgeman Art Library)*

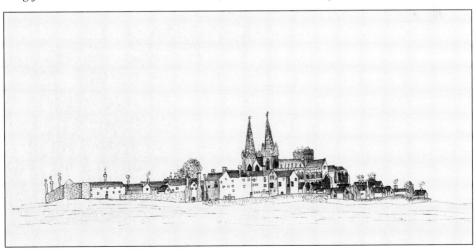

Lichfield Cathedral. *(Bodleian Library, University of Oxford)*

The pulling-down of the Cheapside cross. *(Private Collection/ Bridgeman Art Library)*

Soldiers looting a Catholic church. *(British Library/Bridgeman Art Library)*

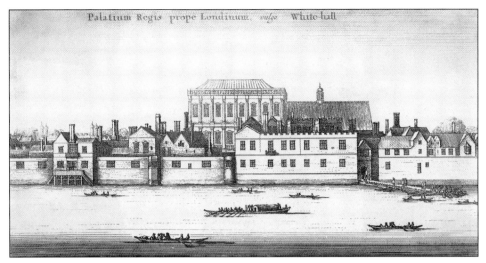

Whitehall by Hollar. *(Mary Evans Picture Library)*

Richard Cromwell. *(Mary Evans Picture Library)*

William Harvey, Royal physician. *(Royal College of Physicians, London/Bridgeman Art Library)*

Matthew Hopkins interrogating two suspected witches. *(Private Collection/Bridgeman Art Library)*

Women being hanged as witches. *(Private Collection/Bridgeman Art Library)*

THE
VVorld turn'd upfide down:
OR,
A briefe defcription of the ridiculous Fafhions of thefe diftracted Times.

By T. J. a well-willer to King, Parliament and Kingdom.

London : Printed for *John Smith.* 1647.

Title page *The World Turn'd Upside Down*, 1647. *(© The British Library)*

John Thurloe. *(Mary Evans Picture Library)*

John Lilburne. *(Mary Evans Picture Library)*

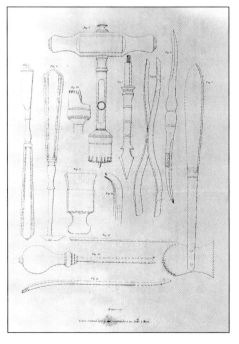

Surgical instruments from Armamentarium
Chirurgicum by Johannes Scultetus.
(Wellcome Library, London)

behaviour', and John Ford of Studland was ordered not to keep company with the wife of Anthony Jollen until his next appearance before the court, but the results of these cases are not recorded. Eighteen charges of adultery were tried in Middlesex between 1651 and 1657 and in every case the prisoners were acquitted – London juries being evidently resolute in their reluctance to condemn their fellow citizens for an offence they may very likely have committed themselves. It was also notoriously difficult to prove.[14] In the spring of 1656 the major-general John Barkstead carried out a sweep of the London brothels – Ralph Josselin heard that 'they took up many loose wenches' who were apparently to be transported to Jamaica – and a few months later three men from Stepney and Ratcliffe Highway were arrested on suspicion of running a bawdy house, but the campaign against sexual immorality remained patchy and, most probably, largely ineffectual.[15]

The success of the major-generals in banning popular sports and pastimes, discouraging drunkenness and profanity and 'suchlike wickedness and abominations' was also patchy, varying according to the zeal of the major-general concerned and his commissioners – groups of local worthies co-opted to assist him in the work of 'securing the peace of the commonwealth'. John Desborough, whose fiefdom covered the south-western counties from Cornwall to Wiltshire, was particularly energetic in the pursuit of order and godliness. A religious radical with Baptist associations, he had a reputation for being 'blunt and honest'. He was noticeably hard on both Quakers and royalists, and as a New Model Army veteran had few reservations about the regime's reliance on military force. After all, it was, as he pointed out, 'blows, not fair words, that settled, and must settle, the peace of England'. Other hardliners included William Boteler, who ruled in Bedfordshire, Huntingdonshire and Northamptonshire. Another Puritan zealot and persecutor of Quakers, he acquired an unpleasant reputation for bullying and bigotry and was later accused of having acted more arbitrarily than the Earl of Strafford, Charles I's detested adjutant. James Berry in Wales and William Packer, Boteler's neighbour in Oxfordshire and

Buckinghamshire, were also religious radicals, as were William Goffe, Charles Worsley, Robert Lilburne, brother of the more famous John, and Thomas Kelsey; but radicalism did not necessarily mean persecution of the sects, those with millenarian beliefs being more likely to show leniency to the Fifth Monarchists, and William Packer was even accused of being 'of one spirit' with some of the Ranters. Only James Berry, though, seems to have had a good word for the Quakers. More moderate major-generals were Charles Howard, who had actually been brought up a Catholic, and Edward Whalley, the Protector's cousin, who, in the spring of 1656, allowed the annual horse race for Lady Grantham's Cup to be run at Lincoln, in the rather touching belief that it was not His Highness's intention in the suppressing of horse races 'to abridge gentlemen of their sport'.[16]

The authorities were, however, rather less tolerant when it came to the sports enjoyed by the general public. There was of course nothing new about the Puritan campaign to outlaw those traditional celebrations associated with the calendar of the Anglican church and, by implication, with popery. These included such cheerful occasions as Shrovetide pancake-tossing, cock-shies, football and wrestling matches; and Easter, when every good Christian took communion and in some parts of the country the young men went 'pace egging' – rolling eggs downhill, a custom said to be symbolic of the stone being rolled from Christ's tomb. May Day, another important spring festival, had nothing to do with the church, the ancient custom of going a-maying being unashamedly pagan in origin and as such a particular target for godly disapproval. Whitsun, a favourite time for church ales, when the church wardens organised the production of a specially potent brew sold to all comers in the churchyard or even in the church itself to raise funds for the parish, was followed by the midsummer bonfires on St John's Eve, the Michaelmas feast of goose fattened on the stubble-fields, and then All Hallows Eve, with its remembrance and propitiation of the souls of the dead. Most villages, too, had their own feast day, usually associated with the patron saint of the parish church. All these were now, in theory at least, to be replaced by a monthly fast day, chiefly marked by sermons, and widely regarded as a poor substitute.

Puritan efforts to suppress play acting, bear baiting, cockfights and frolicking round the maypole – 'this stinking idol' – accompanied by drinking, dancing and other activities inevitably associated with young people scampering about in the woods together in the early morning are all well documented, but probably most notorious was the attempt to do away with Christmas, which traditionally lasted from Christmas Eve to Epiphany or Twelfth Night. The twelve days of Christmas were the nearest thing most people got to an annual holiday break – a time when little could be done on the land and work was more or less suspended while everyone in any position to do so celebrated in an outburst of eating, drinking and hospitality and when manor and farmhouse would be decorated with boughs of holly, ivy, bay, laurel and holm-oak. Nor was this only a country custom. 'Against the feast of Christmas', wrote the London chronicler John Stow, 'every man's house, as also the parish churches, were decked with holm, ivy, bays and whatsoever the season of the year afforded to be green.' On Christmas Day itself everyone went to church before sitting down to the most sumptuous meal the family budget could afford. In the grandest households this was an occasion for serving dishes like boar's head, peacock pie and elaborate sculpted and gilded castles of sugar and marchpane. Humbler folk feasted on beef and mutton, roast or boiled goose, hens and capons, and even the poorest could usually be assured of a good dinner provided by charitable neighbours. Christmas was above all a time for keeping open house for family and friends, when the poorer sort went the rounds singing carols and the mummers performed their antics in the hope of some seasonable reward, while the universities, the Inns of Court and, according to John Stow, 'the house of every nobleman of honour or good worship' still observed the custom of appointing a Lord of Misrule or 'master of merry disports' to preside over the revels – a heathenish custom also much disapproved of by the Puritan tendency.

The whole Christmas carousal had been much disapproved of by the Puritan tendency since Tudor times. Back in the 1550s the godly were lamenting the way in which uninstructed country folk regarded it as almost part of their religion to make merry in this unwholesome fashion 'on account of the birth of our Lord', but it was not until the 1640s that they at last found themselves in a position to do more than preach to the converted and lament the obstinate reluctance of the uninstructed to be reformed. As early as 1642 doubts about the keeping of Christmas were first officially expressed and some London shops remained open on Christmas Day 1643. In 1644 Christmas Day fell on a Wednesday, a day appointed for a Fast and Humiliation, and parliament published an *Ordinance for the better observation of the Feast of the Nativity of Christ.*

Whereas [declared this document] doubts have been raised whether the next Fast shall be celebrated, because it falleth on the day which, heretofore, was usually called the Feast of the Nativity of our Saviour; the lords and commons do order and ordain that public notice be given, that the Fast appointed to be kept on the last Wednesday in every month, ought to be observed . . . and that this day particularly is to be kept with the more solemn humiliation because it may call to remembrance our sins and the sins of our forefathers, who have turned this Feast, pretending the memory of Christ, into an extreme forgetfulness of him, by giving liberty to carnal and sensual delights.[17]

Nevertheless, it was noted that, although parliament sat that day, as indeed it was to do every Christmas Day until 1656, the shops remained shut.

The following year, with Christmas Day on a Thursday, *Mercurius Civicus, or London's Intelligencer* contained a solemn article on the absurdity, if not impiety, of keeping Christmas, adding that in any case it was more probable that the Saviour was born in September. Every good citizen, therefore, was expected to open his shop as usual on the day and see that his apprentices were there behind the counter. If they had to have a holiday, then let them keep 5 November or some other day of that nature which deserved special thanksgiving.[18] Naturally enough, this helpful suggestion was widely ignored, and it was noted that most shops were shut up, 'only one or two open in Cheapside and five or six upon Ludgate Hill'. There was, however, 'some hubbub about those shops that were open', and some were forced to put up their shutters 'by the boys throwing of stones'.[19]

The feelings of the 'poor simple people . . . mad after superstitious festivals', and their stubborn determination to go on enjoying their sirloin of beef, their collar of brawn, their Christmas pies and plum porridge were made clear enough in an anonymous pamphlet which appeared at the end of 1645 entitled *The Arraignment Conviction and Imprisonment of CHRISTMAS . . . And how he broke out of Prison in the Holidayes . . . With an Hue and Cry after CHRISTMAS . . . And what shift he was fain to make to save his life, and great stir to fetch him back again. With divers other Witty Passages. Printed by Simon Minc'd Pie, for Cissely Plum Porridge; and are to be sold out by Ralph Fidler, Chandler, at the signe of the Pack of Cards in Mustard Alley in Brawn Street.*[20] John Taylor, the Water Poet, expressed the same sentiments rather more elegantly when he wrote in his *Complaint of Christmas . . . printed before Candlemas, 1646*: 'All the liberty and harmless sports, the merry gambols, dances and friscols, with which the toiling ploughman and labourer once a year were wont to be recreated, and their spirits and hopes revived for a whole twelvemonth, are now extinct and put out of use, in such a fashion as if they had never been. Thus are the merry lords of bad rule at Westminster.'[21]

In fact it was not until midsummer 1647 that the feast of the nativity of Christ, vulgarly known as Christmas Day, was officially abolished, but when the Mayor of Canterbury proclaimed on 22 December that Christmas Day and all other superstitious festivals should be put down and a market kept on Christmas Day he provoked quite a serious riot, in the course of which several thousand men of Kent passed a resolution that 'if they could not have their Christmas Day, they would have the King back on his throne'. The few shops rash enough to stay open were stormed and ransacked by the mob. The Mayor's windows were broken and the Sheriff was knocked down and 'his head fearfully broke'.

In general, it seems that Christmas survived, even if it went underground, though Ralph Josselin heard in 1652 that Londoners were buying up bays, holly and ivy wonderfully for Christmas, 'being eagerly set on their feasts'. The Commons had just issued another edict 'that no observation shall be had of the five and twentieth day of December . . . nor any solemnity used or exercised in churches upon that day', and John Evelyn would record sadly in his diary on successive Christmas Days that, with no churches open, he was obliged to 'pass the devotions of that blessed day' at home with his family. At Christmas 1657, however, he did find a service he could attend in London, but just as the congregation were receiving the sacrament, they were invaded by soldiers, who arrested the communicants and hauled them away to Whitehall to be interrogated by a panel of senior officers, among others Colonels Whalley and Goffe. Evelyn was asked how he dared to offend against the ordinance forbidding observation of the superstitious time of the Nativity, and particularly to be at Common Prayers, which, he was told, was no more than the Mass in English and, worse still, to pray for Charles Stuart. 'I told them', he wrote, 'we did not pray for Charles Stuart, but for all Christian kings, princes and governors.' In the end, after 'other frivolous and ensnaring questions and much threatening', he was released 'with much pity for my ignorance', and got home late the next day, 'blessed be God'.[22]

By the time the major-generals were appointed most people had become more or less resigned to seeing silent churches and open shops on Christmas Day – at least in those places where the municipal authorities toed the godly line. 'Old Christmas now is come to town, though few do him regard', but in *The Vindication of Father Christmas*, which appeared in 1653, the old gentleman got a warm welcome at a Devonshire farmhouse, where the company sat round the fire roasting apples and drinking lambswool, or spiced ale, while 'the poor labouring hinds, and maid-servants, with the plow-boys, went nimbly to dancing'.[23]

The drinking of ale, spiced or otherwise, was another prime target of the reformers' zeal. Alehouses and taverns led to drunkenness, brawling and swearing. They encouraged idleness, gaming at dice or cards, dancing and sexual immorality. The people haunted alehouses on Sunday when they ought to be in church. Servants gathered there away from their masters' supervision, and in uncertain times they offered a refuge and meeting place for thieves, robbers and 'suspitious persons' of every complexion. Inevitably, therefore, they were regarded by the powers that be as 'the great nurseries of mischief and impiety in this commonwealth'.

The problem of enforcing the regulation of these 'nests of Satan', which were all supposed to be licensed by the local justices, was not a new one, and there was already a raft of legislation fixing the price and strength of ale and beer, forbidding 'tippling' – that is, sitting drinking in an alehouse for more than one hour – and the frequenting of alehouses on Sundays and fast days, plus numerous local orders attempting to restrict their numbers and stipulating that licences should be granted only to men 'of honest life and conversation' who could produce a character reference signed by their local minister and three 'well-affected' neighbours.

No one, of course, was suggesting the suppression of all licensed houses. Inns and taverns on main roads or near market towns, providing accommodation, stabling and refreshment to *bona fide* travellers, filled an obvious social need, but alehouses, which were often little more than a cottager's kitchen, proved next to impossible to regulate effectively. The selling of ale was a useful and long-established sideline which might keep a poor man or woman (many of them were widows) from becoming a charge on the parish, so that the granting and continuance of a licence to such a person could be shown to be in the interest of the parish officers. For this reason many licences were granted, often no doubt to people who would have been hard put to it to provide proof of an 'honest life and conversation', but, however generous the local justices might show themselves, unlicensed houses continued to proliferate, especially in times of dearth.

The arrival of the major-generals marked the beginning of a concerted effort to control the trade and to suppress all unlicensed and superfluous alehouses. Edward Whalley instructed the JPs within his jurisdiction to suppress all alehouses considered to be unnecessary and to send him lists of those they had closed and those allowed to remain. A few weeks later he was reporting that they were now 'depressing alehouses, which were grown to incredible numbers'. Hezakiah Haynes in East Anglia was equally energetic in prodding his justices into action, and in the spring of 1656 they obediently announced their intention not only to 'use all possible diligence and care in the vigorous execution of the laws for the suppressing of unlicensed alehouses' but to cause 'constables and other officers to be dexterous in the discharge of their duties for the discovering, presenting, conviction and punishment of all such offenders'. In Wales, James Berry urged the Caernarvonshire justices to show themselves 'like men that will be found faithful to your trust' by taking action against the 'spreading gangrene' of the alehouse, and similar purges were being undertaken throughout the country in the spring and summer of 1656. In the West Riding of Yorkshire it was decreed that no unincorporated town was to have more than two alehouses and that 'hog feasts, goose feasts and revellings at country weddings' were to be banned – the local clergy were required to inform on parish constables who neglected to enforce these orders; and in London all keepers of inns and alehouses were warned that they would lose their licences if they profaned the Sabbath or allowed 'billiard tables, shovelboard tables, dice, cards, tables, nine pins, pigeonholes, bowling alley or bowling green or any other unlawful game' to be played on their premises. But it was in Charles Worsley's north-west that the campaign was waged most fiercely. In January the petty constables, ministers and 'most honest and religious men' of Lancashire were ordered to meet him and his commissioners, bringing with them a list of all the alehouses in their parishes with the names of those who kept them. As a result two hundred houses in the Blackburn area and several hundred more around Salford were marked down for closure. Prosecutions for alehouse offences rose sharply, and nightly house-to-house searches for drunkards were organised in Chester and other towns.[24]

Unfortunately, though, it was proving as difficult to deprive the Englishman of his ale as it had been of his Christmas beef and plum porridge, and the alehouse, like Christmas, survived, even if in some places it was temporarily forced underground. In Hampshire, where the authorities had been especially active, some enterprising individuals were organising so-called help ales, when a group of friends would club together to buy a barrel of beer and enjoy it on a Saturday evening in the home of one of their number. Of course, not everyone objected to the imposition of the new order. Where the godly tendency was in a majority – or at least where the leaders of the community were of a Puritan persuasion – petitions from groups describing themselves as 'the principal inhabitants', 'the best inhabitants' or 'the honest neighbours' were got up to protest about the multiplicity of alehouses and the prevalence of the drunkenness they encouraged. No doubt these sober citizens, the yeomen farmers, prosperous tradesmen and minor gentry had a point. The Revd Richard Baxter preached against the large numbers of drunkards in his own town of Kidderminster and went on to complain that both there and elsewhere in the country 'still iniquity aboundeth, still drunkards are raging openly in the streets and still the alesellers keep open shop for them'.[25] Other reformers expressed similar frustrations, and in general it does seem that the major-generals and their allies were fighting a losing battle. Although hundreds of alehouses were closed down during the period of their rule, this made little real impression on the tens of thousands of such establishments which existed throughout England and Wales and which continued to provide their customers with refreshment, relaxation and social contacts, just as they had always done. After all, as one such individual remarked, was it 'so great a matter if a man be a little overtaken with drink now and then? There is no man but he hath his faults: and the best of us may be amended.' If neighbours chose to meet at the alehouse, meaning no harm, then surely it was 'good fellowship and a good means to increase a love among neighbours'.

The major-generals were also fighting a losing battle in their efforts to solve the perennial social problem of the poor, both the 'impotent' or deserving variety and the undeserving, that is, the vagrants or 'sturdy beggars'. Edward Whalley in the East Midlands seems to have been the only member of the fraternity to make any serious attempt to improve the lot of the 'good' poor, but they all attacked the other, easier, half of the equation with zest, and in April 1656 Whalley was reporting triumphantly to London that 'you may ride all over Nottinghamshire and not see a beggar or wandering rogue'. As with the alehouses, the major-generals succeeded in stimulating the civil authorities into action, and 1656 saw the issue of a sudden flurry of orders from the justices, requiring the stricter enforcement of the vagrancy laws covering jugglers, tinkers, peddlars, 'Egyptians and counterfeit Egyptians' and all idle persons either begging or pretending to tell fortunes, or using 'any subtle craft or unlawful games or plays'. In London special efforts were made to reduce the swarming vagrant population, 'the vermin of the commonwealth', and 'a competent number of able men under a salary' were recruited to help the unpaid city constables round up the beggars. Unfortunately the law which stated that beggars and vagabonds must be sent back to their native parishes tended to result only in shifting the problem from one place to another. Gaols filled up with sturdy beggars, robbers, horse-stealers, pick-pockets and wandering rogues of all descriptions, and there the drive to rid the commonwealth of its undesirables came to a halt. The original plan had been to deport all those 'fit to grind sugar cane or plant tobacco' to the West Indies, but time passed, no arrangements or transports were forthcoming from the Jamaica Committee in Whitehall, and it seems likely that most of the prisoners were later quietly released.[26]

In addition to all their other tasks, the major-generals had been charged with supervising the work of the Ejectors and Triers, who were to achieve the reform of the parish ministry, something which they all considered to be a matter of prime importance, and during the course of 1656 there was a noticeable burst of activity against those clergy suspected of such crimes as using the Book of Common Prayer and the sign of the cross in baptism, frequenting inns, profaning the Sabbath or being overfamiliar with female parishioners. However, it seems that fewer than 150 parish priests were actually removed from their livings during this period, and again it would appear that the major-generals and the relatively small hardline cliques surrounding them were meeting with a good deal of passive resistance. By no means all the accused ministers were prepared to go quietly and were able to employ effective delaying tactics against the Ejectors, claiming they needed more time to prepare their defence – Walter Bushnell of Box in Wiltshire succeeded in spinning out the proceedings for six months. Nor did the godly always receive the support of congregations, who were often regrettably attached to their 'malignant and scandalous' ministers and reluctant to testify against them. Even Ralph Josselin, whose own godliness was beyond question, felt the major-generals and their commissioners were showing too much rigour and had no joy in seeing ministers put under the lay power, while many a conscientious Puritan official trying to dislodge a scandalous pastor could find himself accused of being 'too busie' or 'precise'.

Conscientious Puritans were continually being saddened and frustrated by the general public's stubborn refusal to take them seriously, to listen to their sermons and to be properly aware of their sins and their souls' danger. There was nothing new about this – the clergy had long been complaining about the invincible ignorance, indifference and irreverence of the lower orders. Richard Baxter believed that 'poor ignorant people' should be treated 'very tenderly . . . for matter of knowledge and defect of expression if they are teachable and tractable', but Adam Martindale, in his Cheshire parish, was defeated by 'the unwillingness of people (especially the old ignoramuses) to have their extreme defects of knowledge searched out, the backwardness of the profane to have the smart plaister of admonition applied'.[27] Ignorance and indifference certainly seem to have been widespread. In 1656 it was said that there were men in Essex as ignorant of Christianity as the Red Indians and 'ignorant heathenish people' were to be found throughout the country. Even when they came to church, and 'sometimes not half the people in a parish [are] present at holy exercises upon the Sabbath day', the behaviour of some members of the congregation left much to be desired. They jostled for places, hawked and spat, farted, made rude jokes, fell asleep and even let off guns. Nor would they hesitate to heckle the preacher. When the rector of Holland Magna in Essex discoursed on the subject of Adam and Eve covering their nakedness by making themselves coats of fig leaves, one wit promptly demanded to know where they had got the thread to sew them, and the long-winded curate at Stogursey in Somerset was told loudly that it was time he came down so that the maids could get to the milking.[28] Clearly the ideal state of 'an ordered and godly commonwealth' where men worked hard, read the Bible, heard the word of God and gave obedience to their betters was still a depressingly long way off.

The second Protectorate parliament was summoned in the autumn of 1656, at least partly at the behest of the major-generals, who believed they would be able to ensure the return of a majority of godly members who would support their purifying campaign. Instead of which, they had provided their enemies with what turned into a perfect opportunity to express their opposition to the rule of the government's 'satraps and bashaws'. The elections held in August were unusually hard fought – 'the greatest striving to get into the parliament that ever was known' – and John Desborough wrote from Cornwall on 12 August to Secretary John Thurloe that 'there are great contendings and strugglings in all parts'. Francesco Giavarina, the new Venetian Resident in London, watched the proceedings with some astonishment. 'The manner in which these elections take place is remarkable,' he reported. 'All those who have a vote . . . meet together and each man calls aloud the name of the person whom he wishes to be elected. In such a large gathering of people it is impossible to know who has the majority of votes, and so the nominees are carried shoulder high out of the meeting followed by all who gave them their votes. These being counted they find out who has the majority and is elected.'[29]

But in spite of the efforts of the major-generals and of preachers such as William Gurnall of Lavenham in Suffolk, who informed his congregation that it was their bounden duty to return those parliament men who would continue the work of godly reformation, the results were disappointing, and even when just over a hundred of the four hundred members elected were prevented from taking their seats, the godly were in a minority. The tide had begun to turn against the swordsmen, and at the end of January 1657 the Commons threw out a bill put forward by major-general John Desborough 'for continuance of a tax upon some people for the maintenance of the militia' – that is, the decimation tax on the royalist population. This effectively put an end to the unloved experiment of government by the military, the memory of which lingered on as a horrid example of unconstitutional, oppressive rule and helped to sow an abiding dislike and distrust of militarism in general and standing armies in particular in the national psyche. But although the experiment certainly failed in its attempt to impose godliness and sobriety on an uncooperative population, the major-generals seem not to have deserved their reputation for tyranny. Rather, they were earnest, often tactless, sometimes autocratic, but undoubtedly sincere in their missionary zeal, and their failure to win hearts and minds was due more to the fact that they had been given an impossible task than to any selfish desire to subjugate their fellow citizens.

The 1656 parliament contained a solid core of experienced conservative gentlemen and they were becoming worried about the future. The regime, after all, was heavily, if not entirely, dependent on one man's life. Cromwell was no longer young – 57 on his last birthday – and his health was beginning to give cause for anxiety.

Rumours that he was about to be offered the Crown were circulating again, and in November Francesco Giavarina heard on good authority that parliament had already 'intimated to the Protector its desire to render that high office hereditary in his family' but that he had declined the offer. However, this was not the end of it. In January, after more scares of royalist plots and risings, one of the county members was suggesting that, if his Highness 'would be pleased to take upon him the government according to the ancient constitution', the hopes of enemy plots would be at an end, and 'both our liberties and peace, and the preservation and privilege of his Highness, would be founded upon an old and sure foundation'. It was also not without significance that a dynasty 'according to the ancient constitution' might prove cheaper than always having to go to the expense of equipping a new Protector. The French ambassador, reporting the suggestion that 'the government should be returned to its old form under a King', with parliament once more composed of Lords and Commons, remarked that 'some supported this proposal and others rejected it but the former seemed to be in the majority'.[30] Finally, on 23 February 1657, Sir Christopher Packe, one of Cromwell's own knights, a former Lord Mayor and a well-respected member for one of the City seats, rose to present a 'Humble Address and Remonstrance of the Knights, Citizens and Burgesses now assembled in the Parliament of this Commonwealth'. This document begged that his Highness

> will be pleased to assume the name, style, title, dignity and office of King of England, Scotland and Ireland and the respective Dominions and Territories thereunto belonging, and the exercise thereof, to hold and enjoy the same with the rights, privileges, and prerogatives justly, legally and rightly thereunto belonging. God who . . . gives the kingdoms of the world to whomsoever he pleaseth, having by a series of Providences raised you to be a deliverer of these nations and made you more able to govern us in peace and prosperity than any other whatsoever.[31]

The Remonstrance, or Humble Petition and Advice as it presently became known, was debated in the Commons over the next month and, although there was determined opposition both from the republican element and the army, most people believed the result would be a foregone conclusion. On 25 March the House divided, voting by a majority of 61 to invite the Protector to accept their offer of the Crown and, on Tuesday 31 March Mr Speaker, attended by the whole House, processed to the Banqueting House in Whitehall to commend to his Highness this 'new model of a kingly government'. His Highness, having expressed a proper sense of obligation at the offer – 'truly I should have a very brazen forehead if it should not beget in me a great deal of consternation of spirit, it being of so high and great importance' – went on to ask that 'I may have some short time to ask counsel of God, and of my own heart . . . And truly I may say this also, that as the thing will deserve deliberation, the utmost deliberation and consideration on my part, so I shall think myself bound to give as speedy an answer to these things as I can'.[32]

The answer was not, however, a speedy one, and it was not until the beginning of May that Cromwell finally refused the Crown, perhaps because, in the last resort, he knew that he could not afford to alienate his oldest allies among the swordsmen. It was, though, the only thing he refused, and he would now, indeed, be king in all but name, with the power to name his successor. Parliament was once more to have an Upper House nominated by him, and his grandeur, status and income were to be raised to a truly royal level. All that now remained was his formal reinvestiture – a ceremony which took place on the afternoon of Friday 26 June, in the presence of the Speaker and members of the House of Commons, the judges and officers of state, the Lord Mayor and Aldermen of the City of London, Garter King of Arms and the other members of the College of Heralds, and staged 'with the greatest pomp and magnificence' that could be contrived. For which great purpose, according to the account of the Revd James Fraser of Phopachy, a visiting Presbyterian Scot, 'they had set up a rich Cloath of state as a

Canapy at the upper end of Westminster Hall and under it a chaire of State placed upon an ascent of two degrees covered over with Carpets where the Protector sat'.[33] Cromwell was vested in a robe of purple velvet lined with ermine, 'being the habit anciently used at the solemn investiture of princes', presented with a Bible 'richly gilt and bossed', a sword and sceptre. 'His Highness standing thus adorned in princely state according to his merit and dignity', the Speaker of the Commons, Sir Thomas Widdington, administered the revised Protectoral oath following the new constitution as set out in the Humble Petition, one of the court chaplains recommended all those present 'to the blessing and protection of God Almighty', and His Highness, sceptre in hand, then sat down in the chair of State – it was, in fact, the Coronation Chair, also known as St Edward's Chair. 'All these Solemn Ceremonies being performed and finished,' says James Fraser, 'a Herald of arms with three Trumpeters in livery sounding Proclaimed him Lord Protector of England, Scotland and Ireland and ye Dominions thereto Belonging.' This was repeated twice more, 'the people with several acclamations and loud shouts crying God Save the Lord Protector'. 'I am not to Judge if this was with all their hearts,' added the disapproving Fraser, 'but sure it was not with mine though a Witness and Spectator.'[34]

Following the 'coronation' – and all that was lacking had been the actual crown – 'the Lord Protector steps out of the hall, accompanied with all these Lords in as great State as ever a King of England was and through the great Court his guards on each side and into St Margarets Church where in great splendour he sat in Seat of honour ordered for him and the Nobles, of Parliament, Lord Mayor and Aldermen in their several seats'. The assembled company listened to the inevitable sermon before returning to Whitehall. 'The train band of London in the streets in arms, bells ringing, bonefires burning and all demonstrations of joy that could be contrived. The Idol of the times being set up Baal and Dagon must be bowed to . . .'[35] There was no doubt as to Fraser's opinion of the proceedings, and Francesco Giavarina was openly hostile, possibly exaggerating the general lack of popular enthusiasm. 'Only when his Highness came out of the doors at Westminster, some soldiers gave some shouts of joy, which were paid for. For the rest it all went off rather sadly . . . This is clear evidence of the dissatisfaction of the people, for although they turned out in countless numbers to see the ceremony, they would not open their mouths to utter what did not come from their hearts.'[36]

In the days following the ceremony at Westminster the newly installed Lord Protector was proclaimed in royal style in the City of London and other towns and cities throughout the country, and within a month he was exercising the royal prerogative of creating a hereditary peerage – the former royalist Charles Howard becoming Viscount Morpeth and Baron Gilsland. About a dozen baronetcies followed, and, as the implacably scornful Lucy Hutchinson commented, he 'wanted not many fools, both of the army and gentry, to accept of, and strut in, his mock titles'.[37] The new Upper, or Other House of Parliament, which met for the first time in January 1658, was entirely nominated by the Protector and consisted of 'life' peers and selected members of the old nobility.

But in spite of the openly expressed disapproval of the usual suspects – among them the irrepressible William Prynne, old-fashioned republicans like Edmund Ludlow and Henry Vane and the lunatic fringe of the Fifth Monarchists – for better or worse the Protectorate had now become a *de facto* monarchy and the Protectoral court had acquired virtually all the trappings of royalty. In the autumn of 1656 it was able to stage two 'royal' weddings for Cromwell's daughters, Frances and Mary, both freely referred to as 'princesses'. This was perhaps fair enough for Frances, since a possible match for her with the exiled Charles II had apparently been quite seriously discussed in some quarters – a proposal which raises some interesting questions of the 'what if' variety. But on Wednesday 11 November Frances was married to Robert Rich, the Earl of Warwick's grandson. This took place at Whitehall, where, according to the new laws on civil marriage, Mr Henry Scobell, Clerk to the Privy Council 'as Justice of the Peace, tied the knot after a godly prayer made by one of his Highness's divines', although it was rumoured that both brides had insisted on a having a private church ceremony according to the Anglican rite. At the wedding feast, held the next day, 'they had 48 violins and 50 trumpets and much mirth with frolics besides mixed dancing (a thing heretofore accounted profane)'. It seems that even the Protectress herself joined in the mixed dancing, partnered by the Earl of Newport, and the occasion was marked by the City's ringing of bells and by the firing of great guns from the Tower.[38] Mary Cromwell's wedding a week later seems to have been a rather quieter affair. *Mercurius Politicus* reported on 19 November that 'yesterday afternoon his Highness went to Hampton Court and this day the most illustrious lady, the Lady Mary Cromwell, third daughter of his Highness the Lord Protector, was there married to the most noble lord, the Lord Fauconberg, in the presence of their Highnesses and many noble persons'.[39] However, the family returned to London the next day, and, according to a letter addressed to the bride's brother Henry, the celebrations continued at Whitehall for several more days and were distinguished by the performance of a musical entertainment with lyrics by Andrew Marvell.

Descriptions of these weddings make it clear just how far the Cromwell family had come and to what extent the great and good of the land had come to accepting the new dispensation. No one in the winter of 1657 seems to have been paying attention to the doomful pronouncements of the Fifth Monarchist seer, Anna Trapnel:

> Spirit and Voice hath made a league
> Against Cromwell and his Crown
> The which I am confident the Lord
> Will ere long so strike down . . .
>   . . . And his posterity
> They shall not sit upon his throne.[40]

SIX

Malignants and Delinquents

There is nothing they [the royalists] have more industriously laboured in than this, to keep themselves separated and distinguish'd from the well affected of this nation.

(Oliver Cromwell, 1655)

Apart from to the Roman Catholics and Church of England clergy, the most seriously disadvantaged minority in republican England were the Quakers, or Children of Light. This was partly due to their perceived connection with the Ranters, who, Richard Baxter had written, made it their business

> to set up the light of nature under the name of Christ in Men, and to dishonour and cry down the Church, the Scripture, the present ministry, and our worship and ordinances; and called men to hearken to Christ within them. But withal they conjoined a cursed doctrine of libertinism, which brought them to all abominable filthiness of life.

Baxter believed that the Quakers were 'but the Ranters turned from horrid profaneness and blasphemy to a life of extreme austerity' and that 'their doctrines were mostly the same with the Ranters'; nor was he alone in maintaining that both would have 'no law but their lusts, no heaven nor glory but here, no sin but what men fancied to be so, no condemnation for sin but in the consciences of ignorant ones'.[1] Certainly in its early days the Quaker movement does seem to have had more in common with the Ranters than its leaders later cared to admit, and George Fox's outburst of 1653 –

133

'O ye great men and rich men of the earth! Weep and howl for your misery that is coming . . . The fire is kindled, the day of the Lord is appearing, a day of howling . . . All the loftiness of men must be laid low' – carries an unmistakable echo of Abiezer Coppe's *Fiery Flying Roll*.[2]

The great majority of early Quakers came from the yeoman and artisan class, and, apart from their dangerously radical opinions, their deliberate failure to observe the accepted codes of conventional good manners had a good deal to do with their unpopularity. 'When the Lord sent me forth into the world,' wrote Fox, 'he forbad me to put off my hat to any, high or low, and I was required to Thee and Thou all men and women without any respect to rich or poor, great or small . . . neither might I bow or scrape with my leg to any one.'[3] This insistence on using 'plain language', and the familiar form of address to all and sundry, caused particular offence. 'We maintain that Thou from superiors to inferiors is proper, as a sign of command; from equals to equals is passable, as a note of familiarity; but from inferiors to superiors, if proceeding from ignorance, hath a smack of clownishness; if from affectation, a tone of contempt . . .'[4] It was certainly taken as affectation by many people. Thomas Ellwood's father was liable to fall on his son with his fists when addressed in 'plain language' and on one occasion was provoked into exclaiming: 'Sirrah, if ever I hear you say "thou" or "thee" to me again, I'll strike your teeth down your throat', while Lady Waller was so enraged at being unceremoniously addressed as 'woman' by the Quaker Ellis Hookes 'that she fell to beating him about the head and pulling his hair, saying she was never called Woman before'.[5]

Even greater outrage resulted from Quaker refusal to remain uncovered in the presence of superiors, the so-called hat honour, observance of which mark of respect was considered fundamental to the preservation of social order. Hats were normally worn indoors and in church, but not during prayers or in the presence of superiors, who included senior members of the family. This caused violent family rows, as recorded by young Thomas Ellwood, who was more unusually the son of a minor country squire and magistrate. Thomas, having been converted by the Peningtons, another gentry family living nearby, had already discarded the lace, ribbons and useless buttons from his clothes and stopped wearing rings, but when he appeared before his father with his head covered, Ellwood senior again fell on him 'with both his fists in a transport of passion, plucked off his hat and threw it away'.[6] The unfortunate Thomas was eventually driven out of his home – he went to London and later became a reader to the blind Milton – but he was by no means the only Quaker convert (they were mostly young men) to be disowned by his family and adopted by the community of Friends.

The Quakers were certainly the strictest in the matter of dress, but all serious Puritans disapproved of any unnecessary adornment of the person and of long hair. 'When Puritanism grew into a faction,' wrote Lucy Hutchinson, 'the zealots distinguished themselves, both men and women, by several affectations of habit, looks and words . . . Among other affected habits, few of the Puritans, what degree soever they were of, wore their hair long enough to cover their ears, and the ministers and many others cut it close round their heads, with so many little peaks as was something ridiculous to behold.' Lucy, having no patience with zealots, went on to make it clear that her own husband, who possessed a very fine thick-set head of hair, 'kept it clean and handsome without any affectation, so that it was a great ornament to him, although the godly of those days, when he embraced their party, would not allow him to be religious because his hair was not in their cut nor his words in their phrase'.[7]

Although there are a number of instances of prosecutions and imprisonment by local justices under the Blasphemy Act, there does not appear to have been any kind of organised persecution of the Quakers during the early 1650s. The Nominated Parliament had been broadly sympathetic, and had indeed come close to abolishing the system of tithes, but the second Protectorate Parliament, which met in the autumn of 1656, was a far more conservative body and not inclined to tolerate religious radicals. It was, in fact, anxious to put an end to the policy of religious toleration and becoming seriously alarmed by the spread of Quakerism, which had been steadily gaining ground in the south and west. It was, therefore, particularly unfortunate that James Nayler should, at this moment of all others, have felt called upon to ride into Bristol in the guise of a Messiah, with women strewing garments before him while singing 'Holy, holy, holy, Lord God of Sabboath'.

Nayler came from a village near Wakefield in the West Riding of Yorkshire, and was a man of some education. He had served in the parliamentary army, where he began his career as a preacher, and by the early 1650s had become a leading figure among the Children of Light, known both for the power and eloquence of his preaching and as a prolific writer of polemical pamphlets. As such he was a natural target for an establishment increasingly hostile to the sects and which now seized the opportunity to make an example. Arrested by the Bristol magistrates, Nayler was asked if he believed he was the Son of God. He replied, 'I am the Son of God, but I have many brethren . . . Where God is manifest in the flesh, there is the everlasting Son, and I do witness God in the flesh. I am the Son of God, and the Son of God is but one.' He added that 'the Lord hath made me a sign of His coming, and that honour that belongeth to Christ Jesus in whom I am revealed may be given to Him as when on earth at Jerusalem'.[8] But while Nayler was careful not to claim divinity for himself, his female followers were less discreet, one of them declaring that she had been right to kneel to him as 'the Son of Righteousness', while another definitely identified him as 'the only begotten Son of God' and went on to assert that she had died in Exeter gaol and he had raised her from the dead.

Somewhat out of their depth, the Bristol magistrates applied to parliament for advice on how to proceed. The Commons promptly appointed a committee to examine and report on 'the great misdemeanours and blasphemies of James Nayler' and ordered him to be brought to London. The committee's report, which was duly read on 5 December, concluded that Nayler had indeed 'assumed the gesture, words, names and attributes of our Saviour Christ' – he was even accused of having grown his hair and beard in order to heighten the resemblance – and its reception was an ominous indication of the mood of the House. Major-General Philip Skippon, now sitting as member for Lyme, a respected veteran of the Civil War and staunch upholder of Presbyterian law and order, spoke of his fears that toleration of the sects could prove more dangerous than any foreign enemy. The Quakers' increase was notorious and 'their principles strike both at ministry and magistracy . . . Should not we be as jealous of God's honour, as we are of our own?' he went on. 'Do not the very heathens assert the honour of their gods, and shall we suffer our Lord Jesus thus to be abused and trampled upon? . . . This offence is so high that it ought not to be passed. For my part, I am of opinion that it is horrid blasphemy, and ought to be punished as blasphemy.'

Skippon was supported by his fellow major-general William Boteler. 'My ears did tingle, and my heart tremble, to hear the report . . . I have heard many of the blasphemies of this sort of people; but the like of this I never heard of. The punishment ought to be adequate to the offence. By the Mosaic law, blasphemers were to be stoned to death.' Other members joined in, calling for an immediate vote that Nayler had committed a horrid blasphemy and should be put to death without further ado, but it was finally agreed that he should first be called to the Bar and allowed to answer the charge, the Lord Chief Justice remarking that, while he would not seek to delay judgment, nevertheless, 'God would have us proceed in a just way, though against the vilest person'.[9] Nayler was therefore summoned the next day and questioned by the Speaker. He insisted that there had never been anything so much against his will and mind as to be set up as a sign in this way, 'for I knew that I should lay down my life . . . I was set up as a sign to summon this nation, and to convince them of Christ's coming. The fullness of Christ's coming is not yet, but He is come now.'[10]

An impassioned debate followed as to whether or not Nayler had indeed committed blasphemy – some more moderate voices pointing out that he had never actually claimed to be Christ, but only a sign of His coming, that he had shown no malice against the Almighty and that he should be regarded rather as being 'under a sad delusion of the devil'. The Instrument of Government of 1653, which had granted a qualified liberty of conscience to 'such as profess faith in God by Jesus Christ though differing in judgement from the doctrine, worship or discipline publicly held forth', was invoked but rejected. Skippon observed that, although the Quakers, Ranters, Levellers and others all sought to shelter under the Instrument, it had never been the intention to allow them the freedom 'to hold forth and practise licentiousness'. 'If this be liberty,' he exclaimed, 'God deliver me from such liberty.'[11] George Downing (he of the Street), member for Carlisle, added his voice: 'As to the Instrument of Government, I hope it shall never be made use of as an argument to let this wretch escape. I am as much for tender consciences as any man; but I deny that this has any share in such liberty.'[12]

Although by no means everybody was satisfied about the legal position – whether or not parliament had the power to act as judge and jury in this case (in fact it did not) – it was eventually decided to go ahead anyway, significantly without troubling the Lord Protector. Nayler having been pronounced guilty of blasphemy without a division, the only question remaining was how to punish him. On 16 December the proposal that a bill should be brought in to provide for the death penalty was defeated by a majority of fourteen, but the final sentence was savage enough. After some argument it was agreed that Nayler should be set in the pillory in the Palace Yard at Westminster for two hours and then whipped by the hangman through the streets to the Old Exchange in the City. Two days later he was to stand in the pillory again for two hours at the Exchange, his tongue was then to be bored through with a hot iron and his forehead branded with the letter 'B'. After that, he was to be sent to Bristol and there whipped again on the next market day. Finally, he would be imprisoned in the Bridewell until released by parliament, kept in solitary confinement, at hard labour and without the use of pen, ink and paper. Brought back to the Commons to hear his sentence read in all its gruesome detail, Nayler was told that the House had mingled mercy with justice, desiring his reformation rather than destruction, and replied simply that 'God has given me a body: God will, I hope, give me a spirit to endure it. The Lord lay not these things to your charge.'[13]

Nayler endured the first part of his ordeal on 18 December. It was an exceptionally cold day and, after standing in the pillory, he was whipped at the cart-tail through the streets, naked to the waist, with only a white cap on his head. His friend and disciple Rebecca Travers, who afterwards washed his wounds, wrote that 'there was not the space of a man's nail free from stripes and blood from his shoulders near to his waist: his right arm [was] sorely striped, his hands much hurt with cords that they bled and were swelled'.[14]

The second part of the sentence was to have been carried out two days later, but a petition begging for a week's respite was granted. On 23 December another petition, signed by eighty-seven sympathisers, was presented to the Commons, praying that the remainder of the punishment might be remitted. This was firmly rejected, George Downing referring to a text in Hebrews 10: 28, 'He that despised Moses' law, died without mercy', being a quotation out of Deuteronomy, speaking of vengeance which God executed by man. 'We', pronounced Downing with some relish, 'are God's executioners, and ought to be tender of his honour. Can any man call this liberty of conscience, a permission to commit such high blasphemy and impiety?' For his part, Downing would rather die on the spot before remitting the sentence already passed.[15] The petitioners then turned to Cromwell, asking him to intervene. The Protector had apparently been watching the proceedings in parliament with some disapproval, and in a letter dated 25 December asked the House to let him know on what grounds and reasons they had acted in a matter 'entered into wholly without us'.[16] This was an implied rebuke, for parliament as now constituted had no legislative power independent of the Protector, and, as John Lambert pointed out, his Highness was 'under an oath to protect the people, both in freedom of their consciences and persons and liberties'. He was therefore bound to inform himself in 'whatsoever he finds encroaching on any of them'.[17] However, since Cromwell was not apparently inclined to press the point, the members of the Commons, having convinced themselves that in the case of Nayler they possessed the necessary judicial powers to proceed – 'I take it we have all the power that was in the House of Lords, now in this Parliament' remarked William Sydenham – stood their ground, voting by 113 to 59 not to suspend the remainder of his sentence.

The diarist Thomas Burton records that on Saturday 27 December he went with a friend 'to see Naylor's tongue bored through, and him marked in the forehead. He put out his tongue very willingly, but shrinked a little when the iron came upon his forehead. He was pale when he came out of the pillory, but high-coloured after tongue-boring. He was bound with a cord by both arms to the pillory . . . Naylor embraced his executioner, and behaved himself very handsomely and patiently. A great crowd of people there.'[18]

Amazingly enough, James Nayler survived the tortures inflicted on him. He was released from prison by the recalled Rump Parliament in September 1659 and died a year later on his way back to Yorkshire. He could, of course, have been tried by an ordinary criminal court under the 1650 Blasphemy Act, but since this would have provided only for a six months' prison sentence for a first offence, such an unexciting course of action had naturally held no appeal to a House of Commons panicked by visions of Quaker multitudes refusing to swear oaths or doff their hats to their betters gathering on the northern moors to the terror of the people, ready to overturn all laws and government and overrun both minister and magistrates.[19] The case had nevertheless revealed a dangerous weakness in the system of a single chamber parliament, as Cromwell himself pointed out in February 1657 when discussing the restoration of an Upper House with a group of reluctant army officers. 'Unless you have some such thing . . .', he said, 'we cannot be safe. By the proceedings of this Parliament, you see they stand in need of a check, or balancing power, for', he warned, 'the case of James Naylor might happen to be your own case.' As things stood, it seemed that by invoking their judicial power the Commons could at any time fall upon 'the life and member' of anyone they considered a danger, and the Lord

Protector, armed only with the Instrument of Government, would be powerless to control them.[20]

While the Friends continued to be unpopular and persecuted at local level – although they were now being careful to try and distance themselves from their more disreputable Ranter connections – at the other end of the scale the royalists, the majority of whom were by both nature and nurture members of the Anglican church, were affected largely in proportion to the fervour of their devotion to the cause of the King and the bishops. Some, though not many, were executed by the Commonwealth as a result of their wartime activities. Far more suffered financial distress and, in some cases, ruin. All wars are expensive, and the idea of making the enemy contribute towards the cost of its defeat was obviously an attractive one, which had occurred to the parliamentary party as early as the spring of 1643, when the county committees were first authorised to seize the personal and real estates of all those who had taken arms for the king, or had in any way assisted his cause. Later that year it was enacted that one-fifth of the value of the property was to be reserved for the maintenance of the delinquent royalist's innocent wife and children, but personal belongings were to be sold at auction and the land let out to tenants, all proceeds apart from the fifths being paid to the state.[21]

On 30 January 1644 parliament issued a Declaration, promising a free pardon to all the King's common soldiers who, 'upon the humble acknowledgement of their former errors, shall offer themselves willingly and speedily to take the Covenant, and shall join heartily and really in the defence of this [the parliamentary] cause, as becometh good Christians and lovers of their country . . . otherwise let them expect the punishment of wilful Delinquents and Malignants'. This offer was extended to those noblemen, knights, gentlemen and citizens who, although supporters of the King, were not to be reckoned 'amongst the prime authors of this unnatural war, nor amongst the malicious and desperate enemies of their religion and country'. They were, however, warned that, since 'a just difference must be made betwixt such persons returning late to their duty, and those that never departed from it', they must expect to make a contribution towards relieving the common burdens of the kingdom. To this end, 'their estates in some proportions should be liable' – the size of the proportions being at the discretion of parliament and its agents, who would be 'as careful to prevent their ruin as to punish their delinquencies'.[22]

This Declaration, which was widely circulated, was the origin of the system of compounding, by which those unfortunates who had suffered sequestration could recover their property on payment of a substantial fine or 'composition'. It was controlled by the Committee for Compounding, which sat at Goldsmiths' Hall in Gresham Street in the City of London, just north of St Paul's Cathedral and was to prove a useful source of ready cash for the winning side. Among the first compounders were Sir Edward Dering and the Earl of Westmorland, who each paid £1,000, Sir Richard Halford, £2,000, Sir John Baker, £3,000, and the Earl of Carlisle, whose fine of £1,000 was later reduced to £500.[23]

After a slow start, the number of those seeking to compound rose sharply in 1646 and again with the apparent collapse of the royalist cause in 1649. The rules of procedure had by this time been fully established, and each intending compounder was required to present a petition to the Committee, setting out the date and nature of his delinquency, together with full details of his estate set out in a book and signed by himself. He also had to provide certificated proof that he had taken the Covenant and the so-called Negative Oath or Oath of Abjuration, in which he promised not to assist the king and to submit to the parliament. These documents were passed to the Counsel for the Committee, who then issued a report on which his fine was assessed. This varied from two-thirds to a tenth of the value of the compounder's estate, according to the perceived seriousness of his delinquency. On payment of the first half, the Committee had the power to suspend the sequestration and to discharge it on payment of the whole.[24]

The two-thirds penalty was imposed only on royalists who had held out to the very end of the war or had been especially active against the parliament (there was a small class which was considered beyond pardon), but even the smaller fines represented a heavy burden to the average landed gentleman, who had probably already contributed plate and money to the King's cause and suffered further losses as a result of the war – rents had gone unpaid, timber had been felled, parks denuded of deer and cattle, and in not a few cases houses pillaged and destroyed. To raise money to pay his composition, anyone without the advantage of rich or influential friends would be forced either to borrow or to sell land at a time when it had everywhere fallen in price and in the months which could pass between sequestration and final settlement of the composition he and his family were often reduced to real penury, as James Wenlock, Justice of the Peace and landowner of Essex, was later to describe. His wife, a gentlewoman, had been forced to turn away all her servants and was unable to hire a poor woman to help her, because of the general reluctance to work for a malignant. She had had to take her children out of school and sell most of the household furniture to buy bread. Finally, she and the children had learnt to spin in order to keep from starving, and even when they managed to buy a cow to provide milk for the children, it was confiscated for non-payment of taxes.[25]

The royalists also suffered in their pride. After 1649 they were excluded from their traditional place in local government, and to hold almost any office or even claim protection of the law, they were obliged to take the Engagement, that undertaking imposed on all adult males to be true and faithful to the Commonwealth without king or House of Lords. Most royalists took this and the other oaths 'for quietness sake', with their fingers crossed behind their backs. They were, after all, in no position to resist. Defeated, discredited and demoralised, most of them wanted only to be left in peace and were in no mood to rally to the standard in 1651 when Charles II made his ill-fated attempt to regain the throne. Cromwell's victory at Worcester seemed to mark the nadir of the royalists' cause, but the regime remained suspicious, well aware that 'necessity rather than good will' was keeping the enemy quiet. The journalist Marchamont Needham put it bluntly when he wrote that 'when a commonwealth is founding, or newly founded . . . upon the ruins of a former government . . . to make no distinction between men but to allow the conquered part of the people an equal right to choose and to be chosen, were not only to take away all proportion in policy, but the ready way to destroy the commonwealth . . .'. Needham believed that 'such as have commenced war, to serve the lust of tyrants against the people's interest, should not be received any longer as a part of the people, but may be handled as slaves when subdued . . . because by their treasons against the majesty of the people . . . they have made forfeiture of all their rights and privileges'.[26] To be fair, had things gone the other way, it is not likely that royalists would have shown any particular generosity to 'the conquered part of the people', as Sir John Gwynne remembered when he was 'seiz'd upon for a malignant and sent with a file of musketeers before the Mayor of Newcastle, who was an exact fanatique . . .' '"Well, had it pleas'd God to give you the victory over us, as it pleas'd his Divine will to give us victory over you,"' remarked this individual, '"ye had call'd us villaines, traytours, sons of whores; nay you had kicked us too." "You are in the right on't, sir,"' replied Gwynne cheerfully, provoking a burst of laughter from the standers-by.[27]

Early in 1652 an ordinance of Oblivion and General Pardon was passed, but contained so many exceptions and caveats as to render it fairly useless for purposes of reconciliation, and any effect it might have had was quickly undone by two further Acts, authorising the sale of a large number of estates forfeited for treason and intended to embrace all those sequestrated properties whose owners had either so far refused to compound or had failed to pay their fines. There was an escape clause, which allowed those who had not yet applied for composition to redeem their property by paying a third of its value, and this flushed out a number of previously obstinate non-compounders. However, many estates were sold, sometimes as a whole but more often broken up into parcels.[28]

There had, of course, always been a class of delinquents considered past redemption, as Margaret Cavendish, wife of the

Marquis of Newcastle, discovered in December 1651. Newcastle, once the King's general in the north, had left England in despair after the disaster at Marston Moor in 1644 and had married Margaret Lucas, a fellow exile, in Paris the following year. A good many of the royalist exiles, impelled by financial necessity to swallow their pride, had now returned home to compound with the dreaded Committee at Goldsmiths' Hall, but Newcastle, branded a traitor to the state, would have faced certain death. His wife, though, could petition to receive her fifth, to which she was surely legally entitled, 'she having no other means of livelihood'. Margaret therefore travelled to London and, escorted by her brother John, duly appeared before the Committee. 'But when I came there,' she wrote, 'I found their hearts as hard as my fortunes, and their natures as cruel as my miseries, for they sold all my lord's estate, which was a very great one, and gave me not any part thereof, or any allowance thereout, which few or no other was so hardly dealt withal.' The Committee gave two reasons for refusing her petition. First, that Newcastle, the greatest traitor and 'an excepted person', was excluded from any possibility of pardon, and, secondly, that Margaret had married him since he became a delinquent, 'so that at the time of marriage he had no estate'. Too shy and too proud to plead her cause before such an ill-bred assembly, she whispered to her brother to conduct her out of 'that ungentlemanly place' and, 'being not a good flatterer', made no further attempt to trouble herself or petition her enemies.[29]

Those royalists forced by sheer financial necessity to take the Engagement and compound could perhaps comfort themselves by reflecting that 'the obligation of subjects to a sovereign is understood to last as long and no longer, than the power lasteth by which he is able to protect them', but bitter resentment over their losses and the other petty restrictions imposed on them burnt corrosively only just below the surface, finding expression in defiant toasts drunk to Charles II, seditious graffiti, and abuse of the regime. One man was fined £20 for saying the Lord Protector and his statesmen were murderers who had beheaded the king and hanged better men than themselves only to get their victims' estates so that they might live in pride. Another was fined for wishing he had the key of the parliament house in his keeping, as he would lock the members and the Lord Protector in till he had cut their throats or they his. Two women had to enter into recognisances for hoping to see Whitehall on fire and the Lord Protector hanged, and once, as he was getting into his coach at Whitehall, a woman in the crowd shouted that bonny heads were cut off while ugly ones did keep on their shoulders.[30] More damaging to the social fabric was the unbridgeable gap, now widening, between the old gentry who had fought for the King and the new men, the 'upstart gentlemen' who had done well out of the war. As the Protector was to remark in 1655, 'there is nothing they [the royalists] have more industriously laboured in than this, to keep themselves separated and distinguish'd from the well-affected of this nation; to which end they have kept their conversation apart as if they would avoid the very beginning of union'. They had, he went on, bred and educated their children by the ejected, Anglican, clergy and even sought to keep their marriage alliances within their own party, 'as if they meant to entail their quarrel and prevent the means to reconcile posterity'.[31] It was not a healthy situation, nor was it improved by the fact that fines were generally assessed and restrictions enforced at local level, which gave plenty of scope for pursuing local vendettas and for the settling of old scores. Certainly the difficulties endured by Sir Roger Twysden of East Peckham in Kent appear to have been exacerbated by the malice of his old enemy Anthony Weldon, chairman of the Kent committee.

Those with the means to do so and without family ties often preferred to go into voluntary exile, and in 1653 a 19-year-old Yorkshireman, John Reresby, decided to abandon his studies at Grays Inn and set off on his travels.

> I found there was little means of improvement for a gentleman as to other respects in England [he recalled in his memoirs], the nobility and gentlemen of the best rank and estates living retired in

the country, to avoid the jealousies of the then suspicious government of every act or word that could be construed in favour of the royal family . . . And such as lived in town were either such zealots in the rebellious, schismatical superstitions of those times, or so very debauched on the other hand, that it was very hard for a young man to avoid infection on one side or the other.[32]

It was not until 1653 that the first definite signs of an organised royalist resistance movement began to appear, with the formation, probably about the end of November, of the celebrated Sealed Knot. This was to consist of six persons 'of general good and confessed reputation, and who of all who were then left alive had had the most eminent charges in the war . . . so that few men could with any reasonable pretence refuse to receive orders from them . . . some of them having, beside their experience in the war, very considerable fortunes of their own to lose, and were relations to the greatest families in England'.[33] The six persons in question were the Lords Belasis and Loughborough, both the younger sons of peers; Sir William Compton; John Russell, Edward Villiers and Sir Richard Willys. These well-connected individuals declared themselves ready to undertake the care of the King's service, and 'as they would not engage in any absurd and desperate attempt, but use all their credit and authority to prevent and discountenance the same, so they would take the first rational opportunity, which they expected from the divisions and animosities which daily grew and appeared in the army, to draw their friends and old soldiers who were ready to receive their commands together, and try the utmost that could be done, with the loss and hazard of their lives'.[34]

Unfortunately, for all its military experience and authority, the Knot turned out to be disappointingly ineffective, both in preventing any 'absurd and desperate' attempts and in finding a rational opportunity to restore the monarchy. It was also penetrated almost immediately by government agents. It has been said that 'Cromwell carried the secrets of all the princes of Europe at his girdle', and the republic's intelligence service is justly famous for its efficiency. Its first director was Thomas Scot, who had entered parliament in 1645 as member for Aylesbury. A member of the panel which had sat in judgment on Charles I and one of the signatories on his death warrant, Scot was also a member of all the Commonwealth councils of state and in July 1649 had been appointed 'to the trust of managing the intelligence both foreign and domestic' and given an allowance of £800 a year to cover his expenses. In his later 'Confession', written in the hope of avoiding the fate of the other regicides, he says he had no knowledge of foreign languages or experience of intelligence matters, but supposed he had been given the job as a reward for his 'known diligence and faithfulness' in the public service. Certainly he was to prove a conscientious and competent operator, employing, among others, a learned Oxford professor of mathematics, who possessed a valuable talent for code breaking, and his success rate was such that Lord Newcastle was heard to remark that he [Scot] dealt with the devil, for 'as soon as things be thought of, you know them'.[35]

After the expulsion of the Rump in 1653, Scot, a staunch Commonwealth man and opponent of the Protectorate, was replaced by John Thurloe, a clergyman's son from Abbess Roding in Essex. Sponsored by the lawyer and politician Oliver St John, Thurloe had risen steadily through the ranks of government service, becoming secretary to the Council of State in March 1652 with a salary of £600 a year, and clerk to the Committee for Foreign Affairs in December. The following July he took over control of the intelligence service and quickly demonstrated his undoubted flair for the job. He had inherited Scot's network of informers and *agents provocateurs* – there was never any shortage of these, 'swarming over all England as Lice and Frogs did in Egypt' – and also employed experts in the arts of intercepting and opening letters. Samuel Morland, another member of his staff, was said to be so skilled a forger that he could copy a letter and send it on to its unsuspecting recipient, while keeping the original as evidence.

Gifted though Thurloe was, his task was made easier by the royalists' lack of organisation and their fatal addiction to gossip. His spies in Paris were certainly helped by the exiles' willingness to chat even to that doubtful character Joseph Bampfield. True, Bampfield seemed to have an impeccable background. He had been a colonel in the royalist army and in 1648 had organised the escape of the young Duke of York from parliamentary custody, but he was also a professional intelligence agent, ready to offer his services to anyone who would pay him a salary. He arrived in Paris in September 1653, and continued to report regularly to Thurloe until the end of the Protectorate. Bampfield survived the Restoration, ending his long, adventurous and disreputable career in exile in Holland in 1685, but another of Thurloe's agents and another royalist renegade was less fortunate. Henry Manning, a Catholic whose father and brother had been killed fighting for Charles I, also turned informer in 1655, but he was careless, suspicions were aroused and he was 'executed' for his treason in a German wood by two senior members of the exiled community.

The information Thurloe was getting from his various sources during the course of 1654 gave him prior knowledge of a plot to assassinate the Protector by 'some desperate people of the king's party'. He was to be ambushed on Saturday 21 May as he travelled from Whitehall down to Hampton Court, his favourite weekend retreat, but, in a convenient last-minute change of plan, decided to go by river as far as Chelsea. The would-be assassins were arrested on the following day and most of their associates had been rounded up by the end of the week. The two ringleaders, John Gerard and Peter Vowell, were executed and several others transported to Barbados. One of those arrested, Thomas Henshaw, escaped to the Continent, possibly with official connivance, and the royalists were soon claiming that the whole affair had been a put-up job invented by the government's 'hired mercenary witnesses'. Very likely *agents provocateurs*, 'trepanners' or 'decoy ducks' as they were known, had been stirring the pot, and Thurloe was presently able to dismiss the episode as having little importance, involving no one of honour or interest that he could hear of.

Potentially more serious than the Gerard Plot, one of those 'absurd and desperate attempts' which the Sealed Knot had been supposed to prevent, was the so-called Penruddock Rising, which took place in the spring of 1655. This had been intended as a countrywide insurrection, with centres reaching from Tyneside to York, from Shrewsbury and the Welsh Borders to the Midlands, the South and the West Country, but lack of leadership and coordination, mistrust between rival groups – the Sealed Knot had been against it from the start – incompetence, delay, poor security and lack of grass-roots support, all combined to ensure an ignominious failure. In the end the only spark of revolt flared in and around Salisbury, where for a few hours on Monday 12 March a few hundred men led by a handful of local landowners – John Penruddock, Hugh Grove, Thomas Mompesson and Richard Thornbury – occupied the town, arresting the Sheriff and a couple of judges, capturing the inns, commandeering any available horses, and unlocking the doors of the gaol, before marching off in the direction Sherborne and Yeovil. But they gathered no recruits, the march turned to flight and by Wednesday it was all over. Penruddock had surrendered, but Charles's friend the Earl of Rochester, sent over from France as designated 'Field Marshal General' of the whole enterprise, was able to make good his escape.

Joseph Bampfield had been dropping hints about a projected royalist rising for some time, but Thurloe got his first definite information in December 1654, and the arrest of the Leveller and republican John Wildman in February had filled in most of the gaps, so that defensive preparations were already well in hand by March. Probably Lucy Hutchinson summed up the situation as accurately as anybody, when she wrote:

> The Cavaliers . . . had not patience to stay till things ripened of themselves, but were every day forming designs, and plotting for the murder of Cromwell, and other insurrections, which, being contrived in drink and managed by false and cowardly fellows, were still revealed to Cromwell, who had most excellent intelligence of all things that passed, even in the King's closet; and

by these unsuccessful plots they were only the obstructors of what they sought to advance.[35]

In spite of the apparent collapse of the Cavaliers, rumours of plots and assassination attempts persisted and the authorities remained in a state of high alert. Troops had been brought over from Ireland, the Tower garrison increased to 1,200 men and cannon placed conspicuously in Whitehall. London that spring was like an armed camp, with soldiers everywhere patrolling the streets, and Thurloe was now beginning a countrywide round-up of leading royalists. On 13 June Sir Ralph Verney was arrested at his Buckinghamshire home and two days later wrote to his son Edmund, 'being just now brought prisoner to town with divers lords and other persons of quality, for we know not what . . . I must confess the soldiers that took me at Claydon on Wednesday last used me very civilly, yet they took all the pistols and swords in the house and carried me to Northampton that very night . . . What shall be done with us, and that multitude of gentry that is secured in every country, we cannot yet imagine.' Sir Ralph and 'at least eleven more of us' were taken first to Lambeth and then St James's Palace, 'where every man hath a guard upon him day and night, but we are not kept up close nor are our friends kept from us. I thank God I am in good air and good health and my innocency keeps me cheerful.' All the same, six weeks later he was complaining: 'we that are restrained have no present hope to enjoy our own houses in haste, patience is an excellent virtue and our new masters are resolved to see how large a proportion we have of it.'[37]

On 18 July the Venetian envoy reported that

the news here consists of the arrests which still continue both in this city and without, chiefly of those who have compounded with the new government after bearing arms for the royalists. A great many of these are in the power of his Highness, and . . . numbers of those of this class, rather than submit to his severity, have preferred to seek refuge in a vagabond life, changing their abode every other night. So one may say that the greatest and richest in England have become the most afflicted and persecuted . . . Although they become even more disaffected they dare not speak or lament their miserable condition.[38]

Paulucci may have been guilty of some exaggeration, but there seems no reason to doubt that, in the aftermath of the failed uprising, life for even the most peaceable royalist sympathisers had become more than usually stressful, especially when the Council reimposed movement restrictions on them in a proclamation dated 6 July commanding anyone who had served with or assisted the forces of the late King or his sons to leave the capital within a week. This meant that those who had no country house of their own would have to find shelter with friends or family, and those unfortunates without any resource at all must give their names and condition to the Justice of the Peace of each parish, who was to keep a register of them and send it up to the Protector. 'This measure will certainly put a stop to any plot to attack the Protector's sway,' observed Paulucci. 'It causes a great outcry,' he went on, 'especially among those who served the late king, who had compounded with the government and believed that, though reduced in circumstances, they would at least be tolerated.'[39] The order was, however, being strictly enforced. 'Diligent search has been made to discover those who have not obeyed or have contrived to remain under some pretext. But the search has had little result as almost all have obeyed, owing to the severity of the proclamation.'[40] Banishment from London was irksome enough, especially so for Catholics, who relied on the chapels of foreign embassies for the practice of their religion, but even country life had lost a good deal of its attractions for gentlemen currently deprived of so many of their normal amusements and, in the summer of 1655, about to find themselves subject to the jack-booted interference of Cromwell's major-generals.

Most of those 'restrained' in the early part of the year had been released by the autumn. Ralph Verney was back at Claydon in

October, but only after he had sealed a bond 'so full of barbarous conditions' that he was ashamed to enumerate them. 'All the favour that could be obtained', he wrote, 'was to get it limited for a year, but 'tis so untowardly penned that I doubt they will continue it longer on us.'[41] Sir Ralph might be home again, but now he and many others were having to face the prospect of the imposition of yet another financial burden. This was the decimation tax, that is, £10 a year for every £100 of landed income or £100 for every £1,500-worth of personal property. This was to be levied on everyone who possessed land worth £100 a year or more and whose estates had previously been sequestered for delinquency, 'who were in actual arms for the late king against Parliament, or for Charles Stuart his son, or have adhered to, assisted or abetted the forces raised against the said Parliament'.[42]

The unenviable task of assessing and collecting the tax fell to the panels of local commissioners working under the major-generals, and soon they were summoning their royalist neighbours to appear before them. All were to bring full particulars of the value of their estates, which would be used to calculate whether or how much they would be required to pay. Ralph Verney's sister wrote from Hampshire to tell him that Major-General Goffe 'hath been in these parts this day fortnight . . . all I hear he hath yet done is to send for all sequestered persons and Romes [*sic*] catholics, and that they must pay the tenth part toward the maintenance of an army besides their usual contribution, but as yet nothing is settled, what more he may do as yet we know not'. His friend Roger Burgoyne in Warwickshire reported how all the principal gentry of the county had been summoned before the 'grand commissioner' and told that 'the tenth part is to be paid to the Lord Protector of all that they have, but if not worth full £1,500 in land and goods, they may escape that shot. However all are to give a security for their peaceable behaviour . . . they are not permitted to have any arms in their houses, not so much as a birding piece, no not a sword, but are to send them to the Chief Commander of the county.'[43]

The business of assessment was to prove a good deal more complicated than had been anticipated, especially when it was discovered how many estates had been conveyed or sold to trustees, who it seems in many cases were acting as agents for the original owners. This resulted in a number of time-consuming legal battles over the precise nature of these trusts, and whether or not they had been set up for the 'use and benefit' of the original owners who now claimed exemption from the tax on the grounds that, although they still lived on the lands, the real owners were the trustees. Other awkward questions arose over whether or not reductions should be allowed for outstanding debts, mortgages and other 'incumbrances' when making assessments, and what about those royalists who owned property in several counties but fell below the £100 threshold in some or all of them?

Then there was the matter of who exactly was liable to pay the decimation tax. Any royalist who could provide the authorities with satisfactory evidence that he had totally renounced his former allegiance and sincerely accepted the new order of things was supposed to be exempt, but the commissioners were also required to include anyone who had ever even indirectly 'adhered to, assisted or abetted' the royalist cause – a definition which allowed for a considerable degree of latitude in interpretation and no doubt offered more tempting opportunities for the settling of old scores. Some unfortunates were decimated simply for having lived in royalist garrisons during the Civil War and Sir Francis Willoughby, who had never been sequestered, found himself 'cast' for the tenth part for having once sent two horses to Charles I.

Ralph Verney, who had never borne arms for the King or done anything to help the royalist cause – he always maintained that his only crime had been his conscientious objection to taking the Presbyterian Covenant – had already fought one long and ultimately successful battle with the authorities over the sequestration of his estate. Now, nearly ten years later, he found himself having to embark on a campaign against decimation. ' I am now in very great trouble', he wrote to his son in March 1656, and in danger to lose the tenth part of my estate, and if I deliver not in a particular of my estate real and personal on Thursday next, they will sequester me. This puts me to an appeal to the Protector and Council, which is not only very chargeable to follow, but the success so hazardous, that I know not which way to turn me. I am now giving over housekeeping, and discharging the most part of my workmen that were building and fitting up my house.[44]

But in spite of a petition to the Protector and several fruitless journeys to Aylesbury to confront the local committee, his decimation was finally confirmed in July and he was forbidden to come to London for six months. Then, in January 1657, came the news that parliament had thrown out the bill for the Continuance of Decimations and hard-pressed royalist squires up and down the country heaved a sigh of relief.

The Venetian envoy was of the opinion that 'as those who fought for the king consisted of the higher classes, that is the more dashing', all the government's energies would be directed 'to enfeebling the strength of that party so that they may be rendered innocuous . . . It cannot be denied', he had reported in December 1655, 'that discontent is great in certain quarters, and if their strength equalled their ill-will some serious conspiracy would break out. But they are so heavily burdened and their fortunes so dilapidated that without money, leaders or support they are better able to grumble than to vindicate themselves.'[45] This was probably a pretty accurate description of the royalists' situation in the immediate aftermath of Penruddock's rising, but by the following spring spirits had begun slowly to revive and during the next two years a loosely organised underground resistance movement was resurrected, its principal, if not its only, hope being focused on the treaty concluded between the exiled King Charles II and Philip IV of Spain in April 1656.

This undertook to return to Spain the island of Jamaica, recently seized by an English expeditionary force, and also contained the inevitable secret clause promising the suspension of the penal laws against the English Catholics. In return, Spain agreed to help Charles recover his kingdom by providing an invasion force of six thousand troops once the English royalists had occupied a port where they could safely disembark. The arrival of the Spaniards, together with some regiments of Charles's own, subsidised by Spain, would then coincide with a general rising of the royalist party, perhaps supported by the Presbyterians and other enemies of the Protectorate. Needless to say, no part of this enterprising scenario ever left the drawing board, although it was to cause the government a good deal of anxiety, and Charles did begin to recruit a small army from among the Irish previously in French service and the swarm of English exiles at a loose end in Flanders. The prospect of action, vague though it was, also offered an outlet for some disaffected young gentlemen still at home, who now started to drift over to the Low Countries in the hope of adventure. One of Thurloe's spies at Bruges reported in the autumn of 1656 that 'diverse runnegadoe English are come . . . to bear company with their king in whoring, swearing and drinking his health, as long as their money last, or that he can give them 6*d* per day'.[46]

Various other schemes continued to be hatched by groups of hopeful activists despairing of the Sealed Knot's inertia, but Thurloe generally experienced little difficulty in dealing with them, especially since he now appears to have been receiving regular inside information from one of the Knot's own members. The exact nature and duration of Richard Willys's treachery remains somewhat unclear, though there seems no doubt that he was playing a double game at least from the late autumn of 1656. The last open manifestation of armed royalist resistance took place at Chester in August 1659. Like its predecessor, it became known by the name of its only effective leader, but George Booth's rising proved as great a fiasco as John Penruddock's, although his force was stronger and the political situation seemingly far more favourable. As before, though, lack of any strong central coordination, disunity, delay, poor communications and a general reluctance to stand up and be counted were to prove fatal. As Charles's faithful councillor Edward

Hyde had remarked when the Spanish project was being discussed: 'If the king should land tomorrow with as good an army as can reasonably be hoped for, he will be overpowered as he was at Worcester, whilst all men sit still and look for the effect of the first battle.'[47]

A settled preference for sitting still and waiting to see which way the wind blew certainly characterised the great majority of royalists. This might be a disheartening attitude for those of an impatient disposition, but it was understandable. Many of the King's supporters had already lost a great deal and were desperate to hold on to what was left. Then again, the King himself was still in his twenties and he had brothers, while the Lord Protector was no longer a young man and his health was said to be poor. There had been so many failures, so many disappointments, surely now it would be wiser, and safer, to wait and hope for better times. So most men seem to have reasoned, and, providing they kept well out of anything political, life was not unbearable. True, whenever there was a security scare another wave of arrests would follow, prominent men could find themselves ordered to furnish a bond for their own and their servants' good behaviour, and more movement restrictions would be enforced. In 1651 Sir Henry Slingsby wrote from Yorkshire that he was occupying his time with gardening, study and teaching his children at home. 'This is all the recreation I have, except it be to hunt, which I can use without exceeding my limits of five miles, though I can make shift to ride 20 or 30 miles in a day's hunting.'[48] While also in Yorkshire in the early 1650s those devoted royalists Richard and Ann Fanshawe were able to rent a house and live an innocent country life, 'minding only the country sports and the country affairs'. Sir Richard spent his time translating Luis de Camoens's long poem 'The Lusiads' from the Portuguese, while his wife found her neighbours 'very civil and kind upon all occasions, the place plentiful and healthful and very pleasant'.[49]

Down in Buckinghamshire, Ralph Verney, relieved of the burden of decimation, was able to turn his attention back to his beloved Claydon, which, lying as it did in the border country between royalist Oxford and parliamentarian Aylesbury, had suffered severely during the Civil War. Ralph was now busy restoring the garden, planting fig and mulberry trees and red roses. '300 Asparagus plants' were ordered from a nursery, together with 'double violets blue and white . . . sweet marjoram and lemon thyme'. There were orders, too, for 'new stone seats, 6 feet 9 inches long and 17 inches broad', and stone stairs in the garden. The inside of the house, which had been in a shocking state after the damage done by relays of soldiers billeted there – linen quite worn out, the feather beds eaten by rats, kitchen equipment all rusted away and the dining room chairs in rags – was now beginning to look comfortable and well furnished again. Friends in London sent down some gilt leather, a fringe for the 'Pentado bed' and some Dutch tiles so that Edmund Verney was able to write in the summer of 1657 that 'of household stuff, I believe few gentlemen have so good or such great store'.[50]

For some families things were gradually beginning to improve, but there was still a strong sense of living under siege, a determination to keep up standards and resist at all costs any attempts by the new 'upstart gentlemen' to infiltrate their ranks. Ralph Verney rather wistfully confessed that he loved old England very well, 'but as things are carried here the gentry cannot joy much to be in it'. In 1656 Dr Laurence Wright, a distinguished member of the College of Physicians and physician-in-ordinary to the Lord Protector, with a large and lucrative practice, was looking for a bride for his son, and his choice had fallen on one of the daughters of Sir Justinian Isham. Dr Wright was a wealthy man and his son said to be 'a tall slender handsome man . . . very gallant, but civil withal – a quality rare enough in these times'. But the staunchly royalist Ishams of Lamport were a leading family, occupying much the same position in their county as the Verneys did in Buckinghamshire, and the Miss Ishams had made up their minds that a mere doctor's son, however wealthy, handsome and gallant he might be, was no fit match for any of Sir Justinian's daughters – Physicke, after all, was the lowest of the professions. They knew nothing of his origins and feared he must be 'ex plebe'. In any case, 'in these degenerating times, the gentry had need to close nearer together, and make a bank and bulwark against that Sea of Democracy which is over running them: and to keep their descents pure and untainted from that mongrel breed, which would feign mix with them'.[51]

Parliament reassembled in January 1658, and, for the first time since before the war, the members of the Commons found themselves being summoned to the Upper House to hear a speech from the head of state. By no means everyone welcomed this development, and a long and acrimonious debate soon began over the title and powers of the new 'Other House'. The republican faction argued passionately against any attempt to resurrect a House of Lords. 'Shall we now rake them up after they have been so long in the grave?' cried Arthur Haslerig. 'Will it not be infamous all the nation over?' In fact, the Protector's second chamber, created as a consequence of the Nayler case, contained only seven peers of the realm out of its sixty-three nominated members and hardly seemed likely to pose a very serious threat to the sacred authority of the people's representatives. But, of course, it was the principle of the thing that mattered, and the ghosts of Pym and Hampden were invoked as the republicans prepared to take their campaign beyond the confines of Westminster. A petition was drawn up in collaboration with some dissident elements in the army, the Fifth Monarchy men and their allies among the sectarian clergy in the City churches. Addressed to 'the Parliament of the Commonwealth of England', this demanded that the House of Commons should ensure a succession of parliaments in which 'the supreme power and trust which the people (the original of all just power) commit unto them, to make laws, constitutions and offices for the government of the whole, and to call officers of justice and ministers of state whatsoever to account, may be so clearly declared and secured against all attempts to the contrary, that no question may henceforth arise concerning the same'. This, of course, meant government by a parliament invested with absolute authority, unlimited by any written constitution, unrestricted by a second chamber or by a

Protector with a veto on the laws it chose to pass. It meant, in short, the end of the Protectorate. A clause providing for liberty of worship, so that 'no tender conscience might be oppressed', was included to appeal to the sects, and another, for the army, requiring that the officers and soldiers who had 'hazarded their lives for the nation's liberty' should not be dismissed from the service without sentence by court martial, which would have deprived the state of any power over military men who engaged in subversive political activity.[52]

Fifty copies of the petition were printed and circulated in London and thousands of signatories were quickly collected – estimates of the actual number range from 2,000 to an optimistic 20,000. The plan was to present it to the Commons on Thursday 4 February, and letters were sent out the day before to all those MPs believed to be sympathetic, urging them to be at the House 'to do service for the army and the nation'. The Republicans had, however, reckoned without the Lord Protector, who had no intention of allowing their plans, far more potentially dangerous than any royalist conspiracy, to go any further. At about ten o'clock on the morning of 4 February he left Whitehall by the back way, intending to go to Westminster by water, but the ice in the river was too thick – it had been a bitterly cold winter, the severest any man alive had known in England, according to John Evelyn – so that he had to turn back. Time was now so short that he would not wait for one of his own coaches to be got ready, but taking the first vehicle that came to hand – a hired hackney drawn by two horses according to one account – and with a scratch guard of footmen and half a dozen soldiers, hurried down unannounced to the Other House. There he paused to refresh himself with a cup of ale and a piece of toast, while those lords in attendance were informed that he intended to dissolve parliament. When his son-in-law Charles Fleetwood tried to protest, Cromwell turned on him angrily. 'You are a milksop! By the living God I will dissolve the house!'

The Commons had been in the middle of one of their interminable debates 'touching the appellation of the Other House' when Black

Rod arrived with the ominous message that his Highness was in the Lords' House and wished to speak with them. After a brief show of defiance – 'What care I for the Black Rod!' exclaimed Arthur Haslerig – the order was obeyed and the members trooped sulkily after the Speaker to hear what his Highness had to tell them. He did not mince his words. There was not a man or woman treading on English ground who could say he had ever sought the office of Protector, which he had undertaken only by their advice and petition, and on condition that

> there might be some other persons that might interpose between me and the House of Commons . . . to prevent tumultuary and popular spirits. It was granted I should name another House, I named it of men that shall meet you wheresoever you go, and shake hands with you, and tell you it is not titles, nor lords, nor party, that they value, but a Christian and an English interest; men of your own rank and quality, who will not only be a balance unto you, but to themselves, while you love England and religion.

He had hoped they would have been on a sure foundation, with 'the power consisting in the two Houses of Parliament and myself'. But now, sadly, it seemed as if 'you have not only disjointed yourselves, but the whole nation . . . through the intention of devising a Commonwealth again; that some of the people might be men that might rule all.' The Protector went on to warn the troublemakers that their efforts 'to divide and break us' tended to nothing else 'but the playing the King of Scots game'. The country was in imminent danger of invasion by Charles Stuart's army, even now gathered at the waterside ready to be shipped to England, 'and while it is doing, there are endeavours from some, who are not far from this place, to stir up the people of this town into a tumulting . . .' Not only were they attempting to pervert the army 'and draw them to state the question about a commonwealth', but some of them were even apparently prepared to join in a royalist insurrection. 'And what is like to come upon this . . . but present blood and confusion . . . If this be the end of your sitting, and this be your carriage, I think it high time that an end be put unto your sitting, and I do dissolve this Parliament: and let God judge between me and you.'

There was no protest, indeed some of the members answered 'Amen', the mace was presently 'clapped under a cloak', the Speaker withdrew and *'exit Parliamentum'*, leaving the Lord Protector once more in possession of the field. It was to be the old warrior's last confrontation with the Commons, that embodiment of all the principles on which his lifework had been founded and which had proved such a consistent disappointment to him over the years.[53]

SEVEN

Coffee Houses and Witches

They have in *Turkey* a Drink called *Coffa*, made of a Berry of the
same name, as Black as Soot, and of a Strong Scent.
(Francis Bacon, *Natural Historie*, 1627)

The Protector's summary dismissal of his second parliament
caused a considerable stir in political circles. His close friends
were surprised and disconcerted, his enemies on the other hand were
delighted, believing it to have been an act of desperation. The
republicans rejoiced at the stillbirth of the new Upper House. 'Thus
the two Houses fell together,' wrote one, 'their father, their good
father, knocking his children on the head, and killing of them,
because they were not towardly, but did wrangle one with another.'
The royalists, too, seized joyfully on the prospect of seeing Old Noll
on the ropes, but, as one of Edward Hyde's correspondents felt
bound to observe, 'any other in his condition would be deemed
irrecoverable, but as the dice of the gods never throw out, so there is
something in the fortune of this villain that often renders ten to one
no odds'.[1]

In fact, as soon became apparent, the Protector had known very
well what he was doing in dissolving parliament. 'This we now see
he was forced to do', wrote Lord Fauconberg, 'lest some turbulent
spirits among them should have put an end to the peace of this
nation by embroiling it in blood and confusions as ever.'[2] The
republicans' designs might have been frustrated, but the disaffection
in the army was still worrying, and two days after the dissolution
Cromwell summoned all the two hundred or so officers stationed in
and around London to a meeting at Whitehall. He and they had

163

always got along together, he said, and he saw no reason why they should differ now. He again justified his present authority, which had not been of his seeking, and went on to explain why, in the interests of public safety, he had been obliged to dissolve parliament. The officers applauded him, promising 'to stand and fall, live and die with my Lord Protector'. Toasts were drunk and a good many bottles emptied in the course of what became a noticeably convivial occasion. 'Deal plainly and freely with me,' said Cromwell; 'if any of you cannot in conscience conform to the new government, let him speak.' This invitation was answered by the colonel of his own regiment of horse, a fanatical Baptist, who declared himself dissatisfied with the present state of affairs, adding that all his troop captains agreed with him. The Protector made several attempts to change their minds over the next few days, but although they said they were willing to stay in the army and follow him for the sake of the 'good old cause', he could not shift their resolute republicanism, and feeling it 'neither for their good nor for the safety of the nation that they should continue in their commands', cashiered all six of them.[3] Again his resolute action paid off. Although the Fifth Monarchists were distributing pamphlets appealing to the soldiers to put an end to the Protectorate: 'Come brethren and fellow-commoners, we are resolved in the strength of the Lord if you will join with us, we will never divide from you, till the foundation of the Beast and its tyranny be overthrown,' the military stayed loyal.[4]

All the same, it was an uneasy spring. The threatened invasion by Charles and his Spanish allies had been frustrated by a naval blockade of Ostend, but the government remained in a state of high alert. All known royalists and Catholics were once more ordered out of London and confined to within a five-mile radius of their homes, while those suspected of involvement in the English end of the invasion plot and projected seizure of a port of disembarkation were successfully rounded up. Yet another, equally hopeless scheme for a royalist rising in London was broken up with almost contemptuous ease – Thurloe had recently acquired another particularly helpful informant in the shape of the former clergyman Francis Corker, who was able to keep him fully up to date on the progress of the conspirators' 'secret' meetings at the Feathers in Cheapside and other popular watering-holes. Having given the ringleaders more than enough rope to hang themselves, the authorities went into action on the morning of 15 May 1658, and some forty arrests were made. The trials continued through May and June, and resulted in five executions – Henry Slingsby and Dr Hewitt, an Anglican clergyman who had been allowed a good deal of licence under the Protectorate to preach and celebrate technically illegal Anglican rites at his church of St Gregory's by St Paul's, were both beheaded on Tower Hill, while of the seven London conspirators tried by the High Court of Justice only three were hung, drawn and quartered 'in several great streets of the city to make the deeper impression on the people'. The Protector's enemies naturally accused him of making a bloody spectacle in the open streets of London – 'we saw and smelt . . . the broiling of human bowels as an offering of a sweet savour to our idol' – but, in fact, although it was doubtless meant as a deterrent to intending plotters, this was a very rare example of the carrying-out of the traditional penalty for treason in Cromwell's England.[5]

Cromwell's life was now drawing to its close. His last months were shadowed by the long-drawn-out, painful illness of his favourite daughter, Betty Claypole, who died, most probably from cancer of the womb or stomach, on 6 August. Her father, a helpless spectator of her sufferings, never recovered from her loss. His own health was already failing, and the stress and sadness of Betty's death seem to have used up the last of his strength. Thurloe reported early in August that he had been very dangerously ill for several days, but he rallied and was even able to go out and take the air 'and finds himself much refreshed by it'.

The court had moved down to Hampton Court early in July, and it was there, one day towards the end of August, that George Fox encountered the Protector riding into Hampton Court Park at the head of his life guard. But, says Fox, 'I saw and felt a waft of death go forth against him; and when I came to him he looked like a dead man'. Fox had come to protest about the continued persecution of the Quakers and was promised an audience next day, but when he arrived he was told the doctors were not willing that he should see his Highness.[6] On 24 August Cromwell was moved back to Whitehall, where he died on 3 September, the anniversary of two of his greatest victories, Dunbar and Worcester, the 'crowning mercy'.

The news that 'the great Beast and murderer' was dead at last naturally produced an upsurge of euphoria in the English expatriate community. In Amsterdam they were mad with joy – 'the young fry dance in the streets at noon-day . . . and the entertainment of the graver sort is only to contemplate the happy days approaching' – and in Paris and Cologne, Brussels, Antwerp and Ghent, wherever the exiled royalists had been eking out a miserable, poverty-stricken existence in cold, uncomfortable lodgings, glasses were being raised and optimistic plans made for the future. But at home all was strangely quiet. 'There is not a dog that wags his tongue, so great a calm are we in,' Thurloe told Henry Cromwell, while Ralph Josselin's entry in his diary for 3 September consisted of one line of almost brutal brevity: 'Cromwell died. People not much minding it.' 'The next morning after the death of Oliver, Richard, his son, was proclaimed his lawful successor,' wrote Lord Clarendon in his *History of the Great Rebellion*. 'The army congratulate their new General and renew their vow of fidelity to him. The navy doth the like. The City appears more unanimous for his service than they were for his father and most counties in England, by their addresses under their hands, testified their obedience to their new sovereign without any hesitation . . . Foreign princes addressed their condolences to him and desired to renew their alliances. And nothing was heard in England but the voice of joy and large encomiums of their new Protector. So that', concluded Clarendon sorrowfully, 'the king's condition never appeared so hopeless, so desperate.'[7]

It certainly looked as if the Protectoral title had passed seamlessly from father to son – although Thurloe did admit to 'some secret murmurings' in the army – but Richard Cromwell was not and never pretended to be the man his father had been. Now in his early thirties, a country squire, though by no means a country bumpkin, for all Lucy Hutchinson described him as 'a peasant in his nature', he was an amiable, well-meaning soul who had never sought, or indeed ever been given the opportunity to hold, public office. Often dismissed as a nonentity and unkindly – and unfairly – nicknamed Tumbledown Dick, he possessed some admirable qualities of courage and good sense, but unfortunately these were not enough. Without his father's spark of genius and essential streak of ruthlessness, Richard Cromwell was not likely to survive for long in the wicked world of high politics, and nor did he.

Outside the world of high politics a number of developments improving the quality of life for some at least of the population were taking place. The 1650s saw the beginning of a rudimentary public transport system, and before the end of the decade stage coaches were operating a regular service on most of the main routes out of London. By the summer of 1657 it was possible to board the coach at Aldersgate on Mondays, Wednesdays and Fridays and travel to Coventry in two days for 25s, to Stone in Staffordshire in three days for 30s and to Chester in four days for 35s. It took two days to reach Oxford, and Edinburgh a bone-shattering six days. None of these journeys was to be undertaken lightly. The coaches themselves were extremely uncomfortable as well as smelly. The only seating was a hard wooden bench, and the floor was ankle deep in muddy straw. They were bitterly cold in winter – such hardy souls as travelled on the roof were liable to freeze to death – and baking hot in summer, and there was, needless to say, nothing to alleviate the jolting over atrocious roads. The state of even the main highways remained a scandal, nothing having been done to maintain them on a national basis since the days of the Romans. Each parish was supposed to be responsible for the upkeep of the stretch of trunk road which passed through it, but in practice this usually meant little more than throwing a few barrow-loads of stones into the worst of the potholes.

In London itself, for those who could not afford their own coach, the only means of transport had for long been the river, where wherries, light two-oared rowing boats, plied for hire like modern taxis. The Thames remained a popular thoroughfare, but by the early 1640s it had become possible to get about by hackney coach drawn by two or four horses – such as the Lord Protector had resorted to in his haste to dissolve Parliament in 1658. These were usually stationed in ranks, waiting for hire, by the better class of inn and cost 6*d* a mile for journeys up to six miles, 10*s* a day for longer journeys in a two-horse carriage or £1 for one drawn by four horses, which could carry up to six passengers. The hackney became so popular that by the end of the century 700 of them had been licensed, although in 1667, when Samuel Pepys was thinking of buying his own coach, he wrote that he was almost ashamed to be seen in a hackney – it was after all advertising the fact that you could not afford to keep your own transport.

The business of transporting people remained in the hands of private enterprise, but when it came to the business of moving letters round the country the government took a close interest. At the beginning of the century the postal service was still a royal monopoly and the monarch's correspondence travelled by special messenger, using teams of horses kept at staging posts, usually inns, along the way. For anyone else with a letter to send who could not afford to employ a private messenger, the only means of delivery was either to bribe one of the royal carriers or to seek out some other obliging traveller going in the right direction. It was Charles I who first opened the royal service to the general public when, in 1635, he founded the Letter Office of England and Scotland, although he was careful to ensure that the service should remain a monopoly: 'His Majesty straightly charged and commanded all his loving subjects whatsoever duly to observe his Royal pleasure therein declared, as they will answer the contrary at their perils.'

From its earliest days, the new Commonwealth was anxious to keep control of the post in state hands, and in March 1650 the Council confirmed the appointment of Edmund Prideaux, MP for Lyme Regis, to the office of Postmaster General. The intelligence value of intercepted letters was, of course, obvious, and little finesse had been wasted on seizing enemy correspondence in the days of the Civil War, but it was not until John Thurloe had taken control of the intelligence service in the summer of 1652 that its value became fully exploited, and in May 1653 control of the Post Office was farmed out to John Manley, brother-in-law of Isaac Dorislaus, one of Thurloe's most valuable assistants.

It was another two years before Thurloe himself, now Secretary of State, was given full charge 'of the postage and carriage of all letters and packets, both foreign and inland'. Detailed instructions for the management of the service were now being laid down. Posts were to travel from one stage to the next at 7 miles an hour from April to September, and 5 miles an hour for the rest of the year. The mail was to be carried in leather bags and the horn sounded on meeting company and four times a mile. Mail to and from London would be carried three times a week and horses changed only at recognised post houses. London postage would be 2d a letter up to 80 miles, and 3d for English addresses beyond that distance, 4d to Scotland and 6d to Ireland, while at no time was any attempt made to conceal the fact that the government reserved the right to intercept any letters which seemed likely to be of interest. 'A Post Office', declared the Postage Act passed by the second Protectorate parliament, 'is the best means to maintain trade, convey despatches and discover dangerous designs.' From Thurloe's point of view, control of the post was a vital tool of his trade and was also a lucrative source of income. Although he paid the government an annual rent of £10,000 for the 'farm' of his office, he is thought to have made a comfortable profit.[8]

Another notable feature of the 1640s and 1650s was the birth of the popular press. Newsbooks or pamphlets, containing mostly foreign news and known as 'mercuries', 'currants' or 'corantos', had been appearing sporadically for some years and grew in readership as distribution became easier via the new postal service, but the outbreak of the Civil War and collapse of the strict censorship imposed by the king's government led to an explosion of print from both sides of the political divide. *Mercurius Aulicus, Mercurius*

Elencticus and *Mercurius Pragmaticus* were all royalist, while *Mercurius Britanicus*, *Mercurius Democritus*, the *Perfect Diurnal*, the *Moderate Intelligencer* and the *Kingdom's Weekly Intelligencer*, to name but a few, supported the parliament and Commonwealth. They mostly appeared weekly and sold for a penny, and in the early days were largely propaganda vehicles. With the end of the war the royalist publications disappeared and in June 1650 the best-known journalist and pamphleteer of the period, Marchamont Needham, brought out his *Mercurius Politicus*, which became the official organ of the new Commonwealth. Five years later, the Protectorate government reimposed a tighter system of censorship and licensing of the press and from then until the end of the decade Needham's *Politicus*, which appeared on Thursdays, and his *Public Intelligencer*, published on Mondays, had the field pretty much to themselves.

As well as its function of government propagandist – 'How sweet the Air of a Commonwealth is beyond that of a Monarchy!' trumpeted the editorial of the issue of 4 July 1650 – *Mercurius Politicus* entertained its readers with a wide range of items of domestic news from around the country. In December 1650 it carried a detailed account of the strange story of Anne Green, an unfortunate young woman in Oxford sentenced to death for infanticide, but who, after hanging for

> near half an hour, in which time she was much pulled by the legs, and struck on the breast by divers other Friends, and other standers by; and above all, received several violent strokes on the stomach by a Soldier with the but-end of his Musket,

was cut down and discovered to be still alive. So much so

> that it pleased God within 14 hours she spake, and the next day talk'd and coughed very heartily, and is now in great hope of recovery. Upon this her reprieve was granted, the Governor of this garrison shewing much wisdom in obtaining thereof, and sense of this

great providence. Thousands of people come from all parts to see her . . . and all seem satisfied of the wenches innocency to the murther.[9]

Other titbits of news, such as one might not be too surprised to encounter in a modern tabloid, concerned 'a very sad and lamentable accident at a place called Church Lawton . . . in the county of Chester', where, 'by the late Thunder and Lightning' of July 1652, several members of the congregation were struck dead during the sermon.[10] And in a follow-up to a story of an explosion and fire in the eastern suburbs of London: 'We had an account that the late lamentable blow at Ratcliff was occasioned by a Cooper, who going to hoop a Gun-powder Barrel, presumed to do it with an Iron Instrument, which lighting upon a Nail, struck fire, and the sparks occasioned that fatal mischief which ensued . . . Among the slain, was found a great-bellied woman, whose belly being immediately opened, the child was taken out alive.'[11]

Mercurius Politicus appears to have been the first newsbook to carry advertisements, and in May 1655 was extolling the virtues of

that Excellent Cordial called the *Countess of* KENT'S *Powder*, approved by long experience of the Nobility, Gentry and best Physitians of this Nation, in any malign disease, *Plague, Small Pox, Burning Fevers, Wind-Collick, Women in Labor, Children newly born, etc.* is now made by one Mistress *Williamson*, living in White-Friers, near the late Countess's house, who was a Servant to her, and for many years compounded it by her Ladies direction . . . This notice is published, because of the many counterfeit powders uttered up and down by Apothecaries and others, under the same name.[12]

'A new invention for a Bedstead, which is of a most admirable use for the ease and infinite convenience of all sick, lame, diseased, wounded or aged persons' was being recommended in January 1659, and, the following June, came an advertisement for 'Chocolate, an excellent *West-India* Drink, sold in Queens-Head Alley in Bishopsgate street by a Frenchman who did sell it formerly in Grace Church street, and in Clements Churchyard; being the first man who did sell it in England'.[13]

Chocolate was not the first exotic new beverage to reach discerning Londoners during the 1650s. 'They have in *Turkey* a Drink called *Coffa*,' wrote Francis Bacon in his *Natural Historie*, 'made of a Berry of the same Name, as Black as Soot, and of a Strong Scent . . . which they take, beaten into Powder, in Water as hot as they can drink it. And they take it, and sit in their Coffa Houses, which are like our Taverns. This drink comforteth the Brain and Heart, and helpeth Digestion.' Bacon is not likely to have had personal experience of coffee drinking, and he most probably sourced his information from the *Relation of a Journey* written by George Sandys, an Englishman who had travelled in the Middle East in the early years of the century, reaching Constantinople in the autumn of 1610. Coffee drinking became popular among the English community trading in the Sublime Porte, and in 1651 a wealthy young Levant merchant called Daniel Edwards, returning home to London from Smyrna and himself a coffee addict, introduced the habit to his fellow citizens.

The first London coffee house, established most likely at some point in 1652, was a modest affair, not unlike a market stall, in St Michael's Alley, a lane leading off Cornhill and conveniently close to the Royal Exchange, where all the City traders gathered on a daily basis. The business was managed by Pasqua Rosee, Daniel Edwards's trusted Greek servant-cum-secretary, and, like all novelties, attracted a great deal of attention, not all of it favourable. To the keepers of taverns and alehouses this foreign interloper, this 'cuphye-house or a Turkish – as it were – alehouse', represented a possibly dangerous threat to their livelihoods, but, in spite of its really rather nasty bitter taste and tendency to produce flatulence, coffee, cuphye or even koffwey had come to stay. To overcome the objections that he was not a citizen or member of a livery company, Rosee's patrons provided him with a partner, Christopher Bowman, who possessed the necessary qualifications, and the business grew and flourished, soon moving into larger premises nearby, where they traded under the sign of Rosee's own head. Soon, too, other coffee houses were appearing, and by the early 1660s there were six of them in the Cornhill ward alone. By the end of the century the coffee-house habit, where gentlemen gathered to drink their 'muddy kind of beverage' greatly deplored by John Evelyn, read the newspapers, gossip, talk business and politics, had become an integral part of City life.[14]

Tea, introduced into Europe by the Dutch in 1610, took longer to become popular in England, although it was advertised in *Mercurius Politicus* in September 1658, when Londoners were informed that the 'excellent and by all psyitians approved China drink called by the Chineans Tcha, by other nations Tay, alias Tee is sold at the Sultaness Head, a Cophee-house in Sweetings Rents, by the Royal Exchange'. Because of a higher excise duty and turf wars between rival trading companies which restricted its import, tea was considerably more expensive than coffee and remained an extravagant luxury in England until the mid-eighteenth century, although, ironically enough, it had been fashionable at the French court as early as 1650 – the widowed Queen Henrietta Maria recommended it to her sister Christine as a wonderful new remedy for colds.

Away from the letter-writing, newspaper-reading, coffee-swilling élite in the capital, life out in the countryside and the little market towns went on very much as it had always done. Despite some improvement in living standards, for the great majority it remained a harsh, precarious world where, only just beneath the sober Christian surface of Puritan pastor and Presbyterian elder, lurked the unquiet spirits of much older gods. It was a world inhabited by ghosts and hobgoblins, by malevolent fairies, by headless horsemen, by hellish hounds with glaring eyes and, of course, by witches. Belief in witchcraft was widespread and had scriptural authority. Witchcraft was also a statutory and capital offence, but not at first in England associated with devil-worship. This was a concept originating in continental Europe and only introduced into English law by an Act of 1604. Most people, however, remained more concerned with simple *maleficium*, that is, the doing of harm to others by the exercise of unspecified supernatural powers.

173

The witch was usually, though not invariably, an old, ill-favoured woman of the poorest class, dependent on her neighbours' charity for survival. If she was refused when she came begging and any misfortune subsequently overtook the uncharitable neighbour, his family or livestock, suspicion of witchcraft would fall on the unfortunate crone – the result of a mixture of resentment, guilty conscience and superstition. At the same time, these outcast old women – or, more rarely, old men – would sometimes deliberately cultivate a reputation for possessing the evil eye, as a means of defence against a hostile world and of extorting blackmail from others afraid of offending them. If a person 'pined away' for no obvious reason, it would generally be put down to their having been 'overlooked' or ill-wished. Similarly, if an apparently healthy individual suddenly dropped dead, there was no medical expert on hand to diagnose a cerebral haemorrhage or coronary, and the popular verdict would be that the deceased had been bewitched.

Although witchcraft trials were not uncommon, there is no evidence of any systematic witch cult in England on the European model or of any sadistic obsession with the subject – except, that is, when Matthew Hopkins, the so-called Witchfinder General, and his associate John Stearne, with the connivance of local magistrate and MP Sir Harbottle Grimston, conducted a reign of terror in the East Anglian counties between March 1645 and September 1647. Little is known of Matthew Hopkins, obscure younger son of a godly Suffolk minister, before the early months of 1645, when he was living in Manningtree in Essex and, according to his own later account, had become troubled by the activities of seven or eight supposed witches living in the town. He would then have been in his early twenties and apparently without any regular occupation, except possibly as a lawyer's clerk, so that when John Rivet, a local tailor, openly accused Elizabeth Clarke, an 80-year-old one-legged widow, living alone and dependent on parish charity, of having caused the mysterious and distressing illness of his wife, Hopkins seems to have seized on the opportunity of making a name for himself as a seeker-out and destroyer of witches.

Old Bess Clarke, hanged with fifteen others at Chelmsford in the following July, was the first of his victims, but by this time Hopkins had widened the scope of his operations and was gaining a fearsome reputation for his ability to extract confessions from suspects. The practice of swimming a witch – if she sank she was innocent and if she floated guilty – was now, officially at least, illegal, and Hopkins seems to have preferred to rely on such time-honoured tactics as days of relentless interrogation and sleep deprivation. A suspected witch would be 'watched' to await the appearance of her familiars or imps – cat, dog, toad, bird or even insect – who were believed to suckle her and bring her instructions from her master, Satan, during which time she would be kept awake, sometimes kept on her feet and walked up and down until the terrified, exhausted creature would confess to anything and believe what she had confessed. Another useful 'proof' of guilt was the existence of a witch's mark. This could be a mole or wart or any unusual excrescences such as haemorrhoids or vaginal polyps – it was noticeable how often these marks were found on the suspects' 'secret parts' – anything, in short, which could be construed as a teat for the familiar to suckle. In order to discover them, women searchers were employed – Mary Phillips, who usually accompanied Matthew Hopkins, being regarded as an especially skilful and successful practitioner of the art.

As the witch fever intensified, Hopkins and Stearne acquired a quasi-official status as witchfinders, and by the end of 1646 their influence had spread throughout East Anglia and as far afield as the Isle of Ely. Exact figures are hard to come by, but it seems likely that between 250 and 300 women and a few men were interrogated or tried as witches and more than 100 hanged – which, in the seventeenth century, meant death by slow strangulation – while this figure does not, of course, include those who died in gaol.

Not everyone succumbed to the general hysteria, which gradually began to subside. Apart from anything else, witch-hunting was an expensive business. Staging the trials was not cheap – suitable board and lodging had to be provided for the judges, their officers and retinues; gaolers had to be recompensed for keeping the prisoners alive, at a rate of 3*d* a day per prisoner, as most of them were too poor to make any contribution themselves; joiners had to be employed to build gallows and hangmen paid for their services. Then, too, the witchfinders demanded their fees and expenses – Matthew Hopkins and Mary Phillips ran up a bill of £4 at the Lion Inn on their visit to Aldeburgh. It all mounted up and was becoming a heavy charge on small boroughs in a time of general dearth, and questions were beginning to be asked about the possibility of wrongful accusations, so that Hopkins felt obliged to publish a self-justificatory tract entitled *The Discovery of Witches.*

The last of the trials took place at Ely in September 1647, by which time Hopkins had recently died 'after a long sickness of consumption' – the persistent tradition that he had himself been swum and executed as a witch being sadly untrue. It had all undoubtedly been a very nasty and brutal business, and Matthew Hopkins was to acquire an almost mythic reputation for evil incarnate, but while he must undoubtedly have been an extremely unpleasant person, he could not have flourished as he did if the general climate of the times had not been propitious. In the immediate postwar period, when many of the normal restraining checks and balances of law and authority were either distracted or absent and society itself was teetering on the edge of anarchy, all the conditions for an outbreak of public paranoia were present – especially in an area where a radical form of godliness had a strong hold on the population. Witchcraft trials continued sporadically for the rest of the century, but acquittals became more frequent as educated opinion grew increasingly sceptical, and although Puritanism and witch-hunting have always been traditionally connected, the so-called Essex witch-hunt remains an isolated episode.[15]

Witchcraft was not necessarily always evil. Virtually every village, small town and city neighbourhood would have its 'cunning man' or 'wise woman', who could count on a steady stream of clients. These 'charmers' offered a wide range of services, from medical and veterinary care to the recovery of lost property, the tracing of missing persons and fortune telling. When it came to recovering stolen property, the cunning man had a high success rate. It often only needed to be known that he had been called in for the missing article to reappear as if by magic. Fortune tellers had to move with circumspection to avoid charges of sorcery, but William Lilly, a noted astrologer, flourished during the Interregnum despite the suspicions of certain Presbyterian divines.

Cunning folk were most widely employed for healing the sick, especially for lifting curses or driving out evil spirits. Their methods usually involved touching the patient and repeating certain magic formulae, many of which were extremely ancient, handed down by word of mouth through countless generations until their original meaning had been lost. Some were debased versions of Christian prayers, and some were the old Latin Catholic prayers, which had by this time acquired a supernatural aura. Many of these magical practitioners were, of course, merely charlatans, while others may well have possessed a useful knowledge of herbal remedies or gift of healing, and such is the power of suggestion that sometimes they were able to achieve cures.

The seventeenth century saw some remarkable advances in medical science. William Harvey's ground-breaking discovery of the circulation of the blood had been published in 1628 but failed to impress his colleagues. John Aubrey, who knew him well in his later years, remembered hearing him say that after his book came out 'he fell mightily in his practice, and that it was believed by the vulgar that he was crack-brained; and all the physicians were against his opinion and envied him'.[16] Other pioneers included Thomas Willis, who published the first monograph on the anatomy of the brain and the spinal cord in 1664, and his assistant Richard Lower, who in 1665 successfully transfused blood from one dog to another and later some ounces of sheep's blood into a man. But in the 1650s the medical profession was still clinging to principles laid down by the ancient Greeks, who held that a person's mental and physical well-being or otherwise depended on the balance of the body's four fluids or humours – black bile, yellow bile, blood and phlegm – and conventional treatment remained confined to blood-letting, purging and drugs of the eye of newt and toe of frog variety; while, in the absence of anaesthesia and antiseptics, surgery necessarily remained of the most basic variety. Surgeons always ranked below physicians in the medical pecking order, and the best recommendation for a surgeon was the speed at which he operated.

Meanwhile the people, the poor in particular, continued to suffer from malnutrition and the diseases resulting from dietary deficiencies, such as scurvy, rickets, sore eyes and 'green-sickness' or anaemia, as well as from those associated with damp, overcrowded, insanitary housing conditions, such as coughs and colds, rheumatics, tuberculosis, typhus or gaol fever. The better-off were more subject to gout and urinary tract infections, which caused the most notorious and painful malady of the Stuart century, stone in the bladder, which led the really desperate sufferer to undergo the procedure known as being 'cut for the stone'. Rich and poor alike suffered from ague or malaria, carried by mosquitoes breeding in the many stagnant pools and undrained marshy areas – quinine, known as 'Peruvian bark', did not arrive in England until about 1665 and was both scarce and expensive, besides remaining suspect by reason of its association with the Jesuits. The general lack of hygiene and sanitation meant that everyone was liable to a variety of stomach upsets and enteric fevers, commonly known as 'griping in the guts', and dysentery, usually referred to as 'the bloody flux'. Babies and small children were particularly susceptible to summer diarrhoea and convulsions.

Infant and child mortality remained horrific – John Evelyn's eldest son Richard died in January 1658 after six fits of a quartan ague, to the 'inexpressible grief and affliction' of his frantic parents, who sent for physicians from London – but the river was frozen and the coach broke down a mile from the house, 'so as all artificial help failing, and his natural strength exhausted we lost the prettiest and dearest child that ever parents had, being but five years, five months and three days old in years but even at that tender age . . . for beauty of body a very Angel, and for endowments of mind, of incredible and rare hopes'.[17]

Only one of the Evelyns' four sons survived into adulthood, but they were certainly not alone in their misfortune. Richard and Ann Fanshawe lost nine out of fourteen children, Lucy Hutchinson miscarried of twins and lost two more children during the war, while of the nine babies born to the wife of William Thornton of East Newton in Yorkshire between 1652 and 1667 only three survived for more than a few weeks, and Alice Thornton wrote of 'the exquisite torment' she suffered in bearing her fifth child 'as if each limb were divided from other' – it was a breech presentation and the baby was born dead.

Midwifery, for the great majority, was still an exclusively female business, although Peter Chamberlen, son of Huguenot refugees, is credited with the invention of obstetrical forceps and probably saved the life of Queen Henrietta Maria at the birth of her first child – another breech presentation. The infant lived only just long enough to be baptised, but the diminutive mother survived her ordeal – Caesarean section, of course, was possible only to remove a living child from a dead mother. Many women did not survive the 'dangerous perils' of childbirth, and many of those who did were still liable to succumb to childbed fever or puerperal sepsis. Ralph Josselin's wife was pregnant almost continuously from 1642 to 1663 and her husband regularly records the 'qualms and weakness incident to her condition'. In September 1647 'my dear wife ill of this child' and in October 1653 'my poor wife very ill, she breeds with difficulty', but although understandably often 'oppressed with fears', Jane Josselin, raised on the biblical edict that 'in sorrow thou shalt bring forth children', would have accepted the physical servitude which had been women's lot from time out of mind without question or complaint. Ralph was an affectionate and attentive husband, summoning the midwife and getting 'fires and all ready', but it would seem that a midwife was not always considered necessary or even desirable, women in labour preferring to rely on their mothers, friends and neighbours for support. In spite of all its perils, a lying-in was always a social occasion, and in spite of everything mother and child did quite often manage to survive. Out of ten live births the Josselins lost one baby at ten days, another at thirteen months and one at eight years old, which was not a bad average.[18]

A virulent strain of smallpox, sometimes still confused with measles, reached epidemic proportions in the seventeenth century. Two of John Evelyn's daughters died of it in their teens, and it killed two members of the newly restored royal family at Christmas 1660. But the most feared disease was, of course, plague or the Black Death. There had been two major epidemics in 1603 and 1625, but ever since its first appearance in 1348, England was seldom if ever completely free of plague, and it remained as great a mystery as it had been in the fourteenth century, no one knowing 'whence it cometh, whereof it ariseth and wherefore it is sent'. Naturally, the most popular explanation was God's punishment for sin, and there was no effective protection against it, apart from attempting to isolate its victims – an infected house would be sealed up, with a cross and the inscription 'Lord have mercy upon us' enclosed in a red circle scrawled on the door.

Plague might be the most dreaded of the ills which could befall them, but illness and pain were, to a greater or lesser extent, constant companions of the great majority of the population. Richard Baxter of Kidderminster suffered, among other things, from a persistent cough, which he feared might be a consumption, 'then very common in the country', a flatulent stomach 'that turn'd all things to wind', a rheumatic head and 'great sharpness' in his blood, which he believed proceeded from latent stones in his kidneys, blurred vision and tormenting toothache. The good Puritan minister Baxter grew to regard his various aches and pains as an 'unvaluable mercy' which greatly weakened temptation and kept him 'in a great contempt of the world'. This did not, however, prevent him from consulting numerous doctors, who, it seemed, only made matters worse, and in the end he found some relief from herbal remedies.[19] Ralph Josselin, too, frequently refers to his various ailments – the sore navel which troubled him for several years, colds, coughs, aguish fevers, bad eyes, sciatica and other miscellaneous 'distempers'.

In general it was only the better-off who were able to turn to the doubtful ministrations of the members of the College of Physicians. The poor either relied on the village medicine man or white witch, or else patronised one of the travelling snake oil merchants who peddled their wares at local fairs and markets. Another resource might be the local lady of the manor with a special interest in the subject and who would consider it her Christian duty to treat the sick of the neighbourhood, dress wounds and even set broken limbs. One such was Elizabeth Gray, Countess of Kent, who published *A Choice Manuall or Rare and Select Secrets in Physick* in 1653. Her prescription for the bloody flux was to 'take the bone of a Gammon of Bacon and set it up on end in the middle of a Charcoal fire, and let it burn till it looks like Chalk and will burn no longer, then powder it and give the powder thereof to the sick'. For the bite of a mad dog, her ladyship recommended the flowers of wild thistles dried in the shade, beaten to a powder and administered in half a walnut shell full of white wine to be taken three times, while to relieve a headache: 'Take the best Sallad oil, and the glass half full with the tips of Poppy flowers which groweth in the Corn, set this in the Sun a fortnight, and so keep it all the year and anoint the temples of your head with it.'[20] But for the vast majority, all medical care began and ended in the home, where the women of the family prepared remedies handed down from mother to daughter through the generations, nursed their feverish children and sick husbands, and prayed for them to get better.

The third and last Protectorate parliament, generally known as Dick's Parliament, gathered in St Stephen's chapel on 27 January 1659. It consisted mostly of the sort of 'conservative' or moderate gentry who had made up its two predecessors, and, like them, it failed either to control the Commonwealthsmen or to satisfy the army, whose pay was now once more heavily in arrears. On 22 April, therefore, the army under its new Lord General, Charles

Fleetwood, forced another dissolution 'without shedding a drop of blood, or making the least confusion in the city and suburbs', and the unfortunate Richard Cromwell was bundled ignominiously out of office and back into private life. The Protectorate was now at an end and it was beginning to look as if the Commonwealth itself might be in danger of disintegration. Little more than six months after Oliver's death, it had become distressingly obvious to what extent the success of the whole revolutionary experiment had depended on the life and towering personality of one man.

Aware of the need for at least a semblance of legal framework, the Council of Officers decided to recall the surviving members of the Purged Parliament or Rump, which had been so summarily dismissed in 1653, desiring them to 'return to the exercise and discharge of their Trust . . . for the improving present opportunity for settling and securing the Peace and Freedom of this Commonwealth'.[21] Fewer than a hundred members were left, available to answer the summons, and it seems that only about sixty-five of these ever took their seats at any one time, but they were to prove as intractable as they had been six years before, and the old battle for supremacy between parliament and the military continued through the summer against a background of rising popular excitement and disquiet. The army, 'the men in buffe', continued to demand their arrears and redress of grievances; the republican faction, scenting a possibly more sympathetic regime, agitated for further reform with a deluge of petitions and inflammatory pamphlets; while out in the country the wildest rumours could result in panic. In July the good people of Tiverton in Devon were roused out of their beds about midnight by one such alarm 'that the Ministers of the town and others fearing God should be all massacred that night'. The local magistrates hastily discussed who should be given arms, 'it being so dangerous a time', while 'neighbors roused each other out of their beds, crying pittifully one to another, *Take Arms, take Arms, else they would have their throates cut in their beds*. And when they came forth of their

Houses, and asked the reason of this Hurlieburlie and feare, the common Replie and general Crie was that *the Anabaptists and Quakers were joyned together, and intended that night to cut the throats of the Ministers, and all the Godly people.*' The more level-headed, 'being wiser than the rest', presently went back to bed, but others took arms and began to patrol the streets as 'the Crie for a while increased and grew higher and higher, to wit, That *the Fifth Monarchie men, Anabaptists and Quakers were joined together, not only to cut the Throats of the Godly in that Town, but the Throats of all the Godly in the Nation that Night*'.

This remarkable incident was reported by *Mercurius Politicus*, which added a warning to those in authority to take heed of 'the secret plotters and cunning designs now everywhere on foot, to ensnare poor people', for it was well known that the Cavaliers in city and country were only waiting for an opportunity to rise for Charles Stuart and did not care how they might reach their malicious end against the government by a Commonwealth.[22]

Exactly how the commotion at Tiverton, which had apparently been started by an indiscreet letter from a parish minister, was to achieve a restoration of the monarchy is not at all clear, but it is true that the abortive rising in Cheshire led by Sir George Booth took place the following month and prompted Dr Denton to write to his friend Ralph Verney from London on 10 August: 'This place was never so near aflame, bustle, confusion which you will, as last night . . . and what will be the issue a few more hours I guess will declare. We have all a mind to be out of the town, but yet hopes, fears and jealousies do so distract us, as that we can resolve of nothing.' Denton was afraid that if fighting were to continue the government's already alarming debts must increase and that 'taxes, free quarter, militia horses, besides the casualty of plunder must and will dock the revenue, and interest as bad as all these will eat like militia horses whilst you sleep'.[23]

In October the army Grandees lost patience with the Rump, which had not only failed to deal with the problem of the soldiers' steadily lengthening arrears of pay or to provide them with a watertight indemnity from prosecution for any acts committed in the course of their military duties, but had also done nothing to address the problem of the controversial Upper House, which the Grandees had wanted converted into a Senate which would include a military presence and reform the law and the church, and guarantee the freedom of the independent congregations. On 13 October, therefore, the soldiers moved in, and, after a brief stand-off between the two regiments who remained loyal to parliament and the majority who had rallied to the Grandees, all access to the Palace of Westminster was blocked.

Power now passed back into the hands of the Council of Officers, who presently appointed a Committee of Safety to run the country, but popular agitation for elections and a free parliament was growing, and a variety of solutions to the Commonwealth's problems, ranging from a renewal of rule by the Saints to the restoration of the monarchy, was being volubly discussed in the London coffee houses. James Harrington, an Oxford educated lawyer, had set up what amounted to a political debating society at the Turk's Head in New Palace Yard, Westminster, and, according to John Aubrey, 'the discourses in this kind were the most ingenious, and smart, that ever I heard . . . and bandied with great eagerness: the arguments in the Parliament House were but flat to it.'[24]

Early in December the *Weekly Post* reported the presentation of a petition to the Lord Mayor and aldermen by a deputation of city apprentices, 'wherein they remonstrate the manifold Troubles and Distractions the Nations are involved in, and the great Decay of Trade: Humbly imploring a speedy and timely Redress of these sad and heavy grievances'. The apprentices subsequently gathered in Cheapside and Cornhill, 'which occasioned the drawing together of several regiments of Horse and Foot, to prevent Commotions and Insurrections, in these times of imminent danger'.[25] Not surprisingly, 'some coales of Dissension were kindled'. The apprentices hurled brickbats and other missiles, and the soldiers retaliated by firing their muskets into the crowd, killing two young men and wounding several others. Nervous shopkeepers put up their shutters, the outraged citizens barred the gates at Temple Bar and the officer in command of the troops found himself being indicted for murder.

This seems to have been an isolated incident, but it illustrates the violent hostility which had come to exist between the civilian population and the military. In fact the uncomfortable truth was that the army, which had successfully brought down the monarchy and subdued both Ireland and Scotland, was now disintegrating into an ill-disciplined, unpaid rabble, rife with internal dissension, its officers more interested in playing politics than looking after the welfare of their men. Colonel Hutchinson and his lady had an unwelcome taste of what the general breakdown of law and order could mean when their home at Owthorpe was invaded by fifty or sixty troopers insolently demanding tax money, and when the Colonel asked 'by what authority they came, they showed their swords, and said, that was their authority'. They openly defied their own officer, who tried to restrain them, laughing at him 'even before Mrs Hutchinson's face', and she later heard that they had taken violently from the neighbourhood above £25 more than they were entitled to collect.[26]

The year came to an end in an atmosphere of general alarm and despondency. 'We had now no Government in the Nation,' lamented John Evelyn, 'all in Confusion; no Magistrate either own'd or pretended, but the souldiers, and they not agreed: God Almighty have mercy on and settle us.'[27] Help, though, was on its way, ironically enough from Scotland, where it had all begun, and where for some months the commander of the English army of occupation had been watching the goings-on in London with growing disquiet. George Monck, a professional soldier all his life, held firmly to the opinion that soldiers should 'receive and observe commands but give none' and that parliamentary resolutions in civil matters should be regarded as 'infallible and sacred'.

Events began to move on Christmas Eve, when the Council of Officers reluctantly reopened the doors at Westminster and the Rump sat again on Boxing Day. Then on New Year's Day came the news that Monck and his small but well-paid and disciplined force was on the march south. No one yet knew for certain what he meant to do. A taciturn individual, he would say only that he intended nothing more than the restoration of the authority of parliament – nothing about the restoration of the monarchy, although it was becoming daily more obvious that this was what the country wanted.

It had been a long, weary journey in wintry conditions, but when he entered the capital on 3 February by way of Holborn and Chancery Lane and along the Strand to Temple Bar, Monck put on a deliberately impressive show, himself on horseback 'gallantly mounted' at the head of his troops. 'After him', reported the *Publick Intelligencer*, 'followed many of his Officers and other persons of honor and quality, and then the Horse in their order. After them marched the Foot which are reputed as good as any in the world, trained up under an excellent discipline.'

Greeted by Speaker Lenthall, brought out of retirement to resume his post, the General advanced to Whitehall to settle into the lodgings prepared for him and where, during the next few days, he received 'particular visits from all the Members of Parliament and hath the like daily from many other persons of the highest rank and quality'.[28] On 11 February, satisfied that opposition from the Grandees had crumbled, he was ready to act, moving his troops into the City and sending a letter to the Speaker requiring parliament to issue writs for elections to make up their numbers. With remarkable short-sightedness it ignored him, but the Londoners openly rejoiced. Samuel Pepys, who had just begun to keep his famous diary, noted that rude boys were now crying '"Kiss my Parliament" instead of "Kiss my arse", so great and general a contempt is the Rump come to among all men good and bad', and when news of Monck's ultimatum reached the streets, the city exploded with relief and delight. His soldiers were everywhere welcomed with open arms and showered with drink and money and blessings. As Pepys made his way home about ten o'clock that night he could hear the clamour of Bow bells and all the bells in all the churches. He counted fourteen bonfires between St Dunstan's and Temple Bar and all along burning and roasting and drinking for rumps – there being rumps tied upon sticks and carried up and down. The butchers at the maypole in the Strand rang a peal with their knives when they were going to sacrifice their rump. On Ludgate Hill there was one turning of the spit that had a rump tied upon it, and another basting of it. Indeed [he wrote], it was past imagination, both the greatness and the suddenness of it. At one end of the street you would think there was a whole lane of fire, and so hot that we were fain to keep still on the further side merely for heat.

When he reached home in Axe Yard, Samuel went out again with his wife to show her the fires and they walked as far as the Exchange before returning 'and so to bed'.[29]

Events now took on a momentum of their own. Before the end of the month the 'secluded members' – that is, those members of parliament excluded in Pride's Purge – were invited to return, and some old familiar faces reappeared at Westminster, among them that battle-scarred veteran William Prynne, who arrived wearing an old-fashioned basket-hilt sword and was greeted with 'a great many great shouts upon his going into the hall'.[30] This remarkable Old Boys' Reunion lasted for three weeks, ending on 19 March, when, almost twenty years since it had first assembled with so many happy expectations in November 1640, the Long Parliament finally dissolved itself. As one irreverent news-sheet put it: 'they went in one day but could not find the way out in twenty years.'

The stage was thus set for the next act in the drama – the holding of fresh elections for the so eagerly desired 'free parliament'. The mood of the electors in the contested constituencies – expressed in shouts of 'no swordsmen' or 'no Rumpers, no Presbyterians' – was unmistakable, and, although no one had yet said so in so many words, no one was in any real doubt that the Convention Parliament – so-called because it had not been summoned by either king or Lord Protector – which assembled on 25 April would indeed vote to restore the monarchy. Negotiations with Charles, still known as the

King of Scots, had been quietly proceeding for some weeks and on 1 May, 'which will be remembered for the happiest May Day that hath been many a year to England', the King's carefully conciliatory Declaration of Breda was presented to both Houses, who responded by passing a resolution formally declaring: 'That according to the ancient and fundamental laws of this kingdom, the government is, and ought to be, by King, Lords and Commons.' Pepys, who was out of town on business connected with the fleet, heard of the great joy all yesterday in London, 'and at night more bonfires than ever and ringing of bells and drinking of the King's health upon their knees in the streets'. Pepys thought this was rather overdoing it, 'but everybody seems to be very joyful in the business . . . And our seamen, as many as have money or credit for drink, did do nothing else this evening.'[31]

But while the country rejoiced – down in Dorset, in the town of Sherborne, they held a mock trial of the effigies of Cromwell and John Bradshaw, President of the Commission which had tried Charles I and who had pronounced the sentence of death – not everyone was quite so happy. Ralph Josselin noted that 'the nation runneth into the King as Israel to bring back David' and could only trust the Lord would 'make him the like blessing to our England, and let God's counsel be in the work'.[32] The influential Presbyterian minister Richard Baxter, summoned to London from his Kidderminster parish, had to be reassured as to his Majesty's firmness in the Protestant religion. He was more than a little scandalised by the scenes of drunkenness and revelry going on in the capital and felt in duty bound to petition General Monck to take care 'that Debauchery and contempt of Religion might not be let loose, upon any men's pretence of being for the King'.[33] Another moderate Presbyterian, the Revd Henry Newcome of Manchester, prayed in roundabout fashion for the King on Sunday 6 May. The following Saturday, he recorded in his autobiography, 'they resolved to proclaim the king in Manchester, and we went first into the church, and sung a Psalm, and after I went up into the pulpit and prayed about half an hour . . . and this one thing I was put on to ask, that the joy of that day might not be blemished by the open intemperance of one person if it were God's will; and I could not hear but the people carried very carefully'. It seems that the proclamation went off soberly enough, but the Revd Newcome was saddened a few weeks later, on a journey into Rutland, to find maypoles in abundance and a morris dance, which he had not seen for twenty years. 'It is a sad sign the hearts of the people are poorly employed when they can make a business of playing the fool.'[34]

Saddest of all at the prospect before him was the blind poet and genius John Milton. 'If we return to kingship and soon repent, as undoubtedly we shall,' he wrote in the spring of 1660, 'we may be forced perhaps to fight over again all that we have fought, and spend over again all that we have spent . . .', and he could only lament the vain sacrifice 'of so many thousand faithful and valiant Englishmen, who left us in this liberty, bought with their lives'. But if people were really prepared 'to prostitute religion and liberty to the vain and groundless apprehension that nothing but kingship can restore trade . . . our condition is not sound but rotten, both in religion and all civil prudence'. Milton had spoken the language 'of that which is not called amiss "the Good Old Cause"' and clung to the hope that he might have spoken persuasively to a future generation of 'sensible and ingenuous men; to some perhaps whom God may raise of these stones to become children of reviving liberty'.[35]

But to the current generation of sensible men the Good Old Cause looked to be dead and buried, and a number of those who had been involved in promoting it were now preparing to make themselves scarce. Of the surviving regicides, Edmund Ludlow sought sanctuary in Switzerland and three more crossed the Atlantic to live out the rest of their lives in Puritan Massachusetts. Richard Cromwell went into exile in France under the name of John Clarke, returning to England at last some time in or about 1680, and dying in 1712 at the age of 85. The rest of the family were not molested, and the erstwhile Lady Protectoress was able to retire peacefully to the Northamptonshire manor of her widowed son-in-law John Claypole.

Meanwhile, across the Channel, the royalist exiles, still slightly stunned by the suddenness and completeness of their enemies' collapse, were preparing to come home. John Evelyn, who had been unfortunately struck down by a 'malignant fever' back in February, was still convalescing at the beginning of May and unable to accompany the delegation now setting off for Holland to invite his Majesty to return and 'assume his kingly government', but his fellow diarist Samuel Pepys was of the party in his capacity of secretary and general factotum to the Admiral Edward Mountagu. He got his first sight of the King at The Hague on 17 May and was able 'to kiss his and the Duke of Yorkes and the Princess Royals hands. The King', he added, seemed to be 'a very sober man'.

Pepys did not fail to notice the number of English persons of quality 'very rich in habit' who were clustering about his Majesty, and was soon hearing that parliament had ordered all those 'that did sit as judges in the late King's death' were to be secured to await trial. He was also finding that the new Court was already growing in self-confidence and that 'the old Clergy talk as being sure of their lands again, and laugh at the presbytery'.[36]

On the morning of Thursday 23 May Charles, with his two brothers, his aunt, the Queen of Bohemia, and his sister Mary, the Princess Royal, came on board the *Naseby*, hastily rechristened the *Royal Charles*, and dined together in a great deal of state 'which was a blessed sight to see'. Later that afternoon, after some affecting family leave-takings, the *Charles* weighed anchor, and with 'a fresh gale and most happy weather' set sail for England. The Restoration had begun.

Restoration

We drank the King's health and nothing else, till one of the
gentlemen fell down stark drunk and there lay spewing . . . and if
ever I was foxed it was now.

(Samuel Pepys, *Diary*, April 1661)

C harles II entered the capital, which he had last seen as a boy of
10, at two o'clock in the afternoon of Tuesday 29 May.

This was also his birthday, and with a Triumph of above 20,000
horse and foot, brandishing their swords and shouting with
unexpressable joy: The ways straw'd with flowers, the bells
ringing, the streets hung with Tapissry, fountains running with
wine: The Mayor, Aldermen, all the Companies in their liveries,
Chains of Gold, banners: Lords and nobles, Cloth of Silver, gold
and velvet everybody clad in, the windows and balconies all set
with Ladys, Trumpets, Musick and myriads of people flocking the
streets . . . I stood in the Strand [wrote John Evelyn], and beheld it
and blessed God. And all this without one drop of blood, and by
that very army which rebelled against him. But it was the Lord's
doing, *et mirabile in oculis nostris*: for such a Restauration was
never seen in the mention of any history, ancient or modern, since
the return of the Babylonian Captivity.[1]

The celebrations went on well into the warm May night.
According to the weekly journal *Mercurius Publicus* (the *Politicus*
had ceased publication and its editor had fled the country), there
were almost as many bonfires in the streets as houses. 'And among

the rest in Westminster a very costly one was made, where the effigies of the old Oliver Cromwell was set up on a high post with the Arms of the Commonwealth, which having been exposed there a while to the publick view . . . were burnt together.'[2] The rejoicings were not confined to London, which remained *en fête* for three days. Norwich kept the party going for nearly a week, and in towns and villages up and down the country bonfires were lit (Melton Mowbray had theirs alight for three days), church bells rung, loyal toasts drunk and maypoles joyfully re-erected.

There is no doubt that the nation was genuinely relieved and delighted by the restoration of the monarchy, but the policy of peace and reconciliation being pursued by the new regime, while politically expedient, left many of those royalists who had suffered for their loyalty frustrated and resentful. The King had no sooner set foot at Dover when he was mobbed by petitioners, and although he did what he could for the most deserving – especially for those who had risked their lives helping him to escape after Worcester – with the best will in the world there were bound to be many disappointments. The widowed Ann Fanshawe had to wait three years for the money owed to her – the arrears of her husband's diplomatic salary plus the nearly £6,000 of his own fortune spent in the King's service. Even then she did not get it all, ending up more than £2,000 out of pocket. 'How far this was from reward, judge ye,' she wrote, 'for near thirty years suffering by land and sea, and the hazard of our lives over and over . . . with the death and beggary of many eminent persons of our family, that when they first entered the king's service had great and clear estates.'[2]

Those whose estates had been confiscated by the Commonwealth were equally embittered, for although most do seem eventually to have got their property back by some means or other, they and sometimes their heirs often faced a long, wearisome wait for repossession, only to find their parks denuded of valuable timber and livestock. The majority, who had been able to compound, had usually been forced either to sell land or to get into debt in order to raise the money, and for them there was no redress.

Those without such problems to contend with were mostly ready enough to settle back into life as it had been lived in pre-Civil War days, and in many ways, in spite of all the upheavals of the past twenty years, the structure of society remained surprisingly unchanged. In spite of the Levellers, the Diggers, the Ranters and the Quakers, there were still privileged and unprivileged, and no sign of manhood suffrage. There were still rich and poor, those with property and those without. Men and women still raised families in wedlock, and husbands' and fathers' authority remained unchallenged in the home. The parish was still the basic building block of the national church, and tithes still had to be paid. But appearances could be deceptive, for of course there were changes. In spite of all the royalist fervour, which had led the King famously to remark that he could not understand why he had not come home sooner since he seemed to have no enemies, the monarchy had changed. The days of divine right had gone for ever, and Charles knew very well that they had.

The swordsmen, too, had gone. Its arrears finally paid off, the New Model was disbanded in January 1661, but it left behind a legacy of England's longstanding aversion to the idea of standing armies. And there was another legacy left behind by the republic. The so-called Cavalier Parliament, which met in the spring of 1661, saw the return of the bishops to the restored House of Lords, but attempts to reach some kind of compromise between the Anglican Episcopalians and the more moderate Presbyterians came to nothing, and a crazy last-ditch act of insurgency mounted by the Fifth Monarchists in January took the authorities by surprise and caused serious alarm. Pepys was woken on the morning of 7 January with news that there had been a great stir overnight by the 'Fanatiques' and that the Lord Mayor and the whole City were up in arms. Samuel nevertheless went to the office as usual and later, with his wife and brother Tom, to the theatre to see a performance of *The Silent Woman*, which he pronounced to be an excellent play. But on their way home they were stopped several times and 'strictly examined, more than in the worst of times, there being great fears of these fanatiques rising again'.

The scare continued over the next couple of days, culminating on Wednesday 9 January with people running up and down, saying that the Fanatiques were coming, so Pepys went out into the street to find 'everybody in arms at the doors; so I returned', he went on, '(though with no great courage at all, but that I might not seem to be afeared) and got my sword and pistol, which however I have no powder to charge, and went to the door'. There he found a neighbour and went with him as far as the Exchange, 'in our way the streets full of trained bands, and great stories what mischief these rogues have done; and I think near a dozen have been killed this morning on both sides'.[3]

In fact, it seems that about fifty Fifth Monarchy men, under their leader Thomas Venner, a London cooper, had first emerged from their meeting house on the evening of 6 January intending to occupy St Paul's, but a hastily mustered party of the local militia and armed volunteers forced them to retreat to Highgate woods, where they regrouped and reappeared in the City on the Wednesday to fight with desperate ferocity against a regiment of militia and royal guards, killing about twenty of them and losing twenty-six of their own. Sam Pepys was astonished that

> so few men should dare and do so much mischief. Their word [he wrote] was 'King Jesus, and the heads upon the gates!' [This was a reference to the recently executed regicides, who included that prominent Saint, Major General Thomas Harrison.] Few of them would receive any Quarter but such as were taken by force and kept alive, expecting Jesus to come and reign here in the world presently, will not believe yet but their work will be carried on, though they do die.[4]

Venner and twelve others were indeed executed and their meeting-house destroyed, but an exaggerated fear and suspicion of the 'fanatiques' persisted in government circles and was reflected in the legislation passed by the Cavalier Parliament. The Act of Uniformity, 1662, restored the Church of England in all its pre-war glory. The

Book of Common Prayer was once more to be the only permitted form of public worship, and all beneficed clergy must publicly declare their 'unfeigned assent and consent' to everything it contained. All schoolmasters were to be licensed by a bishop and conform to the Prayer Book, and all clergy and teachers were required to abjure the Solemn League and Covenant as an unlawful oath. It was now the turn of nonconformist ministers to face ejection, and it is estimated that altogether between 1,700 and 1,800 were removed from their livings in the first two years of the reign. Other punitive measures followed, making it an offence for five or more people not of the same family to worship together, even in a private house, and forbidding any nonconformist preacher to come within five miles of the place of his previous ministry.

All the sects, Presbyterians, Independents, Baptists and Quakers (especially the Quakers) were to suffer in varying degrees as a result, and were temporarily driven underground, but the spirit of noncomformity stubbornly refused to die – we owe the *Pilgrim's Progress* to the son of a Bedfordshire tinker doing twelve years in gaol for unlicensed preaching – and the long tradition of the dissenting conscience, which was to exert such an incalculable influence on the course of eighteenth- and nineteenth-century English life, owes much to that great surge of evangelical energy released by the Great Rebellion.

Another lingering, if diminishing, reminder of the Puritan ascendancy is the British Sunday. Lord's Day Observance was strictly enforced – parish constables could enter private homes without warrant if the inhabitants were suspected of profaning the Sabbath or cooking meat on a fast day – and no fewer than three Acts of Parliament were passed forbidding all forms of sport, pastime or indeed anything which could even loosely be described as recreation. Any kind of outside work or trading or non-essential domestic labour was also banned, as was any form of travel, apart from church-going. Anyone denounced for transgressing these rules could be fined or subjected to humiliating physical punishments – a Quaker girl was set in the stocks for mending her dress on a Sunday and a man and his wife fined 10*s* for going for a walk.

But Puritanism did not stifle the intellectual and cultural life of the period. Apart from John Milton, whose *Paradise Lost* was written between 1658 and 1663, Andrew Marvell and, to a lesser extent, John Dryden were both at work in the 1650s. *The Leviathan*, master work of the political philosopher Thomas Hobbes, was published in London in 1651, and that other classic, Izaak Walton's *Compleat Angler*, was written during the troubles and published in 1653. The physician and scientist William Petty was appointed Professor of Anatomy at Oxford in the 1650s (it was Petty who resuscitated Anne Green, the Oxford servant girl 'hanged' for infanticide in 1650) and went on to become a founder member of the Royal Society. Other Oxford scientists of the time included Robert Boyle, Robert Hooke, John Wilkins, John Wallis the code-breaker and, of course, Christopher Wren, who became a Fellow of All Souls in 1653 at the age of 21. That other giant of the seventeenth century, Isaac Newton, born in humble circumstances on a farm in Lincolnshire in the first year of the Civil War, was still a schoolboy at Grantham at the Restoration (he went up to Trinity College, Cambridge, in 1661), but the education he received during the Commonwealth and Protectorate had clearly prepared him well for his later career.

For all the failed experiments at home, republican England's international reputation had remained high. A successful naval war against the Dutch and another by sea and land, in alliance with France, against Spain in Flanders, ending in the capture of Dunkirk (England's first continental possession since the loss of Calais), had won her the respect of European statesmen; and although Cromwell's Western Design against the Spanish colonies in the West Indies failed in its main objective, the expeditionary force of thirty-eight ships and six thousand men did succeed in capturing the valuable island of Jamaica in May 1655.

All in all, the country to which Charles II had returned was already well on its way to becoming a world power, but that was for the future. In the spring of 1661 most people's attention was focused on the King's coronation, which took place in Westminster Abbey on 23 April, with every detail of its antique pomp and ceremony being scrupulously observed – it was the last occasion on which the sovereign made the Recognition Procession from the Tower to Westminster on the preceding day. Charlotte, Countess of Derby, the Civil War heroine of the siege of Lathom, was present at the ceremony in the Abbey and wrote to her sister-in-law in France that 'it was a very grand and imposing sight, the lords in the robes proper for the occasion which are very becoming. It is the last thing of the kind I shall see; and I have greatly desired to witness it, having prayed with tears to be permitted to behold this crown on the head of His Majesty.'[5]

Sam Pepys was in the Abbey, too, but in spite of having got up at four in the morning and finding a place on a 'great scaffold across the north end of the abbey', he was deeply disappointed not to be able to see the ceremonies conducted in the choir before the high altar. However, he got a good view of the royal procession as it entered Westminster Hall for the banquet, 'and a most pleasant sight it was to see them in their several robes. And the King came in with his Crowne on and his sceptre in his hand – under a Canopy borne up by six silver staves, carried by Barons of the Cinque Ports – and little bells at every end.' He saw the arrival of Dymoke, the King's champion, 'all in armour on horseback . . . And a herald proclaim that if any dare deny Charles Stewart to be lawful King of England, here was a Champion that would fight with him . . .'.

When Pepys and his wife got back to Axe Yard, they found 'three great bonfires, and a great many gallants, men and women; and they laid hold of us and would have us drink the King's health upon our knee . . . which we all did'. This went on for some time and Samuel 'wondered to see how the ladies did tipple'. Eventually he sent his wife home to bed and went off with some friends to the house of the Yeoman of the King's wine cellar, where they proceeded to 'drink the king's health and nothing else, till one of the gentlemen fell down stark drunk and there lay spewing', and Samuel himself admitted that 'if ever I was foxed it was now'. Not surprisingly, he woke next morning with his head 'in a sad taking' and had to settle his stomach with a morning draught of chocolate! But he did not regret it, unconsciously echoing the Lady of Lathom in his diary entry of 24 April: 'Now after all this, I can say that besides the pleasure of the sight of these glorious things, I may now shut my eyes against any other objects, or for the future trouble myself to see things of state and show, as being sure never to see the like again in this world.'[6]

Notes

The Day they Killed the King

1. P. Henry, *Diaries and Letters of Philip Henry, 1631–1696*, ed. M.H. Lee (London, Kegan Paul & Co., 1882), p. 12.
2. *Calendar of State Papers, Venetian*, ed. A.B. Hinds *et al.* (38 vols, London, Stationery Office, 1864–1940), vol. 28, pp. 90–1; *The Kingdom's Weekly Intelligencer*, 30 January–6 February 1649, cited in C.V. Wedgwood, *The Trial of Charles I* (London, Collins, 1964), p. 197.
3. J. Evelyn, *Diary of John Evelyn*, ed. Guy de la Bédoyère (Woodbridge, Boydell Press, 1995), p. 68; Samuel Pepys, *The Diary*, ed. H.B. Wheatley (8 vols, London, G. Bell, 1923), vol. 1, p. 253.
4. A. Barnes, *Memoirs of the Life of Ambrose Barnes*, ed. W.H.D. Longstaffe, Surtees Society (Durham, Surtees Society, 1867), cited in Wedgwood, *Trial of Charles I*, p. 196.
5. R. Josselin, *Diary of Ralph Josselin*, ed. A. Macfarlane (London, Oxford University Press, 1976), p. 155.
6. R. Partridge, '*O Horrable Murder*': *The Trial, Execution and Burial of King Charles I* (London, Rubicon Press, 1998), p. 97.
7. I. Twysden, *Diary of Isabella Twysden*, ed. F.W. Bennit, Transactions of the Kent Archaeological Society, vol. 51 (1939), pp. 129–30.
8. *Mercurius Pragmaticus*, 30 January–6 February 1649, cited in *Making the News*, ed. Joad Raymond (Witney, Windrush Press, 1993), p. 249.

Chapter 1

1. Sir Henry Slingsby, cited in R. Ollard, *This War without an Enemy* (London, Hodder & Stoughton, 1976), p. 42; J. Rushworth, *Historical Collections of Private Passages of State* (7 vols, London, T. Newcomb for J. Thomason, 1659), vol. 4, p. 34.
2. D. Hirst, *The Representative of the People?* (Cambridge, Cambridge University Press, 1975), pp. 13–14.

3. E. Porritt and A. Porritt, *The Unreformed House of Commons* (2 vols, Cambridge, Cambridge University Press, 1909), vol. 1, pp. 29 ff.

4. M. Kishlansky, *Parliamentary Selection* (Cambridge, Cambridge University Press, 1986), p. 11.

5. R.N. Kershaw, 'The Elections for the Long Parliament, 1640', *English Historical Review*, vol. 38, no. 152 (1923), 496–508, at 499–500.

6. *Ibid.*, pp. 504–6.

7. Porritt and Porritt, *The Unreformed House of Commons*, vol. 1, p. 426.

8. *Calendar of State Papers, Venetian*, ed. A.B. Hinds *et al.* (38 vols, London, Stationery Office, 1864–1940), vol. 25, p. 96.

9. Porritt and Porritt, *The Unreformed House of Commons*, vol. 1, p. 584.

10. S. D'Ewes, *The Journal of Sir Simonds D'Ewes*, ed. W.H. Coates (New Haven, Yale University Press, 1942), p. 185.

11. Rushworth, *Historical Collections*, vol. 4, p. 425.

12. D'Ewes, *Journal*, p. 184.

13. *Ibid.*, pp. 186–7; R. Verney, *Notes of Proceedings in the Long Parliament*, ed. J. Bruce, Camden Society, OS 31 (London, 1845), pp. 120–6; Philip Warwick, *Memoirs of the Reign of King Charles I* (London, Chiswell, 1702), p. 202.

14. D'Ewes, *Journal*, pp. 381, 384; Verney, *Notes*, p. 138.

15. Verney, *Notes*, pp. 138–9; D'Ewes, *Journal*, p. 381; Rushworth, *Historical Collections*, vol. 4, pp. 477–8.

16. Bulstrode Whitelocke, cited in Ruth Spalding, *The Improbable Puritan: A Life of Bulstrode Whitelocke* (London, Faber & Faber, 1975), pp. 82–3.

17. C.V. Wedgwood, *The King's War* ([1958], Harmondsworth, Penguin, 2001), p. 277.

18. S.R. Gardiner, *History of the Great Civil War* ([1888], 4 vols, Witney, Windrush Press, 2002), vol. 3, pp. 271–2.

19. B. Whitelocke, *Memorials of English Affairs* (4 vols, Oxford, Oxford University Press, 1853), vol. 2, p. 457.

20. *Ibid.*, pp. 466–7; D. Underdown, *Pride's Purge* (Oxford, Oxford University Press, 1971), pp. 134–5.

21. Underdown, *Pride's Purge*, pp. 138–9; E. Ludlow, *The Memoirs of Edmund Ludlow*, ed. C.H. Firth (2 vols, Oxford, Clarendon Press, 1894), vol. 1, pp. 208–9.

22. Whitelocke, *Memorials*, vol. 2, p. 468.

23. Underdown, *Pride's Purge*, pp. 143–4.

24. Gardiner, *The Great Civil War*, vol. 4, pp. 271–2; Whitelocke, *Memorials*, vol. 2, p. 468.

25. Whitelocke, *Memorials*, vol. 2, p. 471.

26. Gardiner, *The Great Civil War*, vol. 4, p. 273; Underdown, *Pride's Purge*, pp. 148, 153, 162.

27. Ludlow, *Memoirs*, vol. 1, p. 213.
28. Gardiner, *The Great Civil War*, vol. 4, p. 290.
29. S.R.Gardiner, *History of the Commonwealth and Protectorate* (4 vols [1897–1903], Witney, Windrush Press, 1988), vol. 2, p. 3; I. Roots, *The Great Rebellion* (Stroud, Alan Sutton, 1995), p. 142.
30. R. Sidney, *Sydney Papers*, ed. R.W. Blencowe (London, John Murray, 1825), pp. 139–40.
31. Whitelocke, *Memorials*, vol. 4, pp. 5–6.
32. *Ibid.*, p. 6.
33. Ludlow, *Memoirs*, vol. 1, p. 355.
34. *Ibid.*, p. 357.
35. A. Fraser, *Cromwell, our Chief of Men* (London, Weidenfeld & Nicolson, 1973), p. 424; *CSP Venetian*, vol. 29, p. 65.
36. D. Osborne, *The Letters of Dorothy Osborne to Sir William Temple, 1652–54*, ed. Kingsley Hart, Folio Society (1968), pp. 54–5.

Chapter 2

1. *Letters from the Clarendon State Papers* (2 vols, Oxford, Clarendon Press, 1767–86), vol. 2, p. 382.
2. *Reliquiae Baxterianae*, ed. M. Sylvester (London, 1696), part 1, pp. 71–3, cited in A.S.P. Woodhouse, *Puritanism and Liberty*, 2nd edn (London, J.M. Dent, 1974), pp. 387–9.
3. C.H. Firth, *Cromwell's Army* (London, Methuen, University Paperbacks, 1962), pp. 297, 294.
4. C. Carlton, *Going to the Wars* (London, Routledge, 1992), p. 280; I.J. Gentles, *The New Model Army in England, Ireland and Scotland, 1645–1653* (Oxford, Blackwell, 1992), pp. 120–1.
5. W. Clarke, *The Clarke Papers*, ed. C.H. Firth (London, Royal Historical Society, 1992), part 1, pp. x–xi.
6. *Ibid.*, p. 4.
7. Cited in A. Woolrych, *Soldiers and Statesmen: The General Council of the Army and its Debates 1647–1648* (Oxford, Clarendon Press, 1987), p. 58.
8. Clarke, *Clarke Papers*, part 1, p. xii.
9. Woodhouse, *Puritanism and Liberty*, p. 403.
10. *Ibid.*, pp. 404–5, 407–9.
11. Clarke, *Clarke Papers*, part 1, p. 132.
12. *Ibid.*, p. 173.
13. *Ibid.*, pp. 220–1.
14. 'Heads of Proposals', in Woodhouse, *Puritanism and Liberty*, pp. 422 ff.
15. Clarke, *Clarke Papers*, part 1, p. xlv.
16. Woodhouse, *Puritanism and Liberty*, p. 440.

17. *Ibid.*, pp. 429 ff.
18. Clarke, *Clarke Papers*, part 1, pp. 227–8.
19. *Ibid.*, p. 301.
20. *Ibid.*, pp. 303–6.
21. *Ibid.*, pp. 312, 318.
22. *Ibid.*, pp. 322–5.
23. *Ibid.*, p. 377.
24. *Ibid.*, pp. 369, 412.
25. Gentles, *New Model Army*, p. 318.
26. S.R.Gardiner, *History of the Commonwealth and Protectorate* (4 vols [1897–1903], Witney, Windrush Press, 1988), vol. 1, pp. 45–6; Gentles, *New Model Army*, pp. 326–8.
27. *Mercurius Pragmaticus*, 22 May–29 May 1649.

Chapter 3

1. J. Lilburne, 'The Hunting of the Foxes from Newmarket and Triple Heaths to Whitehall', in Baron Somers (ed.), *A Collection of Scarce and Valuable Tracts*, vol. 6 (1809), p. 52.
2. J. Lilburne, 'England's New Chains Discovered', in W. Haller and G. Davies (eds), *The Leveller Tracts* (New York, Columbia University Press, 1944), pp. 161–3.
3. Lilburne, 'England's New Chains', part 2, in *Leveller Tracts*, pp. 172–3.
4. P. Gregg, *Free-Born John: A Biography of John Lilburne* (London, Phoenix Press, 2000), pp. 271–2.
5. A.S.P. Woodhouse, *Puritanism and Liberty*, 2nd edn (London, J.M. Dent, 1974), pp. 367–8.
6. S. Davies, *Unbridled Spirits: Women of the English Revolution, 1640–1660* (London, Women's Press, 1998), p. 77.
7. Gregg, *Free-Born John*, p. 153.
8. Clarke, *Clarke Papers*, part 2, pp. 210–11.
9. *Ibid.*, p. 210.
10. *Ibid.*, p. 211.
11. *A Perfect Diurnal of Some Passages in Parliament*, No. 298, cited in J. Raymond (ed.), *Making the News* (Moreton-in-Marsh, Windrush Press, 1993), p. 393.
12. D. Petegorsky, *Left-Wing Democracy in the English Civil War* (Stroud, Alan Sutton, 1995), pp. 164–5.
13. Clarke, *Clarke Papers*, part 2, p. 223.
14. *Ibid.*, pp. 217–21.
15. *Ibid.*, p. 221.

16. A.L. Morton, *The World of the Ranters: Religious Radicalism in the English Revolution* (London, Lawrence & Wishart, 1970), p. 17.

17. Richard Baxter, *Autobiography*, ed. J.M. Lloyd-Thomas (New York, Dent, Everyman's Library, 1931), p. 73.

18. Morton, *The World of the Ranters*, pp. 70, 76, 77.

19. *Ibid.*, p. 78.

20. *Ibid.*, pp. 87–9.

21. W.C. Braithwaite, *The Beginnings of Quakerism*, 2nd edn, rev. H.J. Cadbury (Cambridge, Cambridge University Press, 1955), p. 20.

22. L. Hutchinson, *Memoirs of the Life of Colonel Hutchinson*, ed. N.H. Keeble (London, Phoenix Press, 2000), pp. 210–11.

23. J. Evelyn, *Diary of John Evelyn*, ed. Guy de la Bédoyère (Woodbridge, Boydell Press, 1995), p. 101.

24. *Acts and Ordinances of the Interregnum, 1642–1660*, ed. C.H. Firth and R.S. Rait (3 vols, London, Stationery Office, 1911), vol. 1, pp. 755–6.

25. A.H. Drysdale, *History of the Presbyterians in England* (London, Presbyterian Church of England Publication Committee, 1889), p. 290.

26. Thomas Edwards, *Gangraena*, cited in C. Hill and E. Dell, *The Good Old Cause: The English Revolution of 1640–60* (London, Lawrence & Wishart, 1949), pp. 319, 320.

27. Evelyn, *Diary*, p. 86.

28. F.P. Verney, *Memoirs of the Verney Family during the Civil War* (2 vols, Longmans Green & Co., 1892), vol. 2, pp. 258–60.

29. R. Josselin, *Diary of Ralph Josselin*, ed. A. Macfarlane (London, Oxford University Press, 1976), p. 236.

30. Evelyn, *Diary*, p. 84.

31. *Acts and Ordinances*, vol. 2, pp. 715–16.

32. *Memoirs of Anne, Lady Halkett and Ann, Lady Fanshawe*, ed. J. Loftis (Oxford, Clarendon Press, 1979), pp. 84–5.

33. *Acts and Ordinances*, vol. 2, pp. 715–16.

34. G.B. Tatham, *The Puritans in Power* (Cambridge, Cambridge University Press, 1913), pp. 256–9.

35. M. Aston, *England's Iconoclasts* (Oxford, Oxford University Press, 1988), vol. 1, pp. 64–5.

36. *Ibid.*, pp. 71, 73.

37. *Ibid.*, p. 69.

38. *Ibid.*, pp. 76, 78.

39. *Ibid.*, pp. 85–6.

40. Tatham, *The Puritans in Power*, pp. 67–8.

41. *Ibid.*, pp. 70–2.

42. Evelyn, *Diary*, p. 102.

43. *Ibid.*, p. 102.

Chapter 4

1. S.R. Gardiner, *History of the Great Civil War* (4 vols [1888], Witney, Windrush Press, 2002), vol. 1, pp. 186–7.
2. B. Whitelocke, *Memorials of English Affairs* (4 vols, Oxford, Oxford University Press, 1853), vol. 2, p. 182.
3. V. Pearl, 'London's Counter Revolution', in G.E. Aylmer (ed.), *The Interregnum: The Quest for a Settlement* (London, Macmillan, 1972), p. 51.
4. *Calendar of State Papers, Venetian*, ed. A.B. Hinds *et al.* (38 vols, London, Stationery Office, 1864–1940), vol. 29, p. 65.
5. Austin Woolrych, *Commonwealth to Protectorate* (London, Phoenix Press, 2000), pp. 112–13.
6. *CSP Venetian*, vol. 29, p. 81.
7. Oliver Cromwell, *Writings and Speeches of Oliver Cromwell*, ed. W.C. Abbott (4 vols, Cambridge, Mass., Harvard University Press, 1937–47), vol. 3, pp. 61–4.
8. 'A Declaration of the Parliament, 12 July 1653', in *Old Parliamentary History*, vol. 20 (1751–66), pp. 184–9.
9. E. Hyde, 1st Earl of Clarendon, *The History of the Rebellion and Civil Wars in England*, ed. W.D. Macray (6 vols, Oxford, Clarendon Press, 1888), vol. 5, p. 282.
10. P.G. Rogers, *The Fifth Monarchy Men* (London, Oxford University Press, 1966), pp. 32–4.
11. John Buchan, *Oliver Cromwell* (London, Reprint Society, 1941), pp. 370–1.
12. Rogers, *The Fifth Monarchy Men*, pp. 41–2.
13. *Calendar of State Papers, Domestic Series, 1649–60*, ed. M.A.E. Green (13 vols, London, Longman & Co., 1875–86), 1653–4, pp. 304–8.
14. *CSP Venetian*, vol. 29, pp. 111–12.
15. *Ibid.*, p. 164.
16. *Ibid.*, p. 184.
17. *Ibid.*, p. 184.
18. *Ibid.*, pp. 185–6.
19. *Ibid.*, pp. 184–5.
20. Woolrych, *Commonwealth to Protectorate*, p. 362.
21. L. Hutchinson, *Memoirs of the Life of Colonel Hutchinson*, ed. N.H. Keeble (London, Phoenix Press, 2000), pp. 256 –7.
22. *CSP Venetian*, vol. 29, p. 185.
23. *Acts and Ordinances of the Interregnum, 1642–1660*, ed. C.H. Firth and R.S. Rait (3 vols, London, Stationery Office, 1911), vol. 2, pp. 18–19.
24. R. Sherwood, *The Court of Oliver Cromwell* ([1977], Cambridge, Willingham Press, 1989), pp. 16–17.
25. *Ibid.*, pp. 18–19.

26. R. Sherwood, *Oliver Cromwell: King in All But Name* (Stroud, Sutton Publishing, 1997), p. 33.
27. Sherwood, *The Court of Oliver Cromwell*, pp. 26–8.
28. Sherwood, *Oliver Cromwell*, p. 26.
29. Hutchinson, *Memoirs*, p. 256, and Sherwood, *Oliver Cromwell*, p. 27.
30. Sherwood, *The Court of Oliver Cromwell*, pp. 135–70.
31. P.S. Seaver, *Wallington's World: A Puritan Artisan in Seventeenth-Century London* (London, Methuen, 1985), pp. 139–40.
32. *Ibid.*, pp. 120–1.
33. *Ibid.*, pp. 141, 140.
34. *Ibid.*, p. 120.
35. *Ibid.*, pp. 87–91.
36. *Ibid.*, p. 167.
37. *Ibid.*, pp. 147–8.
38. *Ibid.*, p. 149.
39. *Acts and Ordinances of the Interregnum*, vol. 1, pp. 26, 1027, 1070–1.
40. Seaver, *Wallington's World*, p. 49.

Chapter 5

1. See S. Porter, *Destruction in the English Civil Wars* (Stroud, Alan Sutton, 1994), chs 4, 5, 6.
2. R. Josselin, *Diary of Ralph Josselin*, ed. A. Macfarlane (London, Oxford University Press, 1976), pp. 316–17.
3. W.A. Shaw, *History of the English Church during the Civil Wars and under the Commonwealth, 1640–1660* (2 vols, London, Longmans & Co., 1900), vol. 2, pp. 284–5, 247; S.R. Gardiner, *History of the Commonwealth and Protectorate* (4 vols [1897–1903]; Witney, Windrush Press, 1988), vol. 3, pp. 19–23.
4. R. Baxter, *Autobiography*, ed. J.M. Lloyd-Thomas (New York, Dent, Everyman's Library, 1931), pp. 83, 84.
5. T. Burton, *Diary*, ed. J.T. Rutt (4 vols, London, Colburn, 1828), vol. 1, pp. xxxii–xxxv.
6. *Calendar of State Papers, Venetian*, ed. A.B. Hinds *et al.* (38 vols, London, Stationery Office, 1864–1940), vol. 30, pp. 31, 32.
7. *Ibid.*, pp. 42–3.
8. Gardiner, *History of the Commonwealth*, vol. 3, pp. 319–20.
9. Burton, *Diary*, p. cxliv, note.
10. L. Hutchinson, *Memoirs of the Life of Colonel Hutchinson*, ed. N.H. Keeble (London, Phoenix Press, 2000), p. 257.
11. Gardiner, *History of the Commonwealth*, vol. 3, p. 332.

12. C. Durston, *Cromwell's Major-Generals: Godly Government during the English Revolution* (Manchester, Manchester University Press, 2001), pp. 40–1.
13. *Acts and Ordinances of the Interregnum, 1642–1660*, ed. C.H. Firth and R.S. Rait (3 vols, London, Stationery Office, 1911), vol. 2, pp. 387–9.
14. F.A. Inderwick, *The Interregum, A.D. 1648–1660* (London, Sampson Low & Co., 1891), pp. 33 ff.
15. Durston, *Cromwell's Major-Generals*, p. 156.
16. See *ibid.*, ch. 3, for a survey of the major-generals' backgrounds and beliefs.
17. *Acts and Ordinances of the Interregnum*, vol. 1, p. 580.
18. W.F. Dawson, *Christmas, its Origin and Associations* (London, Elliot Stock, 1902), p. 208.
19. E.M. Symonds, 'The Diary of John Greene (1635–57). II', *English Historical Review*, vol. 43, no. 172 (1928), 598–604, at 604.
20. M. Harrison, *The Story of Christmas* (London, Odhams Press, 1951), pp. 138–9.
21. Dawson, *Christmas*, p. 206.
22. J. Evelyn, *Diary of John Evelyn*, ed. Guy de la Bédoyère (Woodbridge, Boydell Press, 1995), 25 December 1657, p. 105.
23. Dawson, *Christmas*, p. 212.
24. Durston, *Cromwell's Major-Generals*, pp. 172–6.
25. *Ibid.*, p. 177.
26. *Ibid.*, pp. 168–9.
27. A. Martindale, *The Life of Adam Martindale Written by Himself*, Chetham Society, OS 4 (Manchester, 1845), pp. 122–3.
28. K. Thomas, *Religion and the Decline of Magic* (London, Weidenfeld & Nicolson, 1971), pp. 161 ff.
29. *CSP Venetian*, vol. 30, p. 256.
30. R. Sherwood, *Oliver Cromwell: King in All But Name* (Stroud, Sutton Publishing, 1997), pp.70–1.
31. *Ibid.*, p. 71.
32. Burton, *Diary*, pp. 397, 413, 415–16.
33. Revd James Fraser, cited in J. Raymond, 'An Eye-Witness to King Cromwell', *History Today* (July 1997).
34. *Ibid.*
35. *Ibid.*
36. *CSP Venetian*, vol. 31, p. 82.
37. Hutchinson, *Memoirs*, 257.
38. Sherwood, *Oliver Cromwell*, p. 112.
39. *Mercurius Politicus*, 19 November 1657.
40. B.S. Capp, *The Fifth Monarchy Men* (London, Faber & Faber, 1972), p. 119.

Chapter 6

1. Richard Baxter, *Autobiography*, ed. J.M. Lloyd-Thomas (New York, Dent, Everyman's Library, 1931), p. 73. C. Hill, *The World Turned Upside Down* (Harmondsworth, Penguin, 1991), p. 237.
2. Hill, *The World Turned Upside Down*, p. 234.
3. W.C. Braithwaite, *The Beginnings of Quakerism*, 2nd edn, rev. H.J. Cadbury (Cambridge, Cambridge University Press, 1955), p. 47.
4. Thomas Fuller, *Church History*, cited in Braithwaite, *Beginnings of Quakerism*, p. 493.
5. Braithwaite, *Beginnings of Quakerism*, pp. 492, 488.
6. *Ibid.*, pp. 491–2.
7. L. Hutchinson, *Memoirs of the Life of Colonel Hutchinson*, ed. N.H. Keeble (London, Phoenix Press, 2000), pp. 86–7.
8. Braithwaite, *Beginnings of Quakerism*, p. 253.
9. Thomas Burton, *Diary*, ed. J.T. Rutt (4 vols, London, Colburn), vol. 1, pp. 24–30.
10. Braithwaite, *Beginnings of Quakerism*, p. 258.
11. Burton, *Diary*, pp. 49–50.
12. *Ibid.*, p. 61.
13. Braithwaite, *Beginnings of Quakerism*, pp. 261–2.
14. *Ibid.*, p. 263.
15. Burton, *Diary*, p. 217.
16. Braithwaite, *Beginnings of Quakerism*, p. 264; Burton, *Diary*, p. 370, note.
17. Burton, *Diary*, pp. 255–6.
18. *Ibid.*, pp. 265–6.
19. *Ibid.*, pp. 170–1.
20. *Ibid.*, p. 384.
21. *Acts and Ordinances of the Interregnum, 1642–1660*, ed. C.H. Firth and R.S. Rait (3 vols, London, Stationery Office, 1911), vol. 1, pp. 106–17, 254–60.
22. *Calendar of the Proceeding of the Committee for Compounding, 1643–1660* ed. M.A.E.Green (5 vols, London, Stationery Office, 1889–93), vol. 5, Introduction, pp. vi–vii.
23. *Ibid.*, p. ix.
24. *Ibid.*, pp. ix–x.
25. C.H. Firth, 'The Royalists under the Protectorate', *English Historical Review*, vol. 52, no. 208 (1937), 634–48, at 639–40.
26. Marchamont Needham, *The Excellence of a Free State* (1767 edn), cited in Firth, 'Royalists under the Protectorate', pp. 634–5.
27. *Military Memoirs of Sir John Gwynne* (1822), cited in Firth, 'Royalists under the Protectorate', p. 635.
28. *Committee for Compounding*, vol. 5, Introduction, p. xxx.

29. Katie Whitaker, *Mad Madge: Margaret Cavendish, Duchess of Newcastle* (London, Vintage, 2004), pp. 137–8.
30. Firth, 'Royalists under the Protectorate', p. 645.
31. *Ibid.*, p. 641.
32. J. Reresby, *Memoirs of Sir John Reresby*, ed. A. Browning, 2nd edn (London, Royal Historical Society, 1991), p. 6.
33. D. Underdown, *Royalist Conspiracy in England 1649–1660* (New Haven, Yale University Press, 1960), pp. 76–7.
34. *Ibid.*, p. 87.
35. C.H. Firth, 'Thomas Scot's Account of his Actions as Intelligencer', *English Historical Review*, vol. 12, no. 45 (1897), 116–26.
36. Hutchinson, *Memoirs of the Life of Colonel Hutchinson*, pp. 257–8.
37. M. Verney, *Memoirs of the Verney Family* (London, Longmans Green & Co., 1894), vol. 3, pp. 233–5, 240.
38. *Calendar of State Papers, Venetian*, ed. A.B. Hinds *et al.* (38 vols, London, Stationery Office, 1864–1940), vol. 30, pp. 82–3.
39. *Ibid.*, p. 86.
40. *Ibid.*, p. 88.
41. Verney, *Memoirs of the Verney Family*, vol. 3, p. 251.
42. C. Durston, *Cromwell's Major Generals*, p. 97.
43. Verney, *Memoirs of the Verney Family*, vol. 3, pp. 260–1.
44. *Ibid.*, pp. 268–9.
45. *CSP Venetian*, vol. 30, pp. 147–8.
46. Underdown, *Royalist Conspiracy*, pp. 178–80.
47. C.H. Firth, *Last Years of the Protectorate 1656–1658* (London, Longmans & Co., 1909), vol. 2, p. 55.
48. Henry Slingsby, *Diary of Henry Slingsby*, ed. D. Parsons (London, 1836), p. 136.
49. *Memoirs of Anne, Lady Halkett and Ann, Lady Fanshawe*, ed. J. Loftis (Oxford, Clarendon Press, 1979), p. 134.
50. *Memoirs of the Verney Family*, vol. 3, pp. 408–9.
51. *Ibid.*, pp. 197–9.
52. Firth, *Last Years of the Protectorate*, vol. 2, pp. 30–2.
53. Burton, *Diary*, vol. 2, pp. 464–70; Firth, *Last Years of the Protectorate*, vol. 2, pp. 36–41.

Chapter 7

1. C.H. Firth, *Last Years of the Protectorate 1656–1658* (London, Longmans & Co., 1909), vol. 2, pp. 42–3.
2. *Ibid.*, pp. 43–4.

3. *Ibid.*, p. 45.

4. *Ibid.*, p. 47.

5. *Ibid.*, pp. 76–82; D. Underdown, *Royalist Conspiracy in England 1649–1660* (New Haven, Yale University Press, 1960), pp. 226–9; A. Woolrych, *Britain in Revolution 1625–1660* (Oxford, Oxford University Press, 2002), pp. 690–1.

6. Firth, *Last Years of the Protectorate*, vol. 2, pp. 299–300.

7. E. Hyde, 1st Earl of Clarendon, *The History of the Rebellion and Civil Wars in England*, ed. W.D. Macray (6 vols, Oxford, Clarendon Press, 1888), vol. 6, p. 98.

8. P. Aubrey, *Mr Secretary Thurloe: Cromwell's Secretary of State, 1652–1660* (London, The Athlone Press, 1990), p. 76.

9. *Mercurius Politicus*, No. 28, 12–19 December 1650, cited in J. Raymond (ed.), *Making the News* (Moreton-in-Marsh, Windrush Press, 1993), pp. 182–3.

10. *Mercurius Politicus*, No. 108, 24 June–l July 1652, cited as above, p. 186.

11. *Mercurius Politicus*, No. 370, 2–9 July, 1657, cited as above, p. 196.

12. *Mercurius Politicus*, No. 257, 10–17 May, 1655, cited as above, p. 193.

13. *Mercurius Politicus*, No. 550, 13–20 January, 1659 and No. 572, 16–23 June 1659, cited as above, pp. 200, 201.

14. Markman Ellis, *The Coffee House: A Cultural History* (London, Weidenfeld & Nicolson, 2004), pp. 25 ff.

15. For a comprehensive recent account of the Essex witch hunt, see Malcolm Gaskill, *Witchfinders* (London, John Murray, 2005).

16. John Aubrey, *Brief Lives*, ed. Richard Barber (Woodbridge, Boydell Press, 1982), p. 133.

17. J. Evelyn, *Diary of John Evelyn*, ed. Guy de la Bédoyère (Woodbridge, The Boydell Press, 1995), p. 106.

18. A. Macfarlane, *The Family Life of Ralph Josselin: A Seventeenth-Century Clergyman* (London, Cambridge University Press, 1970), pp. 82, 84–5.

19. F.J. Powicke, *A Life of the Revd Richard Baxter 1615–1691* (London, Jonathan Cape, 1924), pp. 87–8.

20. A.W. Sloan, *English Medicine in the Seventeenth Century* (Durham, Durham Academic Press, 1996), pp. 133–4.

21. 'Declaration of the Officers', *Mercurius Politicus*, No. 566, 5–12 May 1659, cited in Raymond (ed.), *Making the News*, p. 433.

22. *Mercurius Politicus*, No. 580, 21–28 July 1659, cited as above, pp. 437–8.

23. M. Verney, *Memoirs of the Verney Family* (London, Longmans Green & Co., 1894), vol. 3, pp. 450–1.

24. Aubrey, *Brief Lives*, p. 125.

25. *The Weekly Post*, No. 31, 29 November– 6 December 1659, cited in Raymond (ed.), *Making the News*, pp. 444–5.

26. L. Hutchinson, *Memoirs of the Life of Colonel Hutchinson*, ed. N.H. Keeble (London, Phoenix Press, 2000), pp. 270–1.

27. Evelyn, *Diary*, p. 111.

28. *The Publick Intelligencer*, No. 214, 30 January–6 February 1660, cited in Raymond (ed.), *Making the News*, p. 452.

29. Samuel Pepys, *The Shorter Pepys*, ed. R. Latham (London, Book Club Associates, 1986), pp. 14–16.

30. *Ibid.*, p. 19.

31. *Ibid.*, pp. 38–9.

32. R. Josselin, *Diary of Ralph Josselin*, ed. A. Macfarlane (London, Oxford University Press, 1976), p. 463.

33. F.J. Powicke, *A Life of the Revd Richard Baxter 1615–1691* (London, Jonathan Cape, 1924), pp. 190–1.

34. H. Newcome, *The Autobiography of H. Newcome*, ed. R. Parkinson, Chetham Society (Manchester, Chetham Society, 1852), vol. 1, pp. 120–1.

35. C. Hill and E. Dell, *The Good Old Cause. The English Revolution of 1640–60* (London, Lawrence & Wishart, 1949), pp. 462–3.

36. Pepys, *The Shorter Pepys*, pp. 46, 48.

Restoration

1. J. Evelyn, *Diary of John Evelyn*, ed. Guy de la Bédoyère (Woodbridge, Boydell Press, 1995), p. 113.

2. *Memoirs of Anne, Lady Halkett and Ann, Lady Fanshawe*, ed. J. Loftis (Oxford, Clarendon Press, 1979), p. 168.

3. Samuel Pepys, *The Shorter Pepys*, ed. R. Latham (London, Book Club Associates, 1986), pp. 109, 110.

4. B.S. Capp, *The Fifth Monarchy Men* (London, Faber & Faber, 1972), pp. 198–200; Pepys, *The Shorter Pepys*, p. 110.

5. Madame Guizot de Witt, *The Lady of Latham: Being the Life and Original Letters of Charlotte de la Tremoille, Countess of Derby* (London, Smith, Elder & Co., 1869), p. 275.

6. Pepys, *The Shorter Pepys*, pp. 131–3.

Bibliography

Acts and Ordinances of the Interregnum 1642–1660, ed. C.H. Firth and R.S. Rait, 3 vols, London, Stationery Office, 1911

Adair, J. *Puritans: Religion and Politics in Seventeenth-Century England and America*, Stroud, Sutton Publishing, 1998

Aston, M. *England's Iconoclasts*, 2 vols, Oxford, Oxford University Press, 1988

Aubrey, J. *Brief Lives*, ed. Richard Barber, Woodbridge, Boydell Press, 1982

Aubrey, P. *Mr Secretary Thurloe: Cromwell's Secretary of State 1652–1660*, London, Athlone Press, 1990

Aveling, J.C.H. *The Handle and the Axe*, London, Blond & Briggs, 1976

Aylmer, G.E. *Rebellion or Revolution?* Oxford, Oxford University Press, 1986

——. *The State's Servants*, London, Routledge & Kegan Paul, 1973

Bampfield, J. *Col. Joseph Bampfield's Apology*, ed. J. Loftis and P.H. Hardacre, London, Associated University Presses, 1993

Baxter, R. *Autobiography*, ed. J.M. Lloyd-Thomas, New York, Dent, Everyman's Library, 1931

Bossy, J. *The English Catholic Community, 1570–1850*, London, Darton, Longman & Todd, 1975

Braithwaite, W.C. *The Beginnings of Quakerism*, 2nd edn, rev. H.J. Cadbury, Cambridge, Cambridge University Press, 1955

Brunton, D. and Pennington, D.H. *Members of the Long Parliament*, London George Allen & Unwin, 1954

Buchan, J. *Oliver Cromwell*, London, Reprint Society, 1941

Burton, T. *Diary*, ed. J.T. Rutt, 4 vols, London, Colburn, 1828

Calendar of the Proceeding of the Committee for Compounding, 1643–1660, ed. M.A.E. Green, 5 vols, London, Stationery Office, 1889–92

Calendar of State Papers, Domestic Series, 1649–1660, ed. M.A.E. Green, 13 vols, London, Longman & Co., 1875–6

Calendar of State Papers, Venetian, ed. A.B. Hinds *et al.*, 38 vols, London, Stationery Office, 1864–1940

Capp, B.S. *The Fifth Monarchy Men*, London, Faber & Faber, 1972

Carlton, Charles. *Going to the Wars*, London, Routledge, 1992

Clarke, W. *The Clarke Papers*, ed. C.H. Firth, London, Royal Historical Society, 1992

Bibliography

Coward, B. *The Stuart Age: England, 1603–1714*, 3rd edn, London, Longman, 2003

Cressy, D. *Birth, Marriage and Death*, Oxford, Oxford University Press, 1997

——. *Bonfires and Bells*, London, Weidenfeld & Nicolson, 1989

Cromwell, O. *The Writings and Speeches of Oliver Cromwell*, ed. W.C. Abbott, 4 vols, Cambridge, Mass., Harvard University Press, 1937–47

Davies, G. *The Early Stuarts*, 2nd edn, Oxford, Clarendon Press, 1955

Davies, S. *Unbridled Spirits, Women of the English Revolution 1640–1660*, London, Women's Press, 1998

Dawson, W.F. *Christmas, its Origin and Associations*, London, Elliot Stock, 1902

D'Ewes, S. *The Journal of Sir Simonds D'Ewes*, ed. W.H. Coates, New Haven, Yale University Press, 1942

Drysdale, A.H. *History of the Presbyterians in England*, London, Publication Committee of the Presbyterian Church of England, 1889

Durston, C. *Cromwell's Major-Generals: Godly Government during the English Revolution*, Manchester, Manchester University Press, 2001

Earle, Peter. *A City Full of People: Men and Women of London, 1650–1750*, London, Methuen, 1994

Ellis, M. *The Coffee House: A Cultural History*, London, Weidenfeld & Nicolson, 2004

Evelyn, J. *Diary of John Evelyn*, ed. Guy de la Bédoyère, Woodbridge, Boydell Press, 1995

Firth, C.H. *Cromwell's Army*, London, Methuen, University Paperbacks, 1962

——. *The Last Years of the Protectorate 1656–1658*, 2 vols, London, Longmans & Co., 1909

——. 'The Royalists under the Protectorate', *English Historical Review*, vol. 52, no. 208 (1937), 634–48

—— (intro.). 'Thomas Scot's Account of his Actions as Intelligencer during the Commonwealth', *English Historical Review*, vol. 12, no. 45 (1897), 116–26

Fraser, A. *Cromwell, our Chief of Men*, London, Weidenfeld & Nicolson, 1973

Gardiner, S.R. *History of the Commonwealth and Protectorate*, 4 vols [1897–1903], Witney, Windrush Press, 1988

——. *History of the Great Civil War*, 4 vols [1888], Witney, Windrush Press, 2002

Gaskill, M. *Witchfinders*, London, John Murray, 2005

Gentles, I.J. *The New Model Army in England, Ireland and Scotland, 1645–1653*, Oxford, Blackwell, 1992

Gregg, P. *Free-Born John: A Biography of John Lilburne*, London, Phoenix Press, 2000

Hainsworth, R. *The Swordsmen in Power*, Stroud, Sutton Publishing, 1997

Haller, W. and Davies, G. (eds). *The Leveller Tracts*, New York, Columbia University Press, 1944

Hardacre, P. *The Royalists during the Puritan Revolution*, The Hague, Martinus Nijhoff, 1956

Harrison, M. *The Story of Christmas*, London, Odhams Press, 1951

Henry, P. *Diaries and Letters of Philip Henry, 1631–1696*, ed. M.H. Lee, London, Kegan Paul & Co., 1882

Hexter, J.H. *The Reign of King Pym*, Cambridge, Mass., Harvard University Press, 1941

Hill, C. *God's Englishman*, Harmondsworth, Penguin Books, 1990

——. *Society and Puritanism in Pre-Revolutionary England*, London, Secker & Warburg, 1964

——. *The World Turned Upside Down*, Harmondsworth, Penguin Books, 1991

—— and Dell, E. *The Good Old Cause. The English Revolution of 1640–60*, London, Lawrence & Wishart, 1949

Hirst, D. *The Representative of the People?* Cambridge, Cambridge University Press, 1975

Hollings, M. 'Thomas Barret: A Study in the Secret History of the Interregnum', *English Historical Review*, vol. 43, no. 169 (1928), 33–69

Hutchinson, L. *Memoirs of the Life of Colonel Hutchinson*, ed. N.H. Keeble, London, Phoenix Press, 2000

Hutton, R. *The British Republic, 1649–1660*, 2nd edn, Basingstoke, Macmillan, 2000

——. *The Restoration*, Oxford, Clarendon Press, 1985

Hyde, Edward, 1st Earl of Clarendon. *The History of the Rebellion and Civil Wars in England*, ed. W.D. Macray, 6 vols, Oxford, Clarendon Press, 1888

Inderwick, F.A. *The Interregnum, AD 1648–1660*, London, Sampson Low & Co., 1891

James, M. *Social Problems and Policy during the Puritan Revolution 1640–1660*, London, Routledge, 1930

Josselin, R. *Diary of Ralph Josselin*, ed. A. Macfarlane, London, Oxford University Press, 1976

Kershaw, R.N. 'The Elections for the Long Parliament, 1640', *English Historical Review*, vol. 38, no. 152 (1923), 496–508

Kishlansky, M.A. *Parliamentary Selection: Social and Political Choice in Early Modern England*, Cambridge, Cambridge University Press, 1986

Letters from the Clarendon State Papers, 2 vols, Oxford, Clarendon Press, 1767–86

Lockyer, R. (ed.). *The Trial of Charles I*, London, Folio Society, 1959

Ludlow, E. *The Memoirs of Edmund Ludlow*, ed. C.H. Firth, 2 vols, Oxford, Clarendon Press, 1894

Macfarlane, A. *The Family Life of Ralph Josselin: A Seventeenth-Century Clergyman*, Cambridge, Cambridge University Press, 1970

Martindale, A. *The Life of Adam Martindale Written by Himself*, ed. R. Parkinson, Chetham Society, OS 4, Manchester, Chetham Society, 1845

Memoirs of Anne, Lady Halkett and Ann, Lady Fanshawe, ed. J. Loftis, Oxford, Clarendon Press, 1979

Morrill, J.S. *Seventeenth Century Britain 1603–1714*, Folkstone, Dawson, 1980

Morton, A.L. *The World of the Ranters: Religious Radicalism in the English Revolution*, London, Lawrence & Wishart, 1970

Neale, J.E. *The Elizabethan House of Commons*, London, Jonathan Cape, 1949

Newcome, H. *The Autobiography of H. Newcome*, ed. R. Parkinson, Chetham Society, vols 26–27, Manchester, Chetham Society, 1852

Old Parliamentary History, vol. 20, 1751–66

Ollard, R. *This War without an Enemy*, London, Hodder & Stoughton, 1976

Osborne, D. *Letters of Dorothy Osborne to Sir William Temple*, ed. K. Hart, London, Folio Society, 1968

Partridge, R. *O Horrable Murder: The Trial, Execution and Burial of King Charles I*, London, Rubicon Press, 1998

Pearl, V. 'London's Counter Reformation', in G.E. Aylmer (ed.), *The Interregnum: The Quest for a Settlement*, London, Macmillan, 1972

Pennington, D. and Thomas, K. (eds). *Puritans and Revolutionaries*, Oxford, Clarendon Press, 1978

Pepys, S. *The Shorter Pepys*, ed. Robert Latham, London, Book Club Associates, 1986

Petegorsky, D. *Left-Wing Democracy in the English Civil War*, Stroud, Alan Sutton, 1995

Porritt, E. and Porritt, A. *The Unreformed House of Commons*, 2 vols, Cambridge, Cambridge University Press, 1909

Porter, S. *Destruction in the English Civil Wars*, Stroud, Alan Sutton, 1994.

——. *London and the Civil War*, London, Macmillan, 1996

Powicke, F.J. *A Life of Revd Richard Baxter 1615–1691*, London, Jonathan Cape, 1924

Prall, S. (ed.). *The Puritan Revolution*, London, Routledge & Kegan Paul, 1968

Raymond, J. 'An Eye-Witness to King Cromwell', *History Today* (July 1997)

—— (ed.). *Making the News*, Witney, Windrush Press, 1993

Reresby, J. *Memoirs of Sir John Reresby*, ed. A. Browning, 2nd edn, London, Royal Historical Society, 1991

Rogers, P. *The Fifth Monarchy Men*, London, Oxford University Press, 1966

Roots, I. *The Great Rebellion*, Stroud, Alan Sutton, 1995

Rushworth, J. *Historical Collections of Private Passages of State*, 6 vols, London, T. Newcomb for J. Thomason, 1659

Seaver, P.S. *Wallington's World: A Puritan Artisan in Seventeenth-Century London*, London, Methuen, 1985

Shaw, W.A. *History of the English Church during the Civil Wars and under the Commonwealth 1640–1660*, 2 vols, Longmans & Co., 1900

Sherwood, R. *The Court of Oliver Cromwell*, [1977] Cambridge, Willingham Press, 1989

——. *Oliver Cromwell, King in All but Name*, Stroud, Sutton Publishing, 1997

Sidney, R. *The Sydney Papers*, ed. R.W. Blencowe, London, John Murray, 1825

Slingsby, H. *Diary of Henry Slingsby*, ed. D. Parsons, London, 1836

Sloan, A.W. *English Medicine in the Seventeenth Century*, Durham, Durham Academic Press, 1996

Somers, Baron (ed.). *A Collection of Scarce and Valuable Tracts*, vol. 6 (1809)

Spalding, R. *The Improbable Puritan: A Life of Bulstrode Whitelocke*, London, Faber & Faber, 1975

Symonds, E.M. 'The Diary of John Greene (1635–57). II', *English Historical Review*, vol. 43, no. 172 (1928), 598–604

Tatham, G.B. *The Puritans in Power*, Cambridge, Cambridge University Press, 1913

Thomas, K. *Religion and the Decline of Magic*, London, Weidenfeld & Nicolson, 1971

Thornton, A. *The Autobiography of Mrs Alice Thornton*, ed. C. Jackson, Surtees Society, vol. 62, Durham, Andrews, 1875

Twysden, I. *Diary of Isabella Twysden*, ed. F.W. Bennit, *Transactions of the Kent Archaeological Society*, vol. 51 (1939)

Underdown, D. *Pride's Purge*, Oxford, Oxford University Press, 1971

——. *Revel, Riot and Rebellion: Popular Politics and Culture in England 1603–1660*, Oxford, Oxford University Press, 1987

——. *Royalist Conspiracy in England, 1649–1660*, New Haven, Yale University Press, 1960

——. 'Sir Richard Willys and Secretary Thurloe', *English Historical Review*, vol. 69, no. 272 (1954), 373–87

Verney, F.P. *Memoirs of the Verney Family during the Civil War*, 2 vols, London, Longmans Green & Co., 1892

Verney, M. *Memoirs of the Verney Family during the Commonwealth*, 3 vols, London, Longmans Green & Co., 1894

Verney, Sir R. *Notes of Proceedings in the Long Parliament*, ed. J. Bruce, Camden Society, OS. 31, London, Camden Society, 1845

Warwick, P. *Memoirs of the Reign of Charles I*, London, Chiswell, 1702

Wedgwood, C.V. *The King's War* [1958], Harmondsworth, Penguin, 2001

——. *The Trial of Charles I*, London, Collins, 1964

Whitaker, K. *Mad Madge: Margaret Cavendish, Duchess of Newcastle*, London, Vintage, 2004

Whitelocke, B. *Memorials of English Affairs*, 4 vols, Oxford, Oxford University Press, 1853

Witt, Madame Guizot de. *The Lady of Latham: Being the Life and Original Letters of Charlotte de la Tremoille, Countess of Derby*. London, Smith, Elder & Co., 1869

Woodhouse, A.S.P. *Puritanism and Liberty*, 2nd edn, London, J.M. Dent, 1974

Bibliography

Woolrych, A. *Britain in Revolution 1625–1660*, Oxford, Oxford University Press, 2002

——. *Commonwealth to Protectorate*, [1982] London, Phoenix Press, 2000

——. *Soldiers and Statesmen: The General Council of the Army and its Debates 1647–1648*, Oxford, Clarendon Press, 1987

Worden, B. *The Rump Parliament, 1648–1653*, Cambridge, Cambridge University Press, 1974

Wrightson, K. *English Society, 1580–1680*, London, Hutchinson, 1982

Index